Madmen's Ball

The Inside Story of the Lakers' Dysfunctional Dynasties

Mark Heisler

TRIUMPH
B O O K S
CHICAGO

Library of Congress Cataloging in Publication Data

Heisler, Mark.
    Madmen's ball : the inside story of the Lakers' dysfunctional dynasties / Mark Heisler.
        p. cm.
    ISBN 1-57243-681-6
    1. Los Angeles Lakers (Basketball team). I. Title.

GV885.52.L67H45 2004
796.323'64'097494—dc22

2004058019

This book is available in quantity at special discounts for your group or organization. For further information, contact:

Triumph Books
601 S. LaSalle St.
Suite 500
Chicago, Illinois 60605
(312) 939-3330
Fax (312) 663-3557

Printed in U.S.A.
ISBN 1-57243-681-6
Design by Patricia Frey
Production by Prologue Publishing Services, LLC

All photos courtesy of AP/Wide World Photos.

To Dorothy, Nusha, Art, and Kurt

Advertising signs that con you
Into thinking you're the one
That can do what's never been done
That can win what's never been won
Meantime life outside goes on
All around you.

—Bob Dylan, "It's All Right, Ma (I'm Only Bleeding)"

Contents

FOREWORD

WHEN I FIRST CAME TO LOS ANGELES AFTER BEING DRAFTED by the Lakers in 1960, I thought, "My God, this is the most unimportant game in town." We really felt like second-class athletes. The Dodgers and the Rams were on top of the world; we were on the back page of the newspapers, with little or no interest early on.

But Elgin Baylor's greatness, and my development as a player, brought an awful lot of people to the games and helped the franchise. We became very competitive in the early sixties, and I think people started to pay attention, because that basketball was pretty darn exciting.

The thing that most defined the Lakers teams of that era, that created this Jeykll-and-Hyde attitude among our fans, was our losing to the Celtics. We'd play great all during the regular season and then lose to those guys in the Finals. I think for everyone on the team it was probably one of the most painful trials an athlete could ever go through.

In some respects, it was humiliating that they could beat us year after year like that. But realistically, except for two years, we shouldn't have beaten them. They were just better than us. When we weren't able to win in the two years that we should have, either, there was an aura of inevitability to it, like, "OK, they're going to lose again, they're going to lose again, they're going to lose again."

Then late in my career, when I didn't think there was any chance we could win, all of a sudden, we won. And after all that, I thought, "Is that all there is?"

It was fun to be a champion instead of an also-ran, yet it created within me even more of a distaste for all the losses we'd had. I've said it before, and I'll say it again, it left a lot of scars on me, a lot of scars.

The only way to compete in a sport after you've stopped playing is to become part of management. If I could have a different thought process as to what might help the team reach the pinnacle of success on a more consistent basis, that's what I would try to do. And that's exactly what my thought process was. But I think the thing that has driven me all my life was my love for the Lakers franchise. It was everything to me, to the point I almost couldn't stand it.

I loved going to work. I loved the players. The people I worked with were really important to me. But the wins and the losses were sometimes equally painful.

■   ■   ■

When we drafted Magic Johnson and hired Pat Riley as a member of the coaching staff, the next great era of Lakers basketball began.

Pat Riley and I were close. He was a perfect example of what an NBA pro should be. He had a long career as a player but never had the kind of success he'd had in college. Was that disappointing to him? Only he could answer that, but the one thing I know is that no one would ever outwork him. He was committed, dedicated, and always wanted to get better. There was nothing too good for the players. He wanted the best of everything for them, and I think his demeanor drove some of the players further than they thought they could go.

You throw Magic Johnson into the mix, and it was the perfect combination. They were both driven. They had that kind of energy, day in and day out, night in and night out, and our players followed their lead.

I think what we accomplished in the eighties is a great tribute to both of them. But of course, they had one of the truly great players of all time in Kareem Abdul-Jabbar. I've never seen a better professional. When you have that and a young, enthusiastic Magic Johnson and a coach who demanded and got the best out of his players, it was something special to watch.

I just think Riley's contribution was difficult to gauge from a distance, but in person, you knew. He was an intense competitor. Our practices were like our games. Earvin made those like that. It was a combination that worked extremely well.

■ ■ ■

A lot of people ask me, Are the players any different than they used to be?

I say, No, I don't think they are.

Are they more selfish? No. Do they make a lot more money? Yes. I think if there's one major difference, it's money. The other difference is that players come into the league younger. One thing that happens when you have more young people is that you have fewer veterans around to support or endorse appropriate behavior. So they're more susceptible to being influenced by others who have as little experience as them.

On the other hand, some of these kids today are incredibly dedicated athletes from a very early age. They've had a lot of different kinds of coaching, some of it not what you'd want. They've had none of the benefits of collegiate coaching or the well-rounded learning that comes from a college education. As a result, many don't prosper and are unable to fit into the system very well.

Most of them are so confident coming into the league, and it's probably because they've competed against a lot of very good players and can acquit themselves very well in playground-type situations. They think they can go out and play in the NBA, that what they know is enough.

Well, it's not enough. The teams that play together and are unified defensively and offensively are the ones that win and win big.

■ ■ ■

When we were trying to sign Shaquille O'Neal, I talked to him a lot on the telephone, and I really liked him. He was someone who wanted you to talk straight, and that's always what I tried to do. If we hadn't signed him, I still would have been a better person for talking to that young man.

The first time we worked out Kobe Bryant, he was still 17 years old, but I said, "My gosh, this is a kid who's going to make an impact on some level in basketball." I sort of sat there drooling and hoping to find a way to draft a player like that. It was a long shot, at best, I thought, at that point in time. But Jerry Buss said we didn't just want to try to have a team that was going to win 50-some games, he wanted a team that he felt could maybe compete for an NBA championship and do it on a consistent basis. We wound up getting both Shaquille and Kobe that summer, and that gave us a special combination for years to come.

I cared so much for the Lakers franchise. When things were bad, I felt like I was betraying the franchise. And when things were really good, I couldn't even enjoy that.

It was the best thing I ever did in my life, leaving at the time I left. And I think the second-best thing I did was come to Memphis. At times, it's sad to think that I'm not in L.A., but I really believe I did the right thing for me.

The bottom line is maybe sometimes you have to do selfish things in life. From my perspective, it was kind of a selfish thing to do, because I left a lot of wonderful friends and a great situation with the people and the coaching staff they have in place. That was the difficult part of it. But the thing was, it didn't bring me the same good feeling, even when we were winning. It just didn't do it.

—Jerry West
Memphis, July 2004

ACKNOWLEDGMENTS

THE FIRST THING I MUST ACKNOWLEDGE is that Southern California isn't really paradise, although I use it as a metaphor for one. This is not only a handy device but a very California thing to do, even if I, like so many other people here, come from somewhere else (Springfield, Illinois).

Actually, this place is like anywhere else with better weather, worse traffic, higher housing prices, and a love affair with itself, which is a pleasant change.

I grew up yearning to move to the coast, any coast, where it seemed everything started but took years to move inland to us. Like everyone else, I took my cues from the Beach Boys. East Coast girls were hip. The West Coast had the sunshine and the girls all got so tan. All we supposedly had were the Midwest farmer's daughters, and I don't even remember meeting any of those.

I subsequently lived for 10 years in Philadelphia, which was a great place, especially for a sportswriter, but had an inferiority complex, sandwiched as it is between New York and Washington. When I moved there in 1969, a civic group trying to to pump up local pride was running billboards proclaiming, PHILADELPHIA ISN'T AS BAD AS PHILADELPHIANS SAY IT IS.

In Southern California, the local answer to questions (like, say, the slow pace of intellectual life) from anywhere else (like, say, New York) is, "Fine, you stay there and we'll stay here." The *Los Angeles Times'* great Jim Murray (who was from Connecticut) had a standard Rose Bowl column, praying for bad weather lest more midwesterners watching on TV be dazzled by the sun on the San Gabriel mountains looming behind the stadium and decide to move here en masse.

As a new Californian, I quickly fell into the routine. Like, when you call a friend who lives anywhere else, the first thing you say is, "How's the weather back there?"

Of course, there are endemic problems that get saturation coverage, due to their epic nature. After the Northridge quake of 1994, which I felt up close and personally as a resident of Northridge, my friend, Mike Littwin, who worked with me at the *Times* but moved to Baltimore, was kidding me one day about the aftershocks we were getting.

"When the ground stops shaking," I replied, "it'll still be 70 degrees here."

It's easy. Anyone could pick it up in a day.

Appearances notwithstanding, life is the same here. There aren't any more blondes than anywhere else (although that actually struck me as strange when I first got here). We're not all in show business. We're not all even working on screenplays.

As readily as I pass along the popular notion that beauty is indistinguishable from happiness, I don't believe it's an end in itself or an enduring value (which is lucky for most of us). It is, however, another metaphor for paradise.

There are, indeed a lot of good-looking women here but that's because so many come hoping to get into show business, even if they find themselves waiting tables instead. They're tanner, to be sure, and they do tend to head for the fashionable West Side, near the money and the beach.

That's also where NBA players live or stay while they're in town, so if they have a skewed perspective of L.A. in particular, or of life in general, it's understandable.

Unfortunately, the dream inevitably fades, leaving only real life, its own inescapable self.

■　■　■

In the movie *Continental Divide*, John Belushi plays Ernie Souchak, a hardboiled Chicago newspaper columnist. At one point, his editor asks him if he'd like to go up into the Rocky Mountains to interview a woman who works with eagles.

"It would be something new to write about," says the editor.

"I like writing about the old thing over and over," says Souchak.

I'm with that. Happily, although I've spent 14 years around the Lakers and more than 20 covering the NBA, it's never gotten old. It's become more like a carnival ride in which you're always hanging on for dear life.

As anyone who knows me can attest, I've griped every inch of the way, but it has actually been a joy and a privilege. I'm proud of my own small contribution, like the season I started calling the Lakers dysfunctional and Rick Fox picked it up; and the season I trotted out Friedrich Nietzsche's "That which doesn't kill me makes me stronger," and Kobe Bryant started using that.

Best of all, I used to compare Phil Jackson to *Mad* magazine's Alfred E. Neuman, who said, "What, me worry?" and one day Phil said he was taking a what-me-worry approach.

There are lots of people I'm indebted to for their help and friendship over the years. First, there are the guys who covered the beat, especially after 1996 when Bryant and Shaquille O'Neal arrived and coverage became all-Lakers-all-the-time. Here's to you, Tim Kawakami, Scott Howard-Cooper, Jay Adande, Howard Beck, Brad Turner, Kevin Ding, and Marc Stein. I owe special thanks to the talented and relentless Tim Brown, who covered the end of this saga for my paper with such distinction and provided me with a daily account of the forces colliding in the background.

Then there are the old Lakers hands, who, like it or not, know who you are. They not only know where the bodies are buried, but in some cases, helped bury them and remain the living caretakers of Lakers lore. That's Mitch Chortkoff, Doug Krikorian, Joe McDonnell, Scott Ostler, and Steve Springer.

Then there are the Lakers themselves, especially Jackson, O'Neal, Bryant, Fox, Jerry West, Elgin Baylor, Magic Johnson, Del Harris, Mike Dunleavy, Kareem Abdul-Jabbar, James Worthy, Michael Cooper, Byron Scott, Stu Lantz, Keith Erickson, Derek Fisher, Horace Grant, John Salley, Derek Harper, Randy Pfund, Bill Bertka, Kurt Rambis, Jim Cleamons, Frank Hamblen, Larry Drew, Jim Eyen, Lon Rosen, Josh Rosenfeld, Raymond Ridder, and Allison Bogli. A special thank you to John Black, the publicist of the Shaq-Kobe era when the job became Mission: Impossible.

Like everyone who knew them, I miss Wilt Chamberlain, who was more endearing than he came out looking; and Chick Hearn, a giant in his own right.

If the Lakers were different—and if I use words like "madman" and "wacko" to describe them—they were basically just strung-out performance freaks, which I can sympathize with. Of course, they had to handle being rich and famous, too.

I'm indebted to Steve Springer and Scott Ostler for their book, *Winnin' Times*; to Stew Thornley for *Basketball's Original Dynasty*; to Roland Lazenby for *The Lakers*; to Frank Deford, Jack McCallum, and Ian Thomsen of *Sports Illustrated*; Tom Friend and Ric Bucher of *ESPN Magazine*; and Chris Mundy of *Rolling Stone*.

I'm indebted to Jackson for his *Sacred Hoops*; to Chamberlain and David Shaw for *Wilt*; to Johnson and William Novak for *My Life*; to Pat Riley for *Show Time*; to O'Neal for *Shaq Talks Back*; and to Abdul-Jabbar and Peter Knobler for *Giant Steps*. I also used material from my own *Lives of Riley* and *Giants*.

Thanks to everyone else who was so helpful over the years, including Joe Safety, Andy Roeser, and, yes, you too, Donald T. Sterling of the Clippers; Donnie Walsh, Larry Bird, and David Kahn of the Pacers; Larry Brown of the Pistons; John Gabriel, Pat Williams, and Paul Westhead of the Magic; the one and only Jerry Reynolds of the Kings; Danny Ainge and Bob Cousy of the Celtics; Bill Fitch, formerly of the Clippers; Doug Collins of TNT; Jack Ramsay, Bill Walton, and Jim Gray of ESPN; agents Arn Tellem, Dwight Manley, and Leonard Armato; and Pete Newell, the guru, now retired. I talked to Riley a few times off the record when he was a Laker, although that ended when I began doing my book on him, but he was OK after it came out, so I count that as an OK experience. For sure, it was a revealing one.

Thanks to my agent, Steve Delsohn; my bosses at the *Times*, Bill Dwyre and Dave Morgan; and my publisher and editor at Triumph, Mitch Rogatz and Tom Bast.

Thanks to Sam Smith, who tells me what's actually going on while I'm home thinking Big Picture; and to George Kiseda, the greatest basketball writer of all, whom I was lucky enough to work opposite in Philadelphia and who taught me how to cover zanies. Thanks to Littwin, who's always there to tell me it's going to be OK.

Most of all, thanks to Loretta and Emily, for my own slice of paradise.

Introduction

The End of the Rainbow

I grew to love the beauty and informality of Southern California. Everyone there seemed to be "doing his own thing," long before that phrase became fashionable. Girls were prettier and less inhibited and more independent and even the guys seemed more free and open and honest.

—Wilt Chamberlain, *Wilt*

When it came to fine women, Los Angeles was tops. Every team enjoyed coming out to L.A., because even though most of them didn't fare too well when they played us in the Forum, Los Angeles had some of the most beautiful and sexiest women in the country.

—Magic Johnson, *My Life*

■ ■ ■

THIS IS THE CITY.

This isn't really *Dragnet*, so we're not doing that shot of the generic-looking Parker Center. We open on purple-lit Staples Center downtown and pan west to the Hollywood sign, out toward the ocean, with the L.A. basin below us, with all the lights below twinkling like diamonds.

Topographically, this place isn't stunning like San Francisco, but it's beautiful nonetheless, as we pass over the West Side and the glamorous communities of Beverly Hills, Bel Air, Brentwood, Pacific Palisades, and Santa Monica, then down the beach to Venice, Marina del Rey, and the beach cities.

This is the L.A. that NBA players know, from the time their charter flight lands at LAX, 10 minutes by chartered bus south of the Ritz Carlton and the Marriott in the Marina where most teams stay, amid the yachts and the swinging singles.

Aunt Kizzy's Back Porch, a favorite hangout of movie stars and basketball players is right there, tucked away in a corner of the Villa Marina shopping center. Jerry's Famous Deli, open late for postgame, is in there, too, and hot spots like T.G.I. Friday's and Cheesecake Factory, unless the guys are going up to Sunset.

This is a business trip so, sometime in there, they'll bus downtown to the Staples Center for the morning shootaround, returning in the evening for the real deal. Things aren't as simple as they were in Johnson's day, when the Showtime Lakers were taking names and kicking butts in the old Forum, when Sacramento's Jerry Reynolds used to think even the ushers looked down on them, but a night at Staples is still no treat.

In its time, the Forum, ringed by its Doric columns, staked its claim as the greatest or, for sure, the most pretentious arena. The bombastic Jack Kent Cooke, who built it, always called it the "Fabulous Forum," although, due to the pressure of economics, Jerry Buss would rechristen it the "Great Western Forum" in a naming-rights deal with a local bank. The Lakers referred to it that way, anyway; the fans and newspapers didn't.

Nevertheless, the gaudy Forum, with its gold seats, gold free throw lanes, and players in gold uniforms, was a YMCA gym compared to the opulence of Staples. The Staples Center looks like it was built for the suite-holders sitting upstairs and the celebrities sitting courtside at $1,800 a game (Jack Nicholson, Lou Adler, Dyan Cannon, Penny Marshall, Denzel Washington, just to name some you might see in the regular season), with a few of the non-rich and non-famous scattered here and there.

Not that money is a problem for these people; an entertainment lawyer named Steve Jackson, who manufactures Shaquille O'Neal's sneakers, has eight courtside seats, or in other words, $590,400 worth per season.

Above the lower bowl sit three levels of luxury suites, one atop the other, 150 units in all, leased for $200,000 to $340,000 a year, on 5-, 7-, and 10-year plans. No other arena even has two rings of suites so low. It makes the upper bowl so far up, the common people up there should get binoculars or parachutes.

What the design provides in comfort for the few, it surrenders in intimacy or electricity. It's more like an airplane hangar, a vast pleasure dome for stars, agents, studio execs, and other rich people, with a basketball court in the middle. Bruce Springsteen, who opened Staples, looked up at the suites and asked people to "come out of your houses." Los Angeles fans are blasé enough and early-season games are often little louder than practices, so you can hear the sneakers squeaking when the players make their cuts.

Conseco Fieldhouse in Indianapolis, with its steep design and its great sightlines, was built for basketball. Staples is about Having To Be Here, as everyone did, when the Lakers began stringing titles together in 2000, the very season the building opened.

Now, it's like *Lifestyles of the Rich and Famous* during the playoffs, when *everyone* turns out—Sly, Dusty, Steven, Will, Michelle, Pamela, Leo, Heather and Richie, Brad and Jennifer . . .

Etc., etc.

Pat's wife, Chris, who introduced glamour to the coaching profession and became a star as great as any on the silver screen, thought the glitz was so much a part of the Lakers deal, he set about recreating it in Madison Square Garden when he took the Knicks job and succeeded wildly.

Mrs. Riley put the word out through a Manhattan publicist that celebs would be welcomed (i.e., comped), and they poured in. Marketing for all they were worth, the Knicks even provided a nightly list of stars in attendance on their postgame press notes. Gotham was captured and never escaped; 10 years after Riley left, with his team crumbled into ashes, the celebrities were still coming and the Knicks were still playing to 95 percent of capacity.

The Lakers never bothered collecting names, or doing much in general. For years, they were the only team in the NBA that didn't even send anyone to the league's annual marketing meeting. They didn't have to. They were Celebrities R Us.

Indeed, there was little separating the movie stars, rock stars, and rap stars from the Lakers stars. In this context, any Laker who could deliver a line was a star.

In no other dressing room would you have been likely to hear a conversation like this one in 2000, between radio announcer Paul Sunderland and reserve center John Salley.

Sunderland: "Did you see *The Green Mile*?"

Salley: "I read for it."

Rick Fox got to read for the movie, too, but was told he was "too pretty."

Riley, who had never acted unless you count fraternity skits, was offered the lead for the 1988 movie *Tequila Sunrise* by his friend, director Robert Towne. When Riley turned him down, Towne made do with Kurt Russell, although he had Russell slick his hair back, like Riley's. "Riles" even loaned Russell some of his clothes.

Riley's friend, Michael Douglas, did Pat's 'do as Gordon Gekko in *Wall Street*. When Douglas won the Academy Award, Riley telegraphed him, "I have to believe it was all in the hair."

Joe Smith, the Capitol Records president, who sits baseline on the Lakers side of the floor, used to say Johnson was the biggest star in town. Smith reached this conclusion after having lunch with him at Le Dome on the Sunset Strip and seeing the patrons, who made little fuss at the sight of famous actors, go bonkers as Magic walked through the room.

In a five-year period in the nineties, the *Wall Street Journal* counted up four CDs, 17 film credits, and 50 TV appearances among the Lakers. Not even *Variety* could estimate the number of auditions they went to, or the number of producers who pitched them.

At the end of the rainbow, there's a 25-year-old agent in a suit and an open-necked shirt, talking deals rapid-fire on his cell phone on the sideline before a game.

■ ■ ■

It's axiomatic in the entertainment business that no one worships stars like other stars. It's also axiomatic that the actors and the singers want to be athletes (and, of course, athletes want to be singers and actors). Staples is where they all meet.

Just imagine the interactions . . .

Once, a young guy named Anthony Kiedis, who was the singer in a new rock band called the Red Hot Chili Peppers, wrote a song about Magic Johnson and, hoping to get it to him, asked Jack Nicholson to pass the CD along. To which Nicholson is supposed to have replied: "Don't talk to me, kid."

The Lakers' preeminence in the local social scale is actually a relatively recent development, and a remarkable one. They were all but unnoticed when they arrived in 1960 without invitation, as opposed to the Dodgers, who were granted a stadium on a hilltop overlooking downtown in a political fight that lasted years, and were welcomed as conquering heroes.

It was the Dodgers' town back then. Before that, it belonged to the Rams, another Hollywood-saturated outfit, and before that to USC, where John Wayne (né Marion Morrison), not to mention O. J. Simpson, played football.

By Y2K, however, things had changed. College football was a niche sport. The Rams had moved twice, to Anaheim and then St. Louis, which was just too much. The Raiders had been there and gone in 14 years, even while winning a Super Bowl. The once-beloved Dodgers of Sandy, Big D, Smokey, Tommy, Garv, and Fernando were on a long downer and not even a local family concern any more, but a neglected piece of the Rupert Murdoch empire.

Meanwhile, the Lakers kept getting better and more glamorous.

Into this Milky Way of celebrity, they brought their own cast of stars, starting with Elgin Baylor, Jerry West, Chick Hearn (just doing play-by-play was enough to confer stardom, especially if you had as much style as Chick), and Wilt in the sixties and seventies; Magic, Riles, and Kareem in the eighties; and finally Shaq, Kobe, and Phil as the century turned over and things really began to get wild. For a season, they even had Dennis Rodman, who taught them all a thing or two about madness.

The Lakers stars had one thing in common: they were all from somewhere else, literally and figuratively. They all started small, had enough drive, ego, and/or talent to become huge, and had to deal with fame, fortune, and expectations. They all had flaws and took falls.

The bigger they got, the higher the expectations became—and their own were high enough. West, the last of the charter L.A. Lakers, whose drive and angst set their tone for 40 years, could never satisfy his, which finally drove him into retirement.

It was the best of times and the worst of times. Most Lakers stars went just a little out of their gourds somewhere along the line, and some went way out and were never the same.

As Cookie Kelly Johnson described her new hometown in her husband's autobiography, *My Life*:

When you're talking about Earvin and women, the first thing you have to understand is L.A. is a big part of the story. If Earvin Johnson had been drafted by Cleveland, Detroit, Milwaukee, or even New York, we would have been married a long time ago. But L.A. is totally different. It's the land of stars, the land of fantasy.

He was only 20 when he moved there and started meeting all those beautiful people. And many of them really are beautiful. In all my life, I've never seen so many stunning women out to catch somebody. The plastic surgery, the gorgeous clothes, you see it all. . . .

The Forum is like Fantasy Land. It's all so out in the open. . . . The first time I went, I watched as a girl in a bright orange dress, tight and low-cut with her boobs hanging out, strolled and strutted all the way around the court. It was incredible. Men actually wrote numbers on pieces of paper and held them up, like judges in the Olympics. She walked over to where Jack Nicholson was sitting. She bent over and said something to him and then walked back to the guy who brought her and gave him a hug. You could never see that anywhere else. . . .

Showtime wasn't just on the court. Part of the show was all those gorgeous women walking around the Forum on display. And the players noticed, definitely. They'd be at the free throw line and on the bench and they'd look, too. They'd start thinking, Well, I guess this is mine for the taking. And they were right.

It was never the way they dreamed it.

West's name was not only synonymous with *Lakers* but with *NBA*, with the league adopting his lean silhouette as its logo. Even hated rivals adored him. After the 1969 Finals, when he became the only member of a losing team ever named the MVP, John Havlicek told him, "I love you, Jerry." Bill Russell, hardly known for sentimentality, flew out for West's retirement ceremony, announcing to a packed Forum: "The greatest honor a man can have is the respect and friendship of his peers. You have that more than any man I know. . . . If I could have one wish granted, it would be that you would always be happy."

Nevertheless, anyone who thought it was neat to be West was barking up the wrong nervous system. He was not just driven but haunted, unable to enjoy success and blaming himself for failure. At the end, he was so strung out, he couldn't even attend the 2000 Finals as the team he had rebuilt returned to glory, rolling over the Indiana Pacers in no-sweat fashion.

Instead of going to the games, West jumped in his car and drove, getting the score periodically from friends on his cell phone. Once, he says, he got as far as Santa Barbara, a hundred miles away.

Chamberlain was a megalomaniac, if a fun one.

Abdul-Jabbar was his mirror opposite, withdrawn and uncomfortable with his fame.

Johnson was the boy next door when he got there. After several years of getting everything he wanted, he was like a kid in a candy store who wanted everything.

Riley went from abandoned journeyman to radio announcer to assistant coach to coach to superstar coach, bestselling author, and intimate of movie stars so fast, it made his head spin. He got such a case on himself, he lost touch with his players and had to be nudged toward the door before they mutinied for real. He went on to have a similarly stellar and tortured reign in New York, and one in Miami that wasn't as stellar but every bit as tortured.

Jackson was a mystic masquerading as a coach, or the other way around.

O'Neal had everything but seemed happiest when complaining and his number one complaint was his costar, Bryant.

Rodman, of course, had jumped the reservation long before his Laker incarnation, which lasted only 51 days. He often partied with Jerry Buss on Friday nights that ran into Saturday mornings, wobbled home, and called in sick for Saturday practices.

Buss, whose lightbulb went off while reading the "Playboy Philosophy," lived in the style of Hugh Hefner. Or maybe it was Hefner who lived in the style of Buss, it was hard to tell. Hef was more famous and the Playboy Mansion enjoyed a special place in the hearts of the rich and horny, but in L.A., nobody could challenge a Lakers game as the place to be and Buss as the host with the most.

Not that Buss and Hefner competed, since they were friends. Once the *Los Angeles Times*' Steve Springer, doing a profile on Buss, went up to the owner's suite during a game, to find Hef there with seven Playmates.

Just the stuff the players put in their own books or that got on police blotters suggests the Lakers were as kinky as they came, from Chamberlain's claim of sleeping with twenty thousand women (everyone made fun of Wilt, but friends say if he'd just made it ten thousand, he might have been right) to Johnson's confessions of sexual abandon in elevators and board rooms (although he left out the hot tub next to the dressing room where he went before talking to the press after games; no wonder he was always in a good mood).

Norm Nixon, Magic's running mate, claimed a streak akin to Joe DiMaggio's, although Nixon's wasn't for base hits. Then there was James Worthy, busted by two undercover vice cops in Houston for soliciting sex hours before a game.

Worthy was a small-town guy from Gastonia, North Carolina, the son of a deacon and the nicest, most down-to-earth, non-partying–looking man you ever saw. If he was living la vida loca, you could extrapolate from there.

Of course, they also had the most publicly celibate player who ever lived, A. C. Green. Ace was a virgin and proud of it, although he spent a lot of time on the road by himself.

■ ■ ■

Then, of course, there was Bryant.

His name got onto a police blotter, too, in 2003, shaking the latest dynasty to its foundations and, by the way, doing a number on his life.

He was already a herald of a new age, a general in the Children's Crusade that took the game over as players began leaving college early, or skipping it, becoming professionals as teens.

They were not only innocent, they were also rich. Lottery picks now came in with three-year, $5-million guaranteed contracts. Before they made their first pro shot, they got fat endorsement contracts that kept going up and up, through recession and brown-shoe revolution, until they crested at the *pièce de résistance*, LeBron James' $90-million deal with Nike.

Basketball players were now like boxers, surrounded by entourages of agents, endorsement partners, friends, and family, otherwise known as "my peeps." The team was merely one of their sources of revenue, rather than the be-all and end-all of their professional life.

Proving how tricky this proposition was, promising young teams began exploding all over: the Chris Webber Warriors; the Webber–Juwan Howard Bullets; the Jason Kidd–Jamal Mashburn–Jim Jackson Mavericks; the Kevin Garnett–Stephon Marbury Timberwolves.

They didn't merely fail, they blew themselves to smithereens, leaving smoking craters it would take years to dig out of.

The Shaq-Kobe Lakers were the first team built on such young superstars that didn't consume itself before realizing its potential, or at least some of it. Of course, they gave self-destruction a run for three tumultuous seasons before Jackson arrived to chill everyone out. Even with the Zenmeister, they couldn't put off their day of reckoning forever.

Jackson won titles in his first three seasons, laughing everything off as only he could while he and his surrogate children arranged themselves in every possible combination of alliance and feud (Shaq vs. Kobe, Shaq and Phil vs. Kobe, Shaq and Kobe vs. Phil).

Finally dethroned in 2003, they went out and got Karl Malone and Gary Payton, giving them what was supposed to be the greatest array of talent ever assembled. That was when Eagle County D.A. Mark Hurlbert announced Bryant would be charged with sexual assault, and the cheering turned into a hushed silence.

After that, it was psychodrama masquerading as basketball. As wild as it seemed going from West, Baylor, and Wilt to Magic, Kareem, and Riles, they were just warming up for Shaq, Kobe, and Phil.

It wasn't really Paradise, after all. If it seemed like the embodiment of the American Dream, everyone always had to wake up in the end.

That was L.A.

Chapter 1

BUMPKINS

There was really no attention at all. I'll never forget one night the
Laker players went to a Dodger game at the Coliseum. Wally Moon
was hitting his home runs over that little short fence in left field.
We were there en masse, and they introduced us, and it was, like,
no one even knows who in the heck we are.

—Jerry West

■ ■ ■

BEFORE THE BEVERLY HILLBILLIES, there were the Lakers, yokels from a little
farther north.

In the fall of 1960, Bob Short, a Minneapolis trucking magnate—
OK, a guy with a trucking company—moved his basketball team into
the Sports Arena. Actually, it was more like he dropped them off on
the doorstep. Short, himself, was going back home to his day job at the
depot.

The moment, if not the Lakers' arrival, seemed auspicious. The
Sports Arena, next door to the Coliseum, had just opened with the
Democratic Convention that nominated John F. Kennedy after Eugene
McCarthy's rousing speech in favor of Adlai Stevenson.

Of course, no one even knew the Lakers were coming when they
decided to build the arena. The prime tenants were the USC and UCLA
basketball teams. The Lakers were as welcome as any other business that
just drove up; but when there were conflicts, they'd have to go elsewhere, like Cal State–L.A. or the Shrine Auditorium.

The new arena was ultramodern with new gimmicks like a crowd
counter, a sign that flashed the attendance, going up every time someone

1

went through a turnstile. To the Lakers, it was palatial. As Chick Hearn noted later, "They didn't need a fifteen thousand–seat building for two hundred people." Their opener on October 24, 1960, a 111–101 loss to the Knicks, drew a crowd announced at 4,044.

There's an old story of Short calling GM Lou Mohs after each game and asking what that night's attendance was.

"Can't you double it for the press?" Short is supposed to have asked.

"Again?" Mohs is supposed to have answered.

■　■　■

This was still an innocent time in basketball. The college game was still primarily a regional phenomenon, big in the Northeast and rural hotbeds like North Carolina's Tobacco Road and Indiana. The NCAA Tournament wasn't nationally televised yet.

The pro game was a poor cousin to a regional phenomenon. Big-city columnists typically rose from the baseball beat and sneered at the NBA as a YMCA league. Outside its eight cities in the East and Midwest—down from the 11 that started the decade—the NBA was a rumor.

The Lakers had ruled this netherworld in the early fifties with 6'10" George Mikan. The league at that time bore as much resemblance to what would follow as the geeky Mikan, with his glasses held on by an elastic band, would bear to the sleek Wilt Chamberlain.

Years later, Mikan would have been termed a "project," but he happened in a big way, introducing the NBA, which until then was based on guys who cut and weaved, to notions like "domination," not to mention "ego" and "star."

The pro game that Mikan lumbered into in 1947 had a lane six feet across (it's now 16), crowned by the free throw circle called "the key." It would be widened even as Mikan played, in an attempt by the other owners to make it a little more fair (for them).

This established one of the standards for NBA superstars that would be seen over and over: they were so good, they changed the rules.

Players at that time didn't dunk—that was showing off—or dribble between their legs or cross over. They'd have to start using their left hands before they could start crossing over. Years later, Larry Bird, watching films of the great Bob Cousy, would joke, "He could have been in a farm accident and lost his left arm and still been able to play basketball."

Players had begun jumping off both legs to shoot, but it wasn't called a "jumper," much less a "J." It hadn't become everyone's all-purpose weapon yet, but was just part of a repertoire that might include the hook (the old rolling kind), the running one-hander, and the set shot, which could be one-handed or two-handed. Free throws were often shot underhanded.

The word "superstar" didn't exist but if it had, baseball would have had them all. The NFL was an afterthought, to say nothing of the NBA, although professional basketball took a huge step the night the Lakers arrived at (the old) Madison Square Garden to see themselves on the marquee as:

WED BASKETBALL
GEO MIKAN VS. KNICKS

Mikan's Lakers won five titles between 1949 and 1954, inspiring the first national interest. The Dumont Network paid the league $39,000 to televise a 13-game package, but dropped it after one season.

Mikan was an unlikely matinee idol. He had wavy hair, Coke-bottle glasses, and a gentle demeanor, having studied for the priesthood. When he first walked into the Laker dressing room in Sheboygan, Wisconsin, wearing a storm coat and a homburg, the team's star, Jim Pollard, said he was "the biggest-looking dumb character that I'd ever seen for a guy that was barely 23 years old."

Mikan was big, all right. He weighed 265 pounds and, once he got into the spirit of the thing, he was happy to use them all, leading with his off-elbow when he turned into the lane so that he usually wound up getting to where he intended to go.

An apt, if not a graceful student, he could hook with either hand and had a soft touch. His career free throw percentage was 77 percent, which would be impressive for a big man now.

This was no dinosaur. Mikan was the first giant NBA center to walk erect.

"He was one of a kind," says Cousy, describing Mikan's dominance:

I remember Ed Macauley [the 6'8", 220-pound Celtics center before Bill Russell], who had the unenviable task of guarding him when we played them. We'd walk through train stations and he'd walk by one of these huge columns. Macauley had a wry sense of humor and would bump into the column and say, "Oh, excuse me, George." . . .

He just had his way in those days. The Lakers ran no transition. It wasn't unlike what the Sixers did with Chamberlain after a while, the Lakers simply waited for Big George to get down the floor and then the offense started with him getting it. They'd run some splits and things, but basically, he would just overpower you.

He wasn't clumsy. I say awkward and plodding and I suppose that implies clumsy, but he wasn't clumsy. But he wasn't agile either. It was somewhere in between that. He simply was able to go where he chose to go.

Mikan also had the perquisite of stardom: ambition. He may not have been handsome or hip, but he wasn't bashful, either.

"They had a rookie from Tenneesse named Lefty Walther," recalls Pete Newell, the former Cal coach and Lakers GM:

The kid was a real good player.

They're playing a game, and Mikan is in the post, and the guy drives right by Mikan, goes in for a layup. Mikan's got his hand up for the ball, he's the top dog. He gets mad and yells at him.

The next time the kid gets the ball, he drives, and his man and Mikan's man go up to block the shot. The third time he drives, his guy, Mikan's man, and Mikan all go after the shot.

Mikan's thing was, "They're paying you $5,000 to play out there and they're paying me whatever to play in there so when I ask for the ball, darn it, give it to me."

The kid was gone in a few games.

Mikan was gone, too, by 1956, and the Lakers floundered. Elgin Baylor's arrival in 1958 revived them, but they didn't even rule their own little market, which cared more about U of M football and basketball. As if to confirm the local hierarchy, John Kundla, who coached all the Lakers champions, left them for a job at the University.

The Lakers played at the old Minneapolis Auditorium but sometimes had to use the Minneapolis Armory. (Adaptation being key, they took team photos of the players sitting on the National Guard's heavy equipment.) Once Baylor was late because he went to the Auditorium, only to find the game was at the Armory.

When Short sought approval to move to Los Angeles, his fellow owners could only think of the extra expense they'd incur to travel that far. A year after the Dodgers and Giants moved west and were received like kings, Short was voted down, 7–1.

Luckily for Short, Harlem Globetrotters owner Abe Saperstein, who was tired of propping up the NBA with his appearances, announced he was forming his own league with a team in Los Angeles. The NBA owners promptly took another vote. This one was 8–0 to let Short go, after he promised to pay the difference in their travel expenses.

Short offered one of his stars, Vern Mikkelsen, the coaching job, even throwing in a percentage of ownership. This wasn't that staggering since half the businessmen in Minneapolis already had pieces. Mikkelsen turned him down and spent the rest of his life listening to his kids ask him what their share would be worth now.

"I didn't think he'd get the thing to Sioux Falls, much less to L.A.," says Mikkelsen, "but he did."

■　■　■

Los Angeles was just beginning to come on line in sports as air travel improved. In this beautiful setting, with the ideal weather and stars of every other kind, the Rams and Dodgers were naturals, greeted as conquering heroes.

The Rams, coming from Cleveland in 1946, featured a high-scoring style and high-profile quarterback controversies (Norm Van Brocklin, Y. A. Tittle, Bob Waterfield). They were Hollywood-friendly, too, with a galaxy of hunks like Waterfield, who married Jane Russell, and Elroy "Crazylegs" Hirsch, who played himself in the movie, *Crazylegs, All American*.

As popular as they were, the Rams were eclipsed by the Dodgers' arrival in 1958. Owner Walter O'Malley got lease rights for his new stadium on a hilltop overlooking downtown, which required the removal of the people living on it, and was approved in a hotly contested referendum.

The Dodgers then arose from seventh place in 1958 to win the 1959 World Series before horn-blowing, sun-splashed crowds of ninety thousand in the Coliseum. O'Malley proceeded to build the beautiful Dodger Stadium, and the team won two more World Championships in 1963 and 1965, locking the city's heart up for decades.

The Lakers arrived without the negotiations, the referendum, the wrangling, or any fanfare at all.

By the end of their Minneapolis days, the Lakers had begun rebuilding around Baylor, but they had a long way to go. In the meantime, they were so dependent on Baylor, when he had to serve time with his Army reserve unit before his second season, they moved their training camp to Ft. Sam Houston, Texas, so he could work out with them when he was off duty.

"Baylor flew in the night before the opening game in Minneapolis," says teammate Rudy Larusso, a rookie that season. "He had practiced with us five or six days a month earlier. He suited up and got 52 opening night. . . . I had never seen anything like this in my life."

They were Baylor's team, but few teams Baylor was on wouldn't have revolved around him. He dominated everything on court and off, basketball, card games, conversations.

"Elgin was a motor-mouth," said teammate Hot Rod Hundley. "Elgin never shut up. Elgin knew everything—what size a 747 plane was, what horse Willie Shoemaker should be riding. He was an authority on everything."

This was a tender moment in American race relations. The NBA was integrated, but there was still an unofficial quota system, sometimes expressed as, "One at home, two on the road, and three if we're losing." Still, Baylor transcended all social barriers, race included, even on a team with only two other black players.

"It became obvious real quick," says LaRusso. "Elgin Baylor wasn't black—he was Elgin Baylor. He had the respect and admiration of the veteran players that were on the team at that time. It was clear to me, he was the guy."

Of the Lakers superstars, Baylor may have received the least recognition, and may have been the most comfortable in his own skin. It was more than just the basketball. When the Lakers, barnstorming through Charleston, West Virginia, in the 1958 exhibition season, were refused rooms at the Daniel Boone Hotel, Baylor refused to play, turning the standard insult to African Americans into a national story. The game went on, but the Lakers stayed with Baylor in Edna's Rest Home. Baylor got a letter from the mayor, demanding that he apologize, but the team and the league backed Baylor.

Baylor was in the forefront, too, when the players, led by Cousy and Tommy Heinsohn, threatened to boycott the 1964 All-Star Game in Boston unless they got a pension plan. When Short came pounding on the locker-room door demanding to see Baylor and Jerry West, Baylor came out and talked to him. Short went back the way he had come, the owners gave in, and labor peace lasted for decades while baseball and the NFL took strike after strike.

In 1960, Baylor was at his height, averaging 35 points and 19 rebounds in the first season in Los Angeles. At 6'5", 225, he played what today would be called power forward, but he was more like Magic Johnson—he transcended positions. Baylor brought the ball up against presses and challenged Bill Russell at every opportunity, freezing him with fakes—it was said he could hang in the air, which would now be called a hesitation move—and shooting over him.

He posted scoring averages of 25, 30, 35, 38, and 34 in his first five seasons before his knees began deteriorating under him. He began experiencing pain in his sixth season, long before techniques like arthroscopic surgery, or even applying ice for inflammation, had come around. Baylor got heat, which made his knees worse, tried the Mayo Clinic, and even underwent cobalt treatment. He had to be driven to home games because sitting behind the wheel was so painful. Finally in the 1965 playoffs, he went up to shoot, tore his left patellar tendon, and split the kneecap.

He played seven more seasons, but although his numbers were good, he wasn't what he'd been. This was before TV came around, so relatively few fans saw Baylor in his prime. But Chick Hearn used to say Baylor was the original Julius Erving. For some players, everything breaks right, but Baylor wasn't one of those.

■　■　■

There was one significant newcomer, a skinny 6'3" rookie from West Virginia named, providentially enough, Jerry West.

A high-jumping, All-American forward at West Virginia, he had just surprised everyone by moving to guard and becoming one of the stars of the 1960 Olympic team that would be remembered for years as the greatest ever put together, including more famous players like Oscar Robertson and Jerry Lucas.

West had been the second player taken in the draft, after the Cincinnati Royals claimed Robertson as a territorial choice. Jerry arrived in Los Angeles, fresh from his triumph in Rome. He could only stop over in West Virginia briefly before getting on another plane, flying to Los Angeles, and going straight to practice.

"The old Pepperdine [University], over at Inglewood," says West. "I remember it very well 'cause I had just gotten off an airplane at noon and didn't even go to the hotel and went to practice. . . .

"I was whipped. I was so tired. And to get there and have this smog, I wondered what the heck it was. I mean, it hurt so bad to run up and down the court. . . .

"Coming here was an incredible adjustment for me, personally. I probably wasn't as confident as most people I played with."

So, appropriately enough, began the saga of Jerry West, the least confident, most driven great player who ever lived.

"Even to this day," said his Olympic coach, Pete Newell, decades later, "I don't believe Jerry really believes he's as good as he is. He was that way when I had him in Rome and at the trials."

West wasn't simple. He had a raging insecurity, but he also knew he could play this game. He just went back and forth between the two extremes.

He wore his heart on his sleeve, pouring out his emotions to the press, which loved him, and to people he barely knew. However, when he wasn't miserable, tortured, or blaming himself for whatever had gone wrong, he was upbeat, nice as you please, and fun to be around.

John Black, who would become close to West as the team's publicist in the nineties, was once asked if West was the happiest or the most miserable man alive.

"Both," said Black.

Of course, in the fall of 1960, West was leaning more toward his insecure persona. Baylor, who took it upon himself to name all the rookies called him "Zeke from Cabin Creek" and "Tweety," because of his high-pitched voice. West didn't really like being called a hillbilly and, in later years, would pointedly note he wasn't from Cabin Creek but nearby Chelyan, West Virginia, which was even smaller but didn't rhyme with anything. At the time, he was just happy to be acknowledged by The Great Elgin.

As great as West would become, basketball would never just be a game for West but a life's struggle. Born in humble circumstances to a coal-mine electrician, his home was a shack, his first court packed dirt with a hoop nailed to a pole. The youngest child by nine years, he was painfully shy and loved basketball, he noted in his autobiography, because it was a game "a boy could play by himself."

The older he got, the less it seemed like "play" and the more it seemed like "life." He carved his pro career out of body and soul, and he didn't so much retire as collapse from physical and emotional exhaustion.

Every game would leave West spent and wondering how he could summon enough to do this again. By mid-career, the injuries began piling up. He specialized in breaking his nose, after which he'd wear a mask, or pulling hamstrings, so his thighs had to be wrapped like a mummy's, sometimes obliging him to get shot up like a horse, according to the medical practice of the day.

By then, he was wondering how long he could survive and how long he wanted to.

He was popular from the get-go and soon a star with his boy-next-door looks and manners—and it certainly didn't hurt that he was white, either. By the end, he was widely adored, constantly wondering how long he could keep doing this . . . as he would in his three-year coaching career and his 20 years in the front office.

His doubts made him all the more endearing. Everyone felt like his friend, but he felt as if he was all alone. Even looking back years later, he would wonder how he had done it.

"I had so many injuries," West says. "I was tired of having needles stuck in me. Tired of having my nose straightened. . . . Tired of getting stitches, tired of getting my teeth replaced. Seemed like everything that could happen to a player would happen to me. . . .

"I did it [took shots] because I wanted to play, and players wouldn't do that today, and I know that. And I wouldn't ask one of our players to do it because it's the wrong thing to do. . . .

"I could sit in the locker room before a game, I could hold my hand out and sweat would be just dripping off. I don't know if that's the way an athlete's supposed to be, but that's the way I was."

He was restless when he was at play, too, zooming around golf courses or finishing his meal while everyone else was on their salad, and he would soon get itchy for the real action at work.

He suffered defeats keenly and, it seemed, victories more keenly. He wasn't in Boston in 1985, when he was GM and the Lakers finally broke the Celtics curse, winning the title with a Game 6 victory, believing it bad luck to go on the road with the team. The next day, the *Los Angeles Times'* Steve Springer asked him if he was going to the parade, thinking he was only making chit-chat.

"'If I go to the parade,'" Springer remembers West answering in his high-pitched, rat-a-tat twang, "'they'll be cheering me. I'll be a big hero to them. And then if I make a pick in the draft they don't like, they'll boo me.'

"'You know something? I don't need their cheers and I don't need their boos.'"

That all lay ahead of West in 1960. If he and L.A. would one day seem like the same thing, now he was a long way from home for a small-town bumpkin who had only gone as far as the local U.

Although he played well, it would be midseason before Fred Schaus, his own college coach, began starting him, which was standard except for the greatest of players. Of course, one of those was Robertson, already overmatching all who came up against him en route to averaging the league's first recorded triple-double.

No one compared West to Robertson, whom everyone understood to be unique, like Baylor, Russell, or Chamberlain . . . except West, of course. For all his fears, West was used to rising to any challenge the game posed, and this coming-along-slowly stuff wasn't it. He later called it "the worst season of my basketball career."

Of course, he averaged 17.6 points, number two on the Lakers, so the thing wasn't a total write-off. He had a future and, nine months after getting dropped on the doorstep like orphans, so did they.

■   ■   ■

Of course, it was going to take a little while to get to it.

Their opener in the Sports Arena drew 4,044, or that's what they announced, anyway. With Short's reported inclination to multiply the actual count, it might really have been 3,033 or 2,022.

It was a downer. Even in those days, college teams, like West's Mountaineers, played before crowds of ten thousand. There were Indiana high schools that drew more than the Lakers that season.

"It seemed so strange, going from a rabid college situation to come here with little or no fanfare at all," West says. "The Laker organization tried to do everything within the community—appearances, anything that would get some attention in the news media. But we weren't very big news in the media, and I understand."

No one's games were on TV back then, but the Lakers' weren't even on radio. They didn't get a crowd of five thousand until January and listed their season average as 5,045.

They went 36–43, which wasn't the stuff of legend, but it did get them into the playoffs, since six of the eight teams went. Baseball had two leagues, and the NFL had two conferences—and the winners of each played for the title. By comparison, the NBA's playoff format was considered a joke that made the season all but meaningless, though it did bring in enough dollars to ensure the league's survival.

Nevertheless, the playoffs in mid-March brought new interest in a dead spot in the calendar, with the football season over, the euphoria over spring training getting old, and the start of the baseball season still weeks away.

The Lakers split the first four games against the powerful St. Louis Hawks, the 1957 champions, who had Bob Pettit and Cliff Hagan, drawing a crowd of fifteen thousand for the Game 4 victory in the Sports Arena. Excitement was running so high before the deciding Game 5 in St. Louis, Short bought radio time and hired a young announcer to broadcast it back to Los Angeles. That was Chick Hearn. The Lakers lost in overtime, but Chick became a Laker for life.

Hearn was 44, a native of Peoria, Illinois. In those days, when basketball was as obscure an art form as abstract painting, he knew the game, having refereed it in the Midwest. He was also a hot dog with as much ego, style, drive, and stamina as any player. His calls "from high above the western sideline" transported listeners into a little world of his own, with a cast of characters led by the young stars, Baylor and West, in a language all his own ("Dribble drive . . . slam dunk . . . fires from the popcorn machine . . . heartbrrrrreak!").

A spokesman so colorful, who fit so perfectly, was a tremendous advantage in Los Angeles, which liked the action narrated. When the Dodgers were playing the Chicago White Sox in the 1959 World Series, out-of-town writers were amazed to see hundreds, or thousands, of fans with transistor radios (the latest in mobile technology), listening to Vin Scully telling them about what they were seeing. This didn't exist anywhere else, although, of course, it would.

Scully became a star as great as any Dodger. The first man in the organization to make $1 million wasn't Sandy Koufax, Don Drysdale, Maury Wills, Steve Garvey, or Fernando Valenzuela. It was Vin.

Similarly, Lakers fans began bringing their transistors, too. Hearn had to make a nightly announcement—which he loved, of course— asking them to turn them down, lest the accumulated volume from all those little radios go over the air as feedback.

In short order, the Lakers trinity was Baylor, West, and Hearn. In the film, *Blume in Love*, director Paul Mazursky has George Segal driving his Porsche in the Hollywood Hills, listening to Hearn doing a Lakers game as a way of suggesting L.A. life in the sixties and seventies.

And off they went.

Stars began to be spotted in the Sports Arena, with Doris Day as the first celebrity regular, dazzling the players. In 1962–1963, the Lakers' third season, with attendance up to 8,396, they became the first NBA team to make $1 million at the gate.

Short made a $500,000 profit in their fourth season and cashed out, selling the team to Jack Kent Cooke, a dapper, hyper, former encyclopedia salesman from Canada for $5.175 million. Taking no chances, since he'd heard Cooke was tricky, Short made him come up with it in cash, which was physically loaded on a cart and rolled from one New York bank to another.

■　■　■

Thus began a new era, with a front man worthy of their stardom. Grandiose and visionary, Cooke was 180 degrees from Short, who had been far away with shallow pockets. Cooke was involved to a fault, the forerunner of the modern owner, with as much ego as any player and no compunctions about taking it out for a spin.

Cooke loved the sound of his voice and the things he said. There was little he didn't think he could master in 10 minutes—basketball only took him about five—and he didn't lose arguments with people who worked for him. He bore down on everyone under him, so that everyone feared him. This was hard on everyone under him and particularly those who already had enough to worry about, like West.

"He thought he knew," West once said. "He didn't know."

Cooke thought big. Canadian that he was, he wanted the Los Angeles franchise in the upcoming NHL expansion, but the Coliseum Commission, made up of political appointees who ran the Sports Arena, wouldn't give him the dates he needed. They were siding with their prime tenant, Rams owner Dan Reeves, who also wanted the hockey franchise.

"A guy name Ab England was the head of the commission," says Mel Durslag, then a *Los Angeles Herald-Examiner* columnist. "He was a Pontiac dealer from Hollywood. He was a nice guy, but it was just a political plum. They had no idea what they were doing.

"Jack was pestering them for this and that. They had a meeting, and I covered it. Ab says, very knowingly, 'Where's he going?'

"That's all you had to do with Jack."

(For the record, in Cooke's dramatic recreation of the meeting, one of the commissioners laughs in his face—"HAR, HAR, HAR"—and Cooke then tells his lawyers, "Let's depart from this den of inquity.")

Cooke was headed for Inglewood, a working-class town just south of the city, directly in the LAX glide path, which had an available plot of land adjacent to Hollywood Park. There he proposed to build his own $17-million arena.

Eighteen months later, on New Year's Eve, December 31, 1967, there it was, as if transplanted from Athens to Inglewood, the modern Forum, circular instead of rectangular, ringed by 80 unmistakably Doric-style columns, gleaming in its faux splendor. Cooke changed the team colors from the old blue and white to purple (which he insisted was "Forum Blue") and gold. The seats, foul lanes, and home uniforms became gold. Male ushers wore togas and women ushers short skirts. Cooke's new hockey team, the Kings, skated around in gold uniforms, which made them a running joke in the NHL.

Cooke also became the first to move the press table upstairs, unveiling the courtside seats, so movie stars sitting in them could not only see but be seen. Nevertheless, Doris Day didn't make the switch. Informed she would have to pay now, she decided to call it a career.

Cooke, whose pride knew no bounds, called it the "Fabulous Forum" and ordered all employees to make sure they did, too, although no one who wasn't on the payroll did. Hearn claimed he coined the name and told Cooke, who liked it and promised him a little extra in his pay envelope. Chick said that turned out to be a picture of Cooke.

OK, it may not have happened exactly like that, but it sure sounded right.

■　　■　　■

Then, of course, there was the actual basketball, which was high-level, exciting, but not quite good enough.

With Baylor missing almost half the team's second season in town on reserve duty, West broke out, averaging 30.8 points to move right in among the big guys, finishing fifth behind Chamberlain, Walt Bellamy, Pettit, and Robertson.

They made the 1962 Finals against the Celtics but lost in seven games after Lakers guard Frank Selvy, famed for scoring 100 points in a college game, missed an open baseline 15-footer that would have been the series-winner, as time ran out in Game 7.

They then lost in overtime. Later, Ray Felix, trying to cheer the guys up, is supposed to have told them, "We'll get them tomorrow." Hearn told that story for years afterward. Even if it didn't happen exactly that way, it sounded right.

The Lakers and Celtics would meet four more times in the Finals in the sixties in a rivalry that defined the modern NBA and the participants. The Celtics won all the meetings and became lords of all they surveyed. The Lakers were gilded foils, glamorous, admired, but in the end, second best.

This would have been tough in any case, but the Celtics had raised rubbing it in to an art form, with their ceaseless chatter about their tradition and their leprechaun and their parquet floor with the dead spots only they knew about.

Their advantage wasn't just intangible. All those titles made Red Auerbach a power within the league, which he brandished for all it was worth. There wasn't an opposing coach who once didn't complain publicly or privately that Auerbach had the referees intimidated, even, or especially, the great Mendy Rudolph. (If the refs weren't intimidated by Auerbach, it wasn't for any lack of trying. In the 1987 Finals, after Magic Johnson's "junior, junior skyhook" won the pivotal Game 5, Auerbach, who had been out of coaching for 20 years and was now 69, chased Earl Strom to the dressing room and pounded on the door.)

It was hard to tell if the Celtics were worse in defeat than in victory, with Auerbach insulting all comers. "Please, tell me some of those stories about Los Angeles being the basketball capital of the world," he crowed after beating the Lakers in 1963. Worst of all, in a gesture that would start a riot today, he fired up his victory cigars on the bench.

Of course, the entire league roundly hated the Celtics. If the Lakers' suffering seemed particularly acute, it was because they had West, who never hid his pain. (For his part, Baylor said he knew that people thought the Celtics were arrogant, but that stuff never bothered him. Though he really hated losing to them all the time.)

"It was like a slap in the face," West said. "Like, 'We're not gonna let you win, we don't care how well you play.' I always thought it was personal. I got to where I didn't think I was doing enough. I was searching everything that I had ever done in my life for a reason, looking for an answer why. . . . It almost controlled my life."

For all their glamour, it could be hell to be a Laker, especially that Laker.

Nevertheless, they were now a Western power with a palace of their own, befitting stars of their new magnitude. If they weren't yet the toast of the town, at least people knew they were in town.

Chapter 2

ENTER GOLIATH

Some things about Wilt you never forgot. He was such an
awesome physical specimen. To be down there and to look up at him
when he's towering up way over you waiting to dunk, that was a
terrifying picture. . . . When I played him, I kept this foremost in
my mind. Above all, don't make him mad.

—Elvin Hayes, *Houston Chronicle*, 1985

■ ■ ■

TO A FRANCHISE THAT ALREADY seemed maxed out on stardom, and to an
owner who already seemed maxed out in grandiloquence, came Wilton
Norman Chamberlain.

This was an even bigger landmark in franchise history than the
opening of the Forum, at least to everyone but Jack Kent Cooke. An NBA
superstar who was unhappy—and which of them wasn't sooner or
later?—was demanding to be traded to the Lakers, lest he decide to do
something else with his life, or fail to perform up to his standards since
his heart was breaking.

It was a new Lakers day. In moves that would similarly shake the
league, this would happen to them again with Kareem Abdul-Jabbar,
who would also demand a trade, and Shaquille O'Neal, who would
come as a free agent. The bottom line was that the Lakers were suddenly
the NBA destination for superstar centers, which would make them a
force to reckon from that point on.

Of course, it was the Celtics center, Bill Russell—who had overmatched Lakers journeymen like Ray Felix, Jim Krebs, and Darrall
Imhoff all those years—that had been the difference between the two

teams. The Lakers were like the Celtics before Russell arrived in 1956, a good team that never won anything.

At a lithe 6'9", 230, Russell was like the 7'1", 275-pound Chamberlain's little brother, although Russell dominated all other comers and was smart and competitive enough to contain the mighty Chamberlain to a degree. Since the Celtics were usually better than Chamberlain's teams and almost always more cohesive, that was just good enough.

"I think he realized there was no way he [Russell] could have stopped Wilt if he had been fully intent on making it a two-man game," said Elvin Hayes, a great center in his own right. "No one who ever put on a uniform could have done it."

An angry Chamberlain was a sight few forgot, but for better or worse, few saw. He seemed almost gentle on the floor, as if he didn't want to hurt the little fellows around him—except at those rare times, as in 1966 in Boston when 76ers co-owner Ike Richman, whom he was close to, died at courtside.

"The night Ike died at courtside, Dolph [Schayes, the 76ers coach] feels this heavy load on his right arm," says George Kiseda, the *Philadelphia Bulletin* beat writer. "Ike had just had a heart attack. The 76ers had never won in Boston, and Ike Richman used to go up there like a pilgrimage. Every time, he'd say, 'This is the time we do it.' And it never worked.

"At halftime, they got a call from Ike Richman's wife, saying that he's dead, telling them to beat those SOBs.

"In the last three quarters, it was a man against a boy. One time he and Russell got their hands on the ball simultaneously. And Wilt is taking it up. And you can see that Russell had better let go of that ball or he's going to go through the basket. Wilt was just going to take him and everything else and dunk the ball. Russell let go.

"When I look back on the Wilt-Russell games, I divide them into three parts. A third of the time, Wilt outplayed Russell. A third of the time, Russell outplayed Wilt. And there was the other third of the time when Wilt dominated Russell."

The colossus was now coming west, to play with Jerry West and Elgin Baylor in what was deemed the greatest array of talent ever assembled on one team.

Not that things ever went the way everyone thought they were going to for them.

■ ■ ■

In 1968, Chamberlain was at a crossroads. Richman, the co-owner he was close to, had died. Alex Hannum, the coach he liked, had just left. Chamberlain was considering whether to try to be a player-coach, like Russell, or assert his claim to a piece of the team that he insisted Richman promised him, when he went to the West Coast on vacation and decided he wanted to be there year-round.

"Wilt would come by and ask how it was going," says Jack Ramsay, then the 76ers' GM. "I had talked to Frank McGuire, who was at South Carolina. I talked to others but couldn't find anyone I thought was capable of doing the job. And then Wilt said, 'How about if I became player-coach and you'd help me with the Xs and Os?'

"I thought it could work. Koz [owner Irv Kosloff] kind of nodded and said we'd get back to Wilt, who was heading for the West Coast. He got back, came to a meeting, and said he'd decided he was never going to play in Philadelphia again. Said he was going to play in Los Angeles or jump to the ABA team in L.A. So we traded him to the Lakers."

The 76ers took what they could get: Imhoff, Archie Clark, and Jerry Chambers. The Lakers got Chamberlain, giving them three of the game's greatest stars.

Of course, there were lots of stars but only one Chamberlain, a Paul Bunyan character who inspired so many tall tales, it was hard to believe them. Nevertheless, most of them were true, or close.

He may have been the first superstar, a word born in the sixties when a new class of celebrity athletes emerged who transcended their sports, like Muhammad Ali and Joe Namath. Chamberlain was the first, entering the NBA in 1959 after four years of unprecedented coverage of his career with Kansas, the Globetrotters, and even Philadelphia's Overbrook High School.

If Russell was years ahead of his time, Chamberlain was years ahead of Russell. Wilt's full height was 7'1⅟₁₆" (although friend and foe alike swore he was taller). He weighed 275 as a rookie, moved like a guard, and could outrun most of his teammates in his early years. He won a Big Eight high-jump title at Kansas.

He had long arms—"the longest arms of anyone who ever played the game," Baylor says. With his quickness and jumping ability, he was the greatest rebounder the game would ever see and an incredible shot-blocker when he wanted to be one.

He was like an entire new species. When Chamberlain arrived in 1959, the NBA only had two players over 6'10": 7'0" Walter Dukes and 6'11" Ray Felix, both willowy 220-pounders. Chamberlain had skinny legs but a scary upper body, having gotten into weight training decades ahead of the craze. An enthusiast, he sometimes took two 25-pound dumbbells on the road in his shoulder bag. This was no problem for him but hell on bellhops.

If he's remembered more for foibles and failures than heroic deeds, it seems inevitable. He was set up.

He was the first basketball player to get the Big Treatment, with the grown-ups coming around to see the new wonder before he got out of high school, a dizzying experience that didn't make it easier to keep his perspective. Russell entered the NBA as a player, if a celebrated one, but Chamberlain entered as a savior.

The Big Treatment included pampering and plenty of it. When Chamberlain was a junior at Overbrook, NBA publicist Haskell Cohen picked him up in Philadelphia and personally drove him up to Kutsher's in the Catskills for the summer. Chamberlain got a soft job, was coached by Red Auerbach, and dominated college players in pick-up games. According to boyhood friend Vince Miller, he came home with a wad of cash, driving a used Oldsmobile.

In Chamberlain's senior year at Overbrook, Philadelphia Warriors owner Eddie Gottlieb pushed through the territorial draft rule to make sure the hometown team got him, no matter where he went to college. That was the first rules change, and more were forthcoming.

"We had seen tall guys before," says Bob Cousy, laughing. "There was a 7'6" guy in Syracuse, Swede Halbrook. But we had never quite seen anyone like Wilt who was so huge and so big and so agile for that size. I don't know what Wilt measured . . . but I think he was certainly 7'4"."

Thirty years after Chamberlain retired, the NBA record book still reads like his résumé. Of the top 20 scoring games, he had 15. Of the top 15 rebounding games, he had 10.

"Bill Russell interviewed me for TNT," says longtime 76ers statistician Harvey Pollack. "He said 'Harvey, you've been in the NBA all these years, is there one game that stands out in your memory?'

"I said, 'Yeah, the night that Wilt got the 55 rebounds. I think you were there, weren't you?'"

Then there was Chamberlain's mouth, which never stopped.

"He was a guy who dominated every arena he was in," says Kiseda. "By arena, I mean room, restaurant, conversation, dressing room, hall lobby."

Infinitely competitive, at least man-to-man, Chamberlain thought he could do anything, or at least do it better than you could. At Kansas, he once challenged Wes Santee, a world-class miler, to race 440 yards, figuring distance guys weren't really that fast. (In addition to everything else, Chamberlain always had an angle.) Santee beat him by 30 yards.

Being Chamberlain, if he thought it, he said it, for better and often worse. Once, after a monumental outpouring of complaints to *Sports Illustrated*, the magazine put him on the cover with the headline, "My Life in a Bush League." When everyone got upset at him, Chamberlain protested he never said that, after which the *Bulletin*'s Kiseda counted up more than 30 "bush" references in the piece.

This was nothing compared to Chamberlain's claim to have slept with twenty thousand women, which made him a laughingstock. Of course, he may have merely lost count. Pollack, the Sixers statistician, remembers the night the 76ers won the 1967 title in San Francisco, when women queued up outside Chamberlain's room in the Jack Tar Hotel.

"There was a bevy of women of all sizes, shapes, and ages lined up in the hallway," says Pollack. "I happened to be in the room next to Wilt, and they took turns going into the room. The line lasted all night long, far as I know, 'til I went to sleep, and that was deep in the morning."

Being awesome posed problems in basketball, as in life. Russell's game empowered teammates, who scored the points while he watched their backs on defense. Chamberlain's game awed teammates, who waited on him to do everything.

Russell, who looked normal size next to Chamberlain, became the protagonist. Chamberlain, the goateed giant with the big mouth and the impossible expectations, became the bad guy. As Chamberlain put it, "Nobody loves Goliath," and it was God's Own Truth.

■ ■ ■

Of course, the Lakers didn't need to be dominated.

Chamberlain was joining a team with two stars who were there first, not that that seemed to pose a problem. The three had been friendly before and would be after. Unfortunately, there were problems during. It was a perfect triangle. Each thought that despite the strains he felt with the other two, the real problem was between the other two.

In *Wilt*, Chamberlain described problems with West but said he and Jerry remained friends. But Chamberlain took off on Baylor, describing hurtful jokes Baylor made that "fanned the fires of bitterness between us" and a struggle between commanding personalities to see whose team this was. For his part, Baylor remembered one problem, when he took coach Butch van Breda Kolff's side against Chamberlain, but insisted he was never upset at him and they remained friends.

They didn't fit smoothly on the floor, either. Chamberlain liked the low post, clogging the lane Baylor once drove into. Elgin's numbers were fine (he averaged 24 points and 10 rebounds in 1968–1969), but at 34, his knees were gone, and he was a statue on defense. Chamberlain was 32, West 30, and all had heavy mileage on them.

"If we'd had Wilt sooner, earlier in my career, in my prime, don't you think we'd have won many championships?" said Baylor years later. "No doubt, we'd probably have won the championship every year. When Wilt did come, I was certainly past my prime with injuries and everything else. Jerry was probably in the twilight of his years and we were only together a couple of years."

However, age and chemistry paled next to the problem between Chamberlain and Butch van Breda Kolff, who had taken the Lakers to the 1968 Finals in his first season and liked things the way they were, with Imhoff at the high post in his Princeton offense and no prima donnas. A loud, salty, engaging ex-Marine, van Breda Kolff was used to bellowing at college players. He and Chamberlain took one look at each other and went to their respective corners.

The coach's comments would be reported in the morning *Times*, which players began to call "Butch's paper." Chamberlain would reply through Doug Krikorian of the afternoon *Herald-Examiner*, which the players called "Wilt's paper."

Their season, ballyhooed as none had ever been, turned into a months-long prescription for disaster, followed by the disaster itself, their fifth loss of the sixties to the Celtics in the Finals.

The Celtics looked like they were out on their feet by then. Russell was 35, in what would be his final season. They had dropped all the way to number four in the seven-team East.

Meanwhile, the Lakers managed a 55–27 record, best in the West but only tied for second-best in the league, amid rampant reports of trouble. The old foes still managed to make it back into each others' arms in the Finals, where they were tied 3–3 after six games. The teams had played two previous Game 7s in Boston Garden, but this one would be on the Lakers' floor.

Cooke, too full of himself and the moment to worry about contingencies, put balloons up in the Forum ceiling for the postgame celebration, which was planned in detail, with the USC Band set to march out and play "Happy Days Are Here Again."

It said so on the schedule that the Celtics got hold of before the game and read to each other, while grinding their teeth. This wasn't just pride going before a fall, this was megalomania preceding the greatest pratfall the game would ever see.

The Celtics ran up a 17-point lead. The Lakers cut it to eight when Chamberlain the Indestructible, who one season averaged more than 48 minutes a game, banged his knee and took himself out. Chamberlain got up to go back in a few minutes later, but van Breda Kolff snarled at him to sit back down and went the rest of the way with Mel Counts.

The Celtics won, 108–106. Make that 0–5.

Russell, about to announce his retirement, made a speaking appearance at the University of Wisconsin and, in the course of his remarks, said Chamberlain shouldn't have come out if his leg had fallen off. Whether Russell intended it or not, the story went national. He and Chamberlain had been friends through their careers, spurning their gladiator roles, picking each other up at airports and going out to dinner, but this tore it. They wouldn't talk for 20 years.

"We weren't as good," West would say, still suffering his Celtics scars years later. "Luck plays such an element in sports, and people don't want to say that. And I'm not saying the Celtics were lucky to beat us because that's not the case. They were better and they should have won. But we had a couple of opportunities when a good bounce or a basket at the right time, maybe we could have changed the course of history a little bit.

"It's something that probably even today has left some of the scars that I think all of us have. I think today they measure players by the number of championships they've won. I'm not real fond of the fact that we only won one when we played."

They hadn't even won the one at that point, so you can imagine how West felt that night. Every dog had his day, but they were still looking for theirs. Actually, that day was coming. It just wasn't coming right away, and by the time it finally got there, the Lakers would be as surprised as anyone.

■　■　■

Just in case they thought nothing else could go wrong . . . Van Breda Kolff resigned, as everyone knew he had to, taking a coaching job in Detroit. The Pistons were doormats and the winters were miserable, but on the bright side, Chamberlain was two thousand miles away.

The new Lakers coach was mild-mannered, straightlaced Joe Mullaney, a former college coach who announced in his first press conference, "Wilt is special." This pleased Chamberlain, but the unthinkable happened. The man who had never had a major injury suddenly blew out a knee early in the season and underwent reconstructive surgery, the only kind they had back then.

Weightlifter that he was, Chamberlain threw himself into his rehab regimen with more ferocity than he put into some seasons. It was considered a surprise when he made it back for the playoffs, but he was Wilt, he did those things.

The Lakers went 46–36, finishing second in the West to Atlanta, but with Chamberlain back, they swept the Hawks in the playoffs. This set up one of the greatest Finals in NBA history, pitting them against the Knicks, who had risen from joke status and now had Gotham at their feet.

The series lived up to the hype. West tied Game 3 with his famous 63-footer from the other side of half-court as time ran out to tie it, shocking everyone and especially the Knicks' Dave DeBusschere, who was standing under the basket when the ball slammed through and fell on his rear end, as if shot. The Knicks then got back up and won in overtime.

In the storied Game 5 in New York, Knick center Willis Reed tore a hip flexor in the first quarter, finishing him for the night. The devastated Knicks fell 13 points behind, then pulled themselves together to win with a furious second-half rally before a berserk Madison Square Garden crowd.

Back in the Forum for Game 6 with Reed out, the Lakers tied it, 3–3, as Chamberlain went for 45 points and 27 rebounds in one of his old shows of strength.

No one knew if Reed would play in Game 7 until he limped out, 10 minutes after his team had hit the floor, to a thunderous ovation, having needed the extra time to have his hip shot up. It was so dramatic, the Lakers even stopped warming up to watch.

Reed could barely walk, let alone run, but he proceeded to knock down his first two outside shots over Chamberlain. Inspired, the Knicks blew the hollow-eyed Lakers off the floor, leading by 27 at the half. Even West, Mr. Clutch, himself, was overmatched for a night by Walt Frazier, who kept stealing the ball from him en route to 36 points and 19 assists.

That was the night Howard Cosell told Reed he represented "the best, I think, the human spirit has to offer." The Lakers slouched off, all but unnoticed in the merry-making. It didn't even matter if the Celtics were dead. They were still just the foil.

■　■　■

Nor did prospects seem to be improving. The next season, Baylor suffered another knee injury and played only two games. West missed 13. They were old. That stuff happens to old teams.

There was a new kid on the block, too, the Milwaukee Bucks, with a center as great as Chamberlain, Kareem Abdul-Jabbar, who was 10 years younger with two good knees. The Lakers finished 18 games behind Milwaukee, met them in the West finals, and were dispatched 4–1, after which Mullaney was dispatched by Cooke.

The tide had gone out, it seemed. The new coach was earnest, intense Bill Sharman, who had won a title with the Utah Stars, whoever they were, in the American Basketball Association, whatever it was.

Making it all the more awkward, Sharman was a former Celtic, who planned to take this aging, creaky, half-court, non-defending team and turn it into the Celtics. He wanted Chamberlain to forget about offense and concentrate on the defensive end, like Russell. Everyone else was going to apply pressure on defense and chase the opposing players into Russ—, er, Wilt, as if they were John Havlicek, Sam Jones, K. C. Jones, and Satch Sanders.

Sharman, a former USC great, was unusual, to say the least. He wasn't big (6'1", 190 in his playing days) or fast, but he was a fine athlete, making the Brooklyn Dodgers roster before deciding to concentrate on basketball.

He was nice as could be off the floor but a maniac on it, known for flipping out at a moment's notice. An obsessive worker, he led the league in free throw shooting six times in seven years and finished second the other time. If it could be practiced, he would master it.

Normal practices weren't enough. He invented a new one the day of the game, called a "shootaround," in which everyone would go over to the arena around noon to loosen up, take a few shots, and get the feel of the place.

This was a problem for Chamberlain, an insomniac who was used to sleeping in. There's a story about Sharman sending someone to get Chamberlain, who rumbles, "Tell Mr. Sharman I'm only going to the arena once and he can pick which time."

Sharman was smart enough to approach Chamberlain carefully, taking him to lunch at an expensive restaurant to suggest the changes he had in mind. Chamberlain had been asked to concentrate on defense before but that wasn't how he saw himself. He liked measurable exploits, and they didn't even record blocked shots at that time. (If they had, the history of the league might have been different. Out of curiosity, Pollack, the 76ers stat freak, used to detail a helper to count Chamberlain's blocks and remembers the total running as high as 25.) Nevertheless, Chamberlain could be reasonable, when approached humbly, and told Sharman he'd give it a try.

Chamberlain was in a good place. They hadn't won a title, but he'd been through that all his career, except for one season with the 76ers. He loved the West Coast and began building a home worthy of a legend like himself. It sat on three-acre site atop the Santa Monica Mountains, with a 360-degree view of the West Side, the ocean, and, looking north, the San Fernando Valley. It was 8,300 square feet, built with five freight-car loads of redwood, Chamberlain noted proudly in *Wilt,* and 200 tons of Bouquet Canyon stone. There was a 55-foot high fireplace, in case he wanted to barbecue a moose. His bedspread and the rug in the firepit area came from the fur of seventeen thousand wolves, an entire year's bounty. When conservationists protested, Chamberlain replied *he* hadn't ordered the wolves killed, he'd just bought the pelts. It was excessive and mythic. It was him.

Back at the office, things were a little slow. The Lakers were no longer even preseason favorites in the West. Baylor was attempting his third major comeback at 37. The only new Laker who would play 15 minutes a game was a reserve guard named Flynn Robinson.

Nevertheless, they bought into Sharman's program, winning six of their first nine games, which is where they were on October 31, after a 109–105 loss to the San Francisco Warriors.

Sharman wanted more speed. He told Baylor, who'd been having trouble keeping up, he was going to bench him in favor of a second-year forward named Jim McMillian. Baylor went home and decided to retire. It was announced before the next game on November 5. That night the Lakers started their 33-game winning streak, almost doubling the record of 18 the Knicks had set two seasons before.

Suddenly, the parts fit perfectly. Chamberlain led the league in rebounding with forward Happy Hairston at number 11. West became the point guard, freeing the smaller Gail Goodrich, aka "Stumpy," to focus on what he did best, scoring, which he did to the tune of a team-high 25.9 points a game. West was at 25.8, McMillian at 18.8. They scored 121 points a game, with an average victory margin of 12.

Chamberlain would later say his best team was not this one, which set a record of 69 victories, but the 76ers team of 1966–1967, with Hal Greer, Billy Cunningham, Chet Walker, and Luke Jackson. This one was sheer synergy, sweeping the Bulls, 4–0; dumping the 63-win Bucks, 4–2, and overmatching the Knicks in the Finals, 4–1.

It was finally safe to cue that USC band, although a chastened Cooke opted for a routine celebration. There's a picture of West running off the floor, arm in arm with his buddy, reserve guard Pat Riley. Riley looks jubilant, West just intent on getting off the floor.

"When we won the championship, he came into the locker room, had a sip of champagne, shook a few hands, and left," Riley later wrote of West in his book, *Show Time.*

West was never sure how he was supposed to feel in those moments. It was a sentiment that wasn't uncommon among the demon competitors. The thing they liked best about winning, they'd say, was that it wasn't losing.

At least his Lakers weren't losers any more, and had a trophy to prove it.

■　■　■

Greatness, on the other hand, was out of the question.

The standard had been established by the Celtics, who had won 11 titles in 13 seasons, including eight in a row, between the first one in 1956 and the last one in 1969 in you-know-who's arena.

This Lakers title had been a result of the whole exceeding the sum of the parts, but they weren't the Celtics, whose roles were as defined as if Auerbach had brought them down from Mt. Sinai on tablets.

This was Ego City, starting with Cooke, who infuriated the players by giving them $1,500 bonuses, $3,500 less than the year before. The team banquet was an oddly somber affair. Team chemistry depended on Chamberlain, who had mixed feelings about team competition, often lamenting the win-or-else mentality, which may have been an apologia for all his defeats at Russell's hand.

Whether out of pique or disdain, Chamberlain could balk at inconvenient times. His powerhouse 76ers team that won the 1967 title hadn't repeated, either. The next spring, they blew a 3–1 lead over the Celtics and lost Game 7 in Philadelphia, with Wilt taking only two shots in the second half, both tip-ins.

Chamberlain was now 36. West was 34. Hairston, who was 30, would miss most of the season, forcing them to bring in 34-year-old Bill Bridges. In an early-season trip, they were bombed in Boston and New York. Pointing out that West had played poorly in those games, Chamberlain noted in his autobiography, "The only man who could have set the record straight was the Lakers announcer, Chick Hearn. Chick is an extremely knowledgeable basketball man . . . but he has one slight problem: He thinks Jerry West is Jesus Christ."

Somehow they won 60 games, tying the Bucks for first place in the West and made it back to the Finals for another matchup with the Knicks.

This would be no classic. The Knicks were getting old themselves, having been reconfigured since 1970. A declining Reed was now splitting time with Jerry Lucas, who frustrated opposing centers by lurking outside, where they wouldn't follow, and making 20-footers, known as "Lucas layups." In an experiment everyone said wouldn't work but did, Frazier shared the backcourt with his old rival, the old one-on-one legend, Earl Monroe.

The Lakers won the first game, but the Knicks took the next four, with West trying to play with two bad hamstrings and Lucas neutralizing Chamberlain. After that, it was time for farewells. In September, shortly before camp, Chamberlain retired to coach the ABA's San Diego Conquistadores as the last act in his long-running series of contract fights with Cooke. In a tip-off to his mood, he had just finished *Wilt,* in which he would rip just about everyone he had ever met, except his mom and dad.

West, who had also been talking about retiring for years, finally did it, leaving a season later, after the Bucks eliminated them in the first-round, 4–1.

"We had just gotten beat by the Milwaukee Bucks," Riley wrote in his book. "Jerry had a muscle tear that would never get better. . . . Jerry was soaping up in the shower when he turned to me and said, 'This is my last game.'"

The West-Baylor-Chamberlain era was over. The Lakers had had their moments, just not very many of them.

■   ■   ■

Appearances notwithstanding, there would be no seamless transition.

The next superstar eyeing them was none other than the game's greatest player, Abdul-Jabbar, a former UCLA Bruin, himself. He had been Lew Alcindor then, but had since become a Muslim, although his conversion was a source of turmoil. When he was torn between two women, his spiritual advisor, Hamaas Abdul Khaalis, chose for him, selecting the more devout candidate, whom Abdul-Jabbar subsequently divorced, rather than the one he said he loved. Abdul-Jabbar's parents were turned away from the wedding. Abdul-Jabbar donated a house in Washington, D.C., to Khaalis and his followers. There, Black Muslims, who saw them as rivals, staged a massacre that took the lives of seven people, five of them children. The threat extended to Abdul-Jabbar, who was given police protection.

Abdul-Jabbar played through it, taking the Bucks to a title in 1971 and back to the Finals in 1974, when he hit a dramatic sky hook at the end of the second overtime of Game 6, with the fans crowding the court in Boston Garden, ready to stream out to celebrate a Celtics title.

But the Celtics double-teamed him and won Game 7. Oscar Robertson the next season retired, and Abdul-Jabbar missed six weeks after breaking his hand.

The Bucks finished last, and Abdul-Jabbar told management to trade him to New York or Los Angeles, figuring it would be New York. However, the Lakers had more to offer, and on June 16, 1975, the deal went down: Abdul-Jabbar and a backup center named Walt Wesley for Elmore Smith, Dave Meyers, Junior Bridgman, and Brian Winters.

Cooke proudly paraded Abdul-Jabbar out from behind a curtain in the empty Forum, introducing him at the press conference, but all they had beyond their new center were some leftovers. Abdul-Jabbar won his fourth MVP that season, but they didn't even make the playoffs.

The new era was off to a start as dour as its new star. Whatever his failings, Chamberlain had been braggadocio and show business. Abdul-Jabbar was his polar opposite. His interests were intellectual as opposed to material, and he was as introverted as Chamberlain was social.

Chamberlain had once taken the teenage Alcindor under his wing, showing him the bright lights downtown, letting him hang at his West

Side apartment. In those days, the man could still see a kindred body and spirit in the boy, and the boy, flattered by the attention, idolized the man.

However, those days were long past. Abdul-Jabbar had grown up, become a Muslim, hated Chamberlain's pro-Nixon political dabbling, and formally denounced Chamberlain's views on sex after *Wilt* came out.

Chamberlain loved attention. Abdul-Jabbar hated it, especially the part about the press. Wilt enjoyed the exchange, bantering and challenging writers, even letting them have his home number. In Abdul-Jabbar's book, *Giant Steps*, published in 1983 when he was 36 and supposedly mellowed, he conceded there were "some good sportswriters, many more now than when I came into the league," but went on to note:

> For the most part, they were wheedlers, little guys who derived great satisfaction from tweaking the tiger's whiskers or pulling the tiger's tail. You could spot them a mile away, the striped-shirt-and-checked-pants set. I'm sure I intimidated them, as big and quiet and black as I was, and they used whatever power they could muster to make some impression on me or their readers by continually dwelling on the negative.
>
> Sitting by my locker after a game, I started to feel as if a swarm of flies was buzzing around my head. . . . I wanted to get rid of them but they were an occupational hazard. . . . What I did was give them as little as possible. I tried to keep my replies minimal, direct, removed.

If Abdul-Jabbar shunned the press, he was hurt when it shunned him back. In *Giant Steps*, he noted his disappointment at not winning the MVP in his second All-Star Game in 1971 and watching all the writers head for all the other players. That had been 12 years before Abdul-Jabbar's book came out. As he also wrote, "Slights stay with me."

Intelligent and unafraid to speak his mind, Abdul-Jabbar was actually a great interview if he was in the mood, but that mood came over him rarely. The dour impression was exaggerated on the floor by his large goggles and stoic expression. Getting beaten on by lesser centers was another condition of employment he hated and he exploded more than once, as when he cold-cocked Milwaukee's Kent Benson and broke his own hand punching a basket standard in Boston after getting scratched across the eye.

Abdul-Jabbar was a great artist, but fate had set it up so that he was going to be one of the lonely ones who were going to suffer for their craft. In other words, this wasn't going to be easy.

■ ■ ■

West was so miserable in retirement, he agreed to try coaching, which he was sure he'd hate, even if it meant going back to work for Cooke, whom he wasn't crazy about, either.

On the other hand, West had to do *something*.

"You hear about movie stars who have done it all and just go fruit-cake?" West's friend, Gary Colson, then coaching at Pepperdine, told *Sports Illustrated*'s Rich Hoffer. "Here you go. I had this fear, you know, a Marilyn Monroe type of thing. What else was there? What would he do now that the cheering had stopped? He was searching for something. It was a depression that all great actors and athletes go through."

As ill-suited as West thought he was for coaching, and as right as he turned out to be, he showed promise, taking the Lakers from 40–42 to 53–29 in his first season.

That was as good as it got. His second season started with Abdul-Jabbar breaking his hand punching Benson in the opener. It was further disrupted by the punch Kermit Alexander threw that caved in Rudy Tomjanovich's face as the Lakers dropped to 45–37. West's third season had fewer catastrophes, but the bottom line was only 47–35.

Once the writers had protected West, but now when he confided his frustrations with Abdul-Jabbar's cruise-control style, it carried the weight of management and leaked into the papers. Abdul-Jabbar, who could figure out what was going on, eyed West coolly, and West got upset at the writers. For the high-strung West, who had enough problems when he was coddled, this was heavy going.

There were new kids on the block, more physical outfits like the Portland Trail Blazers, who won the 1977 title, and the Seattle SuperSonics, who won in 1979. None of West's three teams got past the second round, and he fled in 1979, after the Sonics stepped on his team 4–1.

That summer, Cooke, who'd holed up in Las Vegas while pursuing a divorce action, got hit with a $41-million settlement and had to cash out. He sold the Lakers, the Kings, and the Forum to a young developer named Jerry Buss, for $57.5 million.

Yet another new day dawned. Happily, it wasn't going to be anything like the others.

Chapter 3

AT LONG LAST, SHOWTIME

[Pat Riley told a group of friends], "I'm not saying I'm a good coach, but if I am, there are two words that explain it. What do you think they are?" My wife said *drive* and *fairness*. Everyone came up with some. And it finally came to Riles, and he said, "*Magic* and *Johnson.*"

—Riley's friend Altie Cohen

■ ■ ■

FAIRY TALES CAN COME TRUE, it happened to them.

The team Jerry Buss bought in 1979 had finished the seventies in a funk and a cloud of dust, having been passed by rising young powers in Portland and Seattle. The Lakers franchise was healthy and their tradition glitzy, but their titles were few.

That season, they arose to rule the West and become a dynasty that would redeem their pain and exact revenge on their archenemies. It was Showtime, the dazzling era that lasted most of the eighties, when the greatness met the glitter. It was Jack Kent Cooke's vision, as executed by the brand-new owner, Jerry Buss, in his own Hefner-inspired interpretation.

It was magic, literally and figuratively, with a new cast of stars even brighter than the ones who'd gone before, and the brightest of all was Magic Johnson.

Earvin Johnson Jr. had just turned 20 when he arrived after his sophomore year at Michigan State, arriving as a child who was ready to lead them. His mere presence seemed to herald a new era for all the grownups around him. Joy bubbled out of him, like a geyser from a fountain on a sunny day. Confidence gushed from him. His game flowed from his personality, which seemed to flow from the heavens.

"He was unique in almost every way, OK?" said Jerry West. "I've seen guys have size advantages, but he probably had the greatest size advantage playing his position of anyone I've ever seen."

It was literally true. The 7'2" Kareem Abdul-Jabbar was only four inches taller than a 6'10" center. Johnson, at 6'9", towered five or six inches over even the tallest point guards and seven or eight inches over most of them; he lobbed the ball into Abdul-Jabbar as easily as if he were sitting next to him at the table, passing him the sugar.

Johnson's size was just the beginning. He had vision, flair, and ball-handling wizardry that enabled a man his size to play the position heretofore reserved for small players.

The great ones change the game, and few had more impact than Johnson, who turned the ball over on every dribble, carving out a new interpretation of the palming rules and setting the stage for future generations of kids who could cover the entire floor in about five bounces and make stunning, 180-degree changes of direction while taking the ball with them.

As great as Johnson was at basketball, however, his real genius lay in his ability to deal with people. He was a pure leader, even when he was the youngest player on the team.

Johnson was actually more complicated than he looked, because he was poised, too, withholding a lot while seeming to withhold nothing. Even his various nicknames suggested carefully monitored levels of entrée. He was "Buck" to his teammates and coaches, but only to them. He liked to be called Earvin by people he knew. He was only "Magic" to the masses, as if that was a made-up person who wasn't real.

He was a delight to be around. It wasn't uncommon for older people around him to hook their careers to his. Pat Riley, who became the coach, used to say that when Magic left, he would, too.

With a couple of good college forwards, Greg Kelser and Jay Vincent, Johnson had taken humble Michigan State to an NCAA title as a sophomore. That was special, too, with the nation transfixed by the looming matchup with Indiana State's Larry Bird. Their meeting in the NCAA Finals got the highest TV rating for any basketball game, before or since.

Now Johnson was here to save the Lakers and the NBA, or at least that was how he saw it. He was 20, so what did he know?

■ ■ ■

Even more than the Lakers—a lot more—the NBA needed some saving.

The league was at a low ebb. The two previous Finals between Seattle and Washington had been ratings disasters. Since the Finals always came up in "sweeps," the TV rating period, CBS didn't even carry them live on weekdays; instead it showed them on tape after the late news.

The Knicks' run that had taken New York by storm was over, and there went the decade. The talk about professional basketball being "the game of the seventies," was like a cruel mockery.

In 1976, the NBA merged with the American Basketball Association, which folded all but three of its teams. Struggling NBA teams packed their carpetbags, too. The Cincinnati Royals, who had come down from Rochester in 1957, skipped across the country like a flat rock, becoming the Kansas City–Omaha Kings in 1972, dropping Omaha in 1976, and leaving for Sacramento in 1985.

Owners traded franchises like baseball cards. In a 1978 deal brokered by the young NBA counsel, David Stern, to make sure the league could keep the Celtics in Boston, owner Irv Levin swapped teams with Buffalo's John Y. Brown. Levin took his new Braves to San Diego, where they became the Clippers, who would last six seasons before moving to Los Angeles.

Worst of all were published reports of rampant drug use by NBA players, casting a sinister light on a league that was now dominated by blacks.

Everyone talked about Johnson's smile, as if he was the first player who'd ever cracked a grin on court. That was Johnson's gift—his joy was so infectious, it was as if he had invented smiling.

With Johnson in Los Angeles and Bird in Boston, restoring their teams to greatness, a renaissance was at hand. After the Washington-Seattle yawners, the league was delighted to get the Lakers or Celtics, representing not only glamour teams but big markets, in every NBA Finals in the eighties. In three of those, they played each other.

Up against the wall as it had been, the NBA had begun a new chapter in labor relations, opening its books to the union to get agreement on a progressive salary cap. The players and owners were now partners, with each getting a defined percentage of revenues.

So much progress would be made in the eighties, with such a change in tone and so many good feelings, it would later loom as a golden era. The league prospered, but it wasn't yet so awash in money that everyone got big heads and began complaining about everything. That would be the nineties.

The Lakers-Celtics rivalry of the eighties would be the best the NBA ever saw, not only exciting but evenly matched, with each breaking the other's heart and other body parts more than once. There were incidents, like the Kevin McHale wipeout of Kurt Rambis that turned the 1984 series in the Celtics' favor; but mostly they just played ball, at a high level.

They lived to beat each other. The Celtics' appearance in Los Angeles during the regular season was like a holiday on the Lakers' schedule. Michael Cooper and his wife, Wanda, customarily held a team party afterward.

In a nice touch, the teams wound up with an abiding respect for each other, led by Johnson and Bird, who hated each other from afar until they met, shooting a Converse commercial one summer. That was when they realized they were different versions of the same guy.

After that, they were buddies. When Bird had a retirement ceremony, Johnson flew to Boston, showed up in Lakers warmups, and tore them off to reveal a Celtics jersey underneath. Bird told him, "Magic, get outta my dreams!"

Johnson, who had deferred his selection to the Hall of Fame by coming back in 1996, tried to get the rules waived so he and Bird could go in together. When that didn't happen, Johnson settled for having Bird present him at his induction.

Of course, the best thing of all was beating the other. Bird remembers a win in the Forum, after which he looked out the bus window and saw Johnson trudging slowly to his car, past fans and well-wishers, looking grief-stricken.

Said Bird: "I thought, 'Suffer, motherf***er.'"

It was the best of times and it started in the summer of 1969.

■ ■ ■

Johnson arrived like a gift from the gods.

The pick itself had come from the New Orleans Jazz three years before, as compensation for signing away the aging Gail Goodrich. Three years later, Goodrich was gone and so were the Jazz, having moved to Utah.

Not that it was an automatic pick. Once the Lakers won a coin toss with the Bulls and learned they'd be number one, there was some discussion about whom they'd take. The front office was in transition from Cooke to Buss, who idolized West and wanted to keep him involved, if not in coaching, in the front office, which was then run by Bill Sharman. West had questions about Johnson and liked Arkansas guard Sidney Moncrief, a more conventional prospect.

However, if Buss was not a basketball man, he had a vision of what he wanted—a team that was not only good but flashy enough to excite the local royalty, the movie stars. He insisted Johnson was their guy.

It didn't take long to see what a prodigy Johnson was.

"There was a uniqueness about that whole year, and that started in the summer pro league," says Michael Cooper, who broke in alongside Johnson:

They were playing that summer pro league at Cal State–L.A. And all of a sudden they said, "Hey, Magic's going to come play with us on a Friday night." They opened up the top. And that had never been open the whole summer.

And you could see the magicalness of it all. The place was full. It was hot. I remember that game so well. That was the time when we got our first Coop-a-Loop. We went over the top, and I got a dunk. You could tell there was going to be something special, not only that young man but what he was bringing to the game of basketball.

That's the way Magic approached it. Every game was fun. And in turn, when the players are having fun, the fans are having fun. He brings them out on the court, even though they can't physically be out there.

He made them part of Laker Showtime, and I think that was the specialness and uniqueness about Magic Johnson. It's very rare that a player can do that, to get everybody excited about playing.

Training camp went the same way. The Lakers already had Norm Nixon, a good, young point guard. It was one reason they wondered if they wanted to take Magic. But from the beginning, it was clear it was going to be Magic's ball and Norm would move to shooting guard, which he did without complaint, at least in the beginning.

Johnson, who knew nothing of being cool, attacked training camp as if it were the Finals. Nixon, a wisened professional, named him "Young Buck," which would be shortened to "Buck." West, who'd been skeptical that a 6'9" player could really play point guard in this league, took one look and decided he could. "You go to training camp, day one and you say to yourself, 'My God, this guy is really unique,'" West said. "He is a guard. He's not some guy who thinks he's a guard. But in watching him, the thing that was really unique early, he didn't really try to be a leader. He was just a leader. He didn't have to try. I mean, that was his niche. He was a leader."

The Lakers needed one, too. Abdul-Jabbar was the game's greatest weapon, but he was aloof and forbidding. Johnson would say later that Abdul-Jabbar barely talked to him for their first five seasons. There were always signs that, despite Kareem's disdain for the system and playing the game, he envied Magic's popularity and resented the attention and favors the owner showered on the rookie.

Nevertheless, each could see what he had in the other. Any rivalry they felt would always be tacit, and any strain they felt would always be kept to themselves.

The era began memorably in San Diego against the Clippers, where Johnson, who was supposed to dribble out and dunk in pregame introductions, tripped on his warmups and fell down.

It wasn't an omen. The Lakers won when Abdul-Jabbar dropped one of his patented sky hooks at the end and Johnson leaped into his arms in a wild on-court celebration. This was a little out of the ordinary for the other Lakers who knew that no one jumped into Kareem's arms.

"We're in our first game, and Kareem hits that sky hook down in San Diego, and Magic is wrapped around his neck," Cooper says. "He's jumping up and down like we've just won a championship. And I know everybody has heard this: Kareem says, 'Hey, what you doing, guy? We still got 81 more games to play.'"

■　■　■

The Lakers also had a new coach, Jack McKinney, but he only lasted 14 games before he fell off the merry-go-round.

McKinney, hired off Jack Ramsay's staff in Portland, actually fell off his bicycle near his Palos Verdes home and suffered multiple injuries, including head trauma, hospitalizing him for weeks.

With a lot of speed now and Johnson to crack the whip, McKinney had put in an attacking fast-break offense, like Ramsay's, that Buss and the players were digging as they started 10–4. Now, however, with doctors saying McKinney would require a long rehabilitation, his young assistant, Paul Westhead, whom everyone had barely met, was thrust into command, 26 days after entering the league.

Westhead had coached at LaSalle, which meant nothing in Los Angeles, and was considered purely interim, working game to game with the front office ready to bring in an experienced coach at the first sign of trouble.

When victory followed victory, Buss decided to go with Westhead until McKinney got back, although he asked Westhead to bring in someone with experience to assist him, like Elgin Baylor. As Buss would learn, Westhead had a mind of his own. Westhead had a candidate no one ever would have thought of—Pat Riley, Chick Hearn's color commentator.

It wasn't that Westhead had detected the makings of a coach in Riley. They had just been hanging out on the road, and Westhead liked him. In any case, it wouldn't be long before McKinney was back, so what did it matter who the assistant was for the next six weeks or so?

It wasn't preposterous to West and Sharman, who knew Riley. But it was to Buss, who already had one neophyte in charge and didn't want another.

"In typical Jerry Buss fashion, he said, 'You should think about that,'" Westhead said later. "Over the years, I've had my ups and down with the Lakers, obviously. I've learned to appreciate Jerry Buss more in hindsight than I did when I was in the thick of things.

"But I realized that was was one of his tricks whenever he didn't think what you wanted to do was the right thing. He would rarely say, 'No, I think that's a bad idea.' He'd say, 'I think you should think that over.'"

So Westhead thought it over, came back, and told Buss he wanted Riley.

"He said, 'Well, it's your decision,'" said Westhead. "And I said yes, and he said OK. But it was not an instantaneous, oh-what-a-great-choice-I'm-glad-you-thought-of-it-and-we-had-that-in-mind-but-you-beat-us-to-the-punch type thing.

"I think they had some people in mind, and I don't know what they were thinking. Obviously, I had coached six games by then and Riles had zippo," Westhead recalled and added, laughing, "We were like the Blues Brothers."

Before Riley could take the job, he had to talk to Hearn, who had rescued him from a year of aimless beach life that followed his retirement. Riley couldn't give up a real job to play assistant coach for a month or two until McKinney got back.

Once more coming to Riley's aid, Hearn made it easy for him, telling him he'd hold the job until he got back. Riley accepted the job, starting one of the most glorious coaching careers on a quiet note indeed.

■　■　■

And they were off.

The players, a high-spirited group, liked the idea of a low-key young coach and a good-guy assistant they already knew and liked. They embraced the new regime, going 50–18 under Westhead. With McKinney recovering slowly, the "interim" appointment lasted the rest of the season.

They rolled through the Western draw and met Philadelphia in the Finals. The Lakers went up 3–2, with a Game 5 victory in the Forum, but lost Abdul-Jabbar, who sprained an ankle, putting him out for Game 6 in Philadelphia.

The Lakers weren't overly concerned, since Kareem was expected back for Game 7, which would be two days later in the Forum. The Philadelphia trip was like a lark and for no one more than Johnson, who boarded the plane, took Abdul-Jabbar's seat, and announced to teammates, "Never fear, E.J. is here."

Frantic 76ers fans reported Kareem sightings all over the Delaware Valley. Sixers coach Billy Cunningham said he'd believe Abdul-Jabbar wasn't coming "when the game ends and I haven't seen him."

Westhead, who knew Kareem really wasn't coming, had a little show-stopper of his own. Johnson was going to jump center. He wasn't going to actually play center, that would be Jim Chones, but this would definitely get the 76ers' attention.

What ensued was one of the most eye-popping performances in NBA history. Johnson scored 42 points, with 15 assists, and seven rebounds as the Lakers wrapped the title up right there and then.

Said Buss, the first-year owner, in the dressing room, hugging the Larry O'Brien Trophy and wiping champagne out of his eyes, "You don't know how long I've waited for this."

■　■　■

Well, it's not that easy.

With one year's experience, Buss was still basically a rookie and proceeded to prove it in a series of mistakes that popped the dream like a soap bubble.

Buss was now forced to choose between the coach who'd won a title and the coach who'd set the program up. McKinney, who was understandably eager to return, bugged the front office for months, while the doctors urged a go-slow approach.

Awkward as it was, there's no hero like today's hero, so it wasn't a close call for Buss, who had fallen for Westhead and now made him the coach. Determined not to say anything critical about McKinney, Buss said he had chosen Westhead because he wanted someone he could "run and chum with."

Buss did a lot of running and chumming, indeed, but even if Westhead was younger and looked hotter than McKinney, he was a devout Catholic and as straightlaced as McKinney.

Trying to smooth things out, Buss got his business partner, Frank Mariani, who had purchased the Indiana Pacers, to hire McKinney. Everyone was supposed to live happily ever after, but the Westheads and McKinneys, who'd been lifelong friends, took years to get past it.

The man Buss really was running and chumming with was Johnson, and it was making everyone else on the team crazy.

The Magic-as-favorite thing had gotten old fast. In his second season, Johnson missed 45 games with a knee injury, and some teammates rolled their eyes when management celebrated his return by passing out THE MAGIC IS BACK buttons.

The whole thing went boom in the first round of the 1981 playoffs. Before the last game, there was a dressing-room confrontation between Johnson and Nixon after Nixon complained about all the sacrifices he'd made for Johnson in the *L.A. Times*, stating, "Anyway, 15 years from now, everyone will have forgotten Magic."

They were then ousted in the deciding Game 3 in the Forum by a Houston team that had gone 40–42. It ended, appropriately enough, with Johnson, who'd missed 13 of 15 shots, breaking off a play for Abdul-Jabbar and throwing up a last-second air ball.

Within weeks, Buss announced he was giving Magic a $25-million "lifetime" contract, and the veterans went bonkers. Abdul-Jabbar went public with his objections, although he couched them diplomatically— "Some members of the team wondered if their value lay in competing for the affection of the owner, rather than what they do on the court." It wasn't just Kareem who was mad, but Nixon, who was always sure management had it in for him, and Jamaal Wilkes.

The next season was even worse, or at least the 11 games that Westhead lasted. The players' favorite was actually coaching now and was no longer such a favorite. They didn't want a lot of direction, but Westhead, who had a Ph.D. in English, was given to parables, like the story he told at the halftime of a game they were losing about being adrift in a boat and needing all hands to pull together. It ran so long, they couldn't even warm up before the second half.

"Here we are, down by 18," Nixon later told the *Times'* Steve Springer, "and he's in some damn boat with no oars."

Westhead was determined to improve their half-court execution to get ready for the playoffs, which meant slowing the game down to go into Abdul-Jabbar. This had the other 11 players on the verge of mutiny, and the pirate who finally popped his head up turned out to be Johnson, who went off after a victory in Utah—their fifth in a row—demanding to be traded.

This prompted a full-scale circling of the wagons back home, after which Westhead was shot off his magic carpet 18 months after it had swooped down and picked him up.

For the record, it was later asserted that the firing had been in the works for a week or two, so that Magic's outburst had (snicker) nothing to do with it. In fact, the haste with which the front office sprang into action the next morning resulted in a few omissions, like a clear understanding of who was taking over.

West, who had returned as a consultant and was now GM, was summoned to Buss' Pickfair home, the famous mansion built by Mary Pickford and Douglas Fairbanks. Buss said he "begged" West to coach again, giving no thought to Westhead's assistant, Riley. As far as Buss was concerned, Pat would stay or go, at West's pleasure.

West, who had no intention of ever going Down There again, turned Buss down and nominated Riley. When Buss asked West to help Riley get the offense back up to speed, West said he would.

Unfortunately, Buss came out of the conversation thinking West had agreed to a two-coach system, in which West would be "offensive captain" and Riley would be "coach." Since West was West and Riley was only Riley, Buss assumed the actual chain of command would take care of itself.

This resulted in a never-to-be-forgotten press conference in which Buss tried to explain his scheme to stunned reporters, who just wanted to ask about Magic firing his coach, after which West came up and lateraled the job to Riley, right in front of everyone.

It went like this:

BUSS [*stepping to the podium*]: We have appointed Jerry West offensive captain for the Lakers. His duties will begin immediately. Pat Riley will remain with the Lakers as coach.

QUESTION: Doctor, offensive coach, does that mean head coach?

BUSS [*pausing for a drag of his cigarette*]: I did not specifically make someone head coach and someone else assistant coach. That was not accidental. I did it the way I announced on purpose. I feel that Pat is very capable of running the Laker team. However, I feel that we need a new offensive coach. I asked Jerry if he'd take the job, and fortunately, because of his relationship with Pat, I feel the two of them will coach this team together, with Jerry being in charge of the offense in particular.

QUESTION: Jerry, there'll be a game tomorrow night. The game will end. Will two coaches come out and talk to us? Or will they choose which one it's going to be from game to game?

BUSS [*grinning*]: We discussed that. In that I'm really making this change to change the offense, and since Jerry West will be in charge of the offense, he will be the one you will question. [*Smiling*] You can, however, talk to Pat whenever you want, as well.

QUESTION: Jerry, who picks the starting lineup?

BUSS [*grinning uneasily now, as he senses this thing isn't flying*]: Oh, which one of these two? Uh, I think there are some things along the line, not only the starting lineups but other considerations as well—uh, potential trades, etcetera, etcetera—that Pat and Jerry are going to have to sit down and work out what their responsibilities are. Fortunately we're dealing with a situation of two men who have worked together on and off for years and years and therefore, I've decided to leave that up to them, the division of duties.

That had been an interesting two minutes, indeed.

West, standing behind Buss, had just heard he would be a co-coach, would handle the press, and his present duties, like "potential trades, etcetera, etcetera," were now to be divided up with Riley.

If Buss was going to reinvent the wheel, he would have to do it on his own time. With the owner standing next to him, West spelled out the real deal, declaring, "First of all, I want to clear up one thing. I'm going to be working for Pat Riley."

In other words, despite what Buss had just said, Riley, not West, was the coach.

Fortunately for the Lakers, this farce wouldn't get the attention it deserved, since it was merely a sideshow. The big story was Johnson's effrontery. Magic was denounced at home and abroad. The *Times* ran an expanded letters column, with most readers blasting him: "It has taken him only two seasons to go from Magic to Tragic" . . . "His next contract should be with Gerber's baby food."

Riley, the human afterthought, finally took the microphone at what had just become his introductory press conference. When he would tell the story in ensuing seasons, he'd claim he said, "If no one else wants it, I'll take it." This would have been a good line but didn't make it onto the videotape.

However, Riley did handle the Keystone Kops act as gracefully as it could have been handled. He didn't abandon his old boss to the mob, insisting Westhead didn't deserve his fate, calling the firing "an over-reaction," but going on to express confidence in himself, promising a better tomorrow, and directing everyone's eyes to the future.

Riley had been hanging out with the writers for years as radio guy and assistant, so they were all glad for him. To lighten the mood, one asked, "Are you going to keep combing your hair that funny way?"

Riley had just begun moussing his hair and combing it back. It would become His Look and start a new fashion in executive grooming, although no one would have believed that at that moment, starting with Riley. It was a lesson in the prerequisites of charisma. For years, Riley had been part of the scenery. Now, with power, he seemed to give off a glow.

Buss was nervous and his voice quivered. West was glum, as he would be whenever he had to fire a coach. Riley looked as if this was his bar mitzvah, which it was, because until that moment, he was nobody.

■ ■ ■

Riles?

There was no one who didn't know him or like him. It was just that no one had ever thought of him in this context. He was Lakers family, having played five of his nine seasons with them, before becoming Hearn's color commentator and Westhead's assistant.

Riley was friendly and easy-going and, as far as Buss was concerned, a piece of furniture that came with the team. Asked years later what his first impressions had been, Buss recalled that Riley had been a "friendly, very good, loyal-type human being, pro-Laker." He added, "Admittedly, I didn't spend a lot of time with the color man on the radio."

For Riley, the radio gig was like heaven dropping down a ladder. Before that, he'd been an unemployed former player, hanging out at the beach in Santa Monica, writing his memoirs, and they weren't happy ones.

After college stardom at Kentucky, he'd had a journeyman career that ended in 1976 when he was 31 and failed the Phoenix Suns' physical, sending him into retirement that felt more like exile. His teammates had been his friends, but he didn't fit with them anymore. Once Abdul-Jabbar invited him over, but when Riley got there, Kareem was hurrying around, doing stuff, and answering the phone. Feeling hurt, Riley never went back.

Another time after a Lakers game, Riley tried to get into the press lounge where Buss, his friends, and all manner of hangers-on hung out, but the guard at the door wouldn't let him in. When Riley explained who he was, the guard explained former players weren't allowed in. Riley slunk home like a snake.

He grew a beard like Jeremiah Johnson's. At a New Year's Eve party, he offered to let friends take whatever they wanted from his expensive wardrobe, since he said he wouldn't need that stuff anymore in his new life.

He had no idea what to do. A friend offered him a job in a clothing store in Beverly Hills, where Riley used to shop, but even that fell through. He thought about coaching, although he didn't know where to start. Idell Cohen, the wife of Pat's beach friend, Altie Cohen, said she knew someone at Ventura County Junior College she could call for him.

It had been a long year when Lynn Shackelford left as Hearn's color commentator to take an anchor job at Channel 9. Riley jumped at the suggestion this might be something he could do.

Chick was an old friend. Early in Riley's career, when Pat had been in danger of being cut in Portland, he had asked Hearn if he could do anything for him. Hearn, who had the title of assistant GM, mentioned it to GM Fred Schaus, who agreed they could use a hard-working, non-complaining bench player and brought Riley to the Lakers.

Now Hearn brought Riley in to make a tape they could show to Cooke, who would have to sign off. "He was pretty nasal at the time," Hearn said, "and I thought, 'Oh, Jesus,' to myself, 'Cooke will never accept this guy.' . . . After we did it many, many times—Cooke didn't even know I was interviewing him—I said, 'Here's a tape I think we can take in to Cooke.'

"So I took it in. I thought we'd get thrown out of his office. And Cooke says, 'My Gawd, Chick! This boy is wonderful! Just what we need!'

"So we hired him."

Riley became color commentator and gofer, doubling as traveling secretary, which meant he got the tickets from the travel agency (this was long before charters) and passed them out to the players—here, Kareem; here, Jamal. If someone didn't want to sit next to someone else, Riley would have to sort it out.

Nevertheless, he was delighted at returning to The Life. He was branching out into production, learning how to shoot features, and would have lived quite contentedly if that lightning bolt hadn't struck, knocking McKinney off that bicycle in 1979 and opening a job on the bench next to Westhead.

In Riley's days as a lost boy on the beach, he'd been unassuming to the point of anonymity. Their friends thought his striking, long-legged wife, Chris, was the looker in the family. Years later, when Pat became a matinee idol and women, who thought he was so sensitive, too, would remark on how hot he was, Idell Cohen would think to herself, What did I miss?

Whatever else awaited him, Riley's days of being overlooked were over.

■ ■ ■

Cue another honeymoon.

The attention was not on Riley but on Johnson, who was booed at home as they went out to play their first game against a San Antonio team that had recently beaten them by 26. Riley was so wired, he made 45 pages of notes for his pregame speech.

The Lakers blew the Spurs away with a night of furious fast-breaking that had the Forum rocking as Johnson, digging in to reclaim his standing, started off by scoring 20 points with 16 assists and 10 rebounds.

And they just went from there.

"We had a team that could really play together," West said later. "It was an easier transition for Pat because he didn't inherit a bad team. . . . They were going to be on their best behavior. It was like a crusade for those players, not to hear about them getting someone else fired."

This was fortunate for Riley, who had all the transition he could handle. In the beginning, he didn't even want them to call him *coach*. It sounded like some grown-up, like Adolph Rupp, his coach at UK. He wanted everyone to keep calling him *Riles*.

His humility was his saving grace. He turned his players loose and stayed out of their way, which was just how they liked it. Nixon agreed:

A little of that was there. That's why I say, look at the team. I watch tapes, it was amazing to watch that team play, how quick we scored on people, the passes. . . . The ball would never hit the floor. Bam, bam, bam, layup. Magic tip one in, Kareem, [Bob] McAdoo comes off the bench, just the foot speed!

We knew in our heads, we had a whole thing, we tried to break teams. We tried to make 'em hit that wall because, couldn't nobody keep up. That's why teams would stay with us for two quarters, three quarters and we'd reach a point where we'd score 16 straight points and the game would be over. . . .

You'd see the teams, they'd go, "F***, we can't run with these guys." And we'd blow 'em out and go to the bench and get oxygen 'cause we were dying, too. But we knew we could take teams. We pushed the rock on 'em all the time and tried to make 'em quit.

It wasn't a matter of how ready Riles was. We, again, didn't want anybody who could come in and change the systems that we had. . . . We made a deal with him. We actually had a meeting. We said, "Riles, shorten the practices, and we're going to give you everything we've got. We'll give you everything for an hour and 15 minutes. Nobody's going to walk around. We're going to push the ball every time, and we're going to pick each other up full-court every time." And we actually made the deal. . . .

The best coaches leave the players alone. The years I was there, Riley knew how to get us in shape and he put the systems in. And man, he just let us play.

It was a tour de force with everyone on board. The players were happy to be rid of Westhead, the press loved Riley, and the fans were worn out from cheering. The only skeptic was Buss, who'd been burned once. The owner was now noticeably noncommittal, suggesting he felt little investment in Riley and would have dropped him like a hot rock if things hadn't worked out so well.

West was only on the bench for a week before high-tailing it back upstairs where he belonged. The Lakers won 11 of Riley's first 13, going from 108 points a game to 119. By early January, when his record was up to 20–6, the Lakers were so far out ahead, they locked up his job as coach of the West All-Stars.

The prevailing view, which would last for years, was that Riley was the luckiest man alive. As the acerbic Celtics coach, Bill Fitch, put it, "Two years ago, Pat carried the bags of West and Goodrich. In 1982, he's coach of the West. The way he's going, in 10 years he'll probably be president of the United States."

Buss said nothing about bringing Riley back until they blitzed through the first two rounds of the playoffs, sweeping the Suns and Spurs, 4–0. Acknowledging his doubts ("My reaction was like being from Missouri, you know"), Buss said Riley was no longer just an interim coach.

The Lakers then polished off the 76ers in a 4–2 Finals. The Showtime stars, who would rule the eighties, were now in place, and their time was almost at hand.

Chapter 4

THE RISE AND FALL OF RILES

Pat, let's face it, he wasn't just the coach. He was as big as Magic. It wasn't just a bunch of superstars with a coach. It was the L.A. Lakers coached by Pat Riley.... He had the whole image. He played it to the hilt. He didn't just play it, he lived it.

—Gary Vitti, Lakers trainer

So in '87, it was like, "Hey, this guy thinks we can, we can." We won in '88, and I think that's where he says, "S***, I am the s***!" He believed it. And I think that's when the parting of the so-called Red Sea began.

—Michael Cooper

■ ■ ■

NOW ABOUT THEIR ANCIENT SCOURGE.

With two titles in the first three years of the eighties, the Lakers had a foothold on the decade, but their archenemy loomed just around the corner once more.

Larry Bird, entering the league with Magic Johnson, had found himself in humbler surroundings. Nevertheless, if they were different in so many ways, it seemed to come out the same in the end. They weren't merely superstars but transcendent players, the kind who come along once in a generation, except that theirs had produced non-identical twins, whose rare playmaking ability and leadership changed everything from the moment they arrived.

In his first season, Bird took a 29–53 Celtics team to 61–21, then the biggest jump in NBA history. The next season, while Johnson and his teammates were dealing with the issues that came with success, it was Bird's turn to succeed, taking the Celtics to the 1981 title.

The Lakers won in 1982, with Pat Riley, and the 76ers squeezed in a moment of their own as the Moses Malone–led powerhouse swept the limping Lakers in the 1983 Finals.

Then, finally, in 1984, came the one everyone had been waiting for: Lakers vs. Celtics, Bird vs. Magic, the rematch.

Of course, Jerry West was rabid on the subject of the Celtics, but it was the failure that haunted him, rather than the actual Celtics. They had been respected foes who respected him back.

For his part, Riley hadn't been on any of the Lakers teams that lost to Boston, but he'd heard the stories. He was Pure Lakers when it came to the Celtics, seething at the thought of them. But with Riley, it came out different. He hated the Celtics themselves.

Of course, Riley would say hello to Red Auerbach in the hall. It was sports hatred as opposed to real hatred, but there was nothing Riley would ever put beyond Red. Once Riley had the Lakers' Gatorade barrel in Boston Garden dumped, out of fear Auerbach had put something in it.

The hardest working man in Showtime, Riley was now in his third season of pouring his entire being into the job. To him, basketball was war, the enemy was the personification of evil, and his job was to make sure the troops, er, players understood that.

"I had to educate my players who the Celtics were," he wrote in *Show Time*. "One day in practice, I asked if anyone knew. Finally, Kareem raised his hand. He said they were a warring race of Danes who invaded Ireland. I had to explain they were also a cunning, secretive race.

"We had to learn to overcome the mythology of the Celtics."

Of course, Riley was Irish and would turn out to be pretty cunning and highly secretive, himself.

Did he care that the Celtics, meanwhile, were comprised of several races and didn't have a single Irishman or Dane? Most of the players were African Americans. Auerbach was Jewish. Danny Ainge was Mormon. Nevertheless, as far as Riley was concerned, the day they put on those black sneakers, walked out on that parquet floor, and began spouting that Celtics Pride BS, they were evil.

On the other hand, Riley and the Lakers knew, as they knew their own names, that this was a new day. They had Magic Johnson and Kareem Abdul-Jabbar, still the ultimate low-post weapon at 37. As a bonus, they had young James Worthy, the top pick in the 1982 draft, a windfall from a 1979 deal in which they'd sent a forward named Don Ford, remembered only for his flowing blond hair, to Cleveland and swapped future No. 1 picks as an afterthought. Michael Cooper, a sub, was becoming one of the league's top defenders. Bob McAdoo, a five-time All-Star, was coming off their bench.

They were not only good, but cohesive. Johnson and Abdul-Jabbar, who coexisted for years, were becoming friends as Abdul-Jabbar opened up. Nixon, who'd had the toughest time with Magic's fame—which was all mixed up because they were buddies—was gone, replaced by a born-to-run rookie named Byron Scott, the No. 4 pick in the 1983 draft. They had it all, talent, youth, experience.

The cunning Auerbach had worked another one of his tricks, separating Robert Parish and the draft pick that became Kevin McHale from the Warriors, but the Celtics guards, Ainge and Dennis Johnson, couldn't shoot, so you could sag off them.

The Lakers were finally the better team, and all they had to do was claim what was theirs.

■ ■ ■

Well, they certainly tried, didn't they?

The Lakers won the opener in Boston and led Game 2, 113–111, going into the last minute when Worthy misunderstood Riley and called a timeout. Then, in-bounding the ball, Worthy threw a lollypop that Gerald Henderson picked off and took in for the tying basket. The Celtics wound up winning in overtime.

Back in the Forum, the Lakers turned their anguish into fast breaks, scorching the Celtics in Game 3, 137–104. Bird, feeling the need for something drastic, told the press they needed "12 heart transplants."

How about a nice garroting, instead?

In the third quarter of Game 4, McHale, who was often accused of not being mean enough, put a chokehold on Kurt Rambis, going in for a layup. A mêlée ensued, in which Bird and Abdul-Jabbar had to be separated.

The Lakers still led, 113–108, with :57 left, but the Celtics stole this one out of their mouths, too, winning after Johnson, who lived for moments like these, let the 24-second clock run out in regulation and missed two key free throws in overtime.

The Lakers had now led all four games going into the last minute of regulation, but the series was tied 2–2, and the Celtics had recaptured the home-court advantage.

Worse, Riley thought the Lakers' manhood had been challenged and must now be defended. Whenever the two teams met, the Celtics would be depicted as the blue-collar, lunch-pail–carrying working men from the hardscrabble East, while the Lakers were the flashy guys from the West Coast with their chi-chi Hollywood friends. This carried the suggestion that the Lakers were more talented but softer and the Celtics smarter and tougher. Take it a step further, as some did, and the Lakers were the black team and the Celtics, with Bird, Mchale, Ainge, and their Irish motif, the white team.

That was innuendo that didn't have to be dignified, much less addressed. However, Riley didn't bear slights to their manhood, or his, lightly. He felt it like a cloud that followed him around. "I don't think there's any doubt," he said, "that Southern California and Hollywood and L.A. are considered to be filled with people who are soft and have no values and couldn't work a day in their lives."

Now he perceived McHale's attack as the traditional slap across the cheeks, which had to be answered. Riley even compared the teams to warring gangs who "both say bare fists and one of them shows up with zip guns."

Instead of Lakers speed versus Celtics execution, the rest of the series became a rumble, in which the Lakers no longer had an edge. The Celtics' home-court advantage held. They won Game 5 in the Garden as Abdul-Jabbar wilted on a steamy Sunday afternoon that turned the Garden into a sauna. Then after the Lakers tied it in the Forum, the Celtics won Game 7 back in the Garden, holding off a Lakers rally, with Dennis Johnson taking the ball off Magic on a fast break after the Lakers had cut a 14-point lead to 105–102.

The Lakers only thought they had suffered before.

Riley, spent and devastated, held an impromptu wake back at their hotel with Chris, assistant coach Bill Bertka, and Bertka's wife, later calling it "the longest night of my life."

Nor did Riley spin the awful truth—"We choked"—or try to pretend he'd made the right decisions. "You looked at Pat afterwards, and, I mean, it looked like he hadn't eaten for three days, hadn't slept," said Dave Wohl, Riley's assistant. "You were looking at a person who was ravaged by the loss."

West was still haunted.

"It was a loss that never should have happened," he said years later. "It was probably the worst loss in Lakers history. We should have won in four straight games. It made me crazy. It was just unforgivable. But I'd been through all that before, and I know what it's like to lose when you don't want to lose."

Johnson stayed up all night in the hotel after Game 7 with pals Isiah Thomas and Mark Aguirre. Back home, Johnson shut himself up in his house for days and wouldn't even take calls from his mother. Johnson still remembered the hurt years later:

The whole series was a disaster for me. I let the clock run down in Game 2. We go back there for Game 7, another crucial play, I had James open, I could have gotten it to him, and DJ took it from me. . . .

It hurt so bad. We hurt. All of us hurt. It was just heartbreaking. . . . He [Riley] was like a crazy man. We knew we were better than them, and to lose to them!

But when we got out of there, we learned a valuable lesson. Only the strong survive and that's something we didn't know until then. Talent just don't get it. We realized it's not all about talent and that's the first time the Lakers ever encountered that, someone who was stronger minded.

So we said, "OK, we got to be stronger."

■ ■ ■

If suffering builds character, they'd had enough.

The entire 1984–1985 season was a penance for their sins and a warmup, they hoped, for their chance at redemption, starting in camp when Riley made the no-layup rule he'd proclaimed in the Finals permanent. There was a new emphasis on defense, with Lakers players now required to bump all cutters, even in practice.

Left unsaid was the feeling shared by all: let the Celtics win the East, and give us another shot at them. The shame they felt couldn't be expunged by a victory over mere 76ers or Bucks. Happily for the Lakers, everything worked as planned, and in the spring, the Celtics came back around again.

Unhappily for the Lakers, there would be more suffering required of them.

In Game 1 in Boston Garden, afterward known as the "Memorial Day Massacre," the Celtics slaughtered them like lambs in purple livery, 148–114. The Lakers' ancient curse not only lived and breathed, it seemed about to become holy writ.

It was a horrific pounding, highlighted by the Celtics center, Parish, beating the venerable Abdul-Jabbar, 38, downcourt time after time for layups. For the Lakers, who were already up to here with suggestions they were soft, or psyched out, it was the opener from hell.

Riley now had 48 hours to turn their heads around because Game 2 was coming. In later years, Riley would say misery was actually the best state, because it was then that you would find out what you had inside. He would talk about his father, Lee, a minor league baseball player and manager, who was left embittered by his experience in the game. Lee told him that one day he'd have to make a stand, with the corollary that seemed to go with it: make sure you do it better than I did. Avenge me.

Riley had actually made a lot of stands, or tried to. Anything he hadn't achieved hadn't been through lack of desire or effort. As a player, he just hadn't been one of the chosen ones. Now he had a new career, one he liked, but any way you cut it, that day was here.

It was an eerily silent Riley who welcomed the players to a meeting at their hotel the next morning. Everyone noted that Abdul-Jabbar took a seat, right in front of the video screen. The room went dark. Michael Cooper recalls what followed:

It was just like a 30-minute video but [Riley] sat there and replayed it. Every time you f***ed up, he'd rewind it five times. You just sat there and saw yourself f***ing up five times.

It literally stayed on Kareem. And he would say, "Cap, look at how this guy is beating you down the floor!" I thought he had literally gone crazy, just totally lost it, 'cause he wasn't maniacal, he was silent. . . . I was waiting for Kareem to say, "Hey, Riles, f*** this, let's get on," but he never said anything. He'd just shake his head and continue to watch.

And he went down the line—Kareem, Magic. He went through all the starters. He went systematically to everybody. Once the video was over, the guy stood up, put the [remote] down and he proceeded to go off on us verbally. Tried to put his fist through the back of the chalkboard. The chalk went flying. People who were sitting up front looked like they were at the movies when it gets scary. Things were happening!

Fifteen years later, Johnson still remembered it:

He came out and he started, *"You guys call yourselves the Three Musketeers? You guys ain't crap!"* He was talking about the guards. *"DJ's kicking your ass, Buck! Danny Ainge is just intimidating you, Byron!"*

Down the line, he just made you feel like you were this tall.

And Kareem, he got to Kareem, just called him every name in the book. *"You're supposed to be our captain, our f***ing leader! You didn't even show to play! This is the world championship! They just took it to you! And what makes it worse, Greg Kite came in and did it to you!*

"And what makes things worse, Buck, you foul DJ and then you pick his ass up! We're down 40 points. If one man picks up a Celtic, $500 fine! If there's one layup—one layup!—another fine! No box out, another $500!

At the ensuing practice, Riley went back to his eerie silence, giving instructions in a cold, detached manner, as if talking to pond scum.

"He was so mad, I mean, I was scared to talk to him, and I usually talk to him," Johnson said. "I tell you what, it was the greatest coaching strategy that I've ever seen, because when we came out the next night, we were ready. Kareem was ready. You know what I'm saying?"

It was a Lakers crossroads and a lot of individual Lakers' crossroads, as well. When they boarded the bus at their hotel, Abdul-Jabbar asked Riley if it was OK for his father, known as Big Al, to ride with him.

Riley had long rigidly enforced a rule that kept everyone but the traveling party off the bus. Now, he saw Kareem, who'd had his issues with his father, asking to keep his dad next to him and was moved to make an exception. In Riley's pregame speech, he recalled Lee's order to make that stand and told his players to remember what their dads had told them. As trainer Gary Vitti would note, "We were into, like, this father thing."

It was May 30, 1985, the night the Lakers' world changed.

Johnson had a way to see if Abdul-Jabbar was into a game—"when he bends down real low when he posts up and he stays low. He doesn't stand straight up like he does when he's tired or whatever. He stays down low"—and that was how Kareem was that night. He wouldn't let Parish push him off the block. At the other end, he challenged the Celtics whenever they came into the lane with a ferocity he rarely showed. He finished with 30 points, 17 rebounds, 8 assists, and 3 blocks. The Lakers led by 18 at the half and won, 109–102.

The rest of the series was furious and waged on even terms, but this time, when the Lakers had leads at the end of the game, they kept them. They went back to Boston for Game 6, leading 3–2, and expecting the usual heroic defense, not only from the Celtics, but the inflamed citizenry that once dumped the tea in the harbor and now hated them worse than any redcoats.

The Lakers always suspected that Auerbach had turned up the heat on them the year before, or had switched off the air conditioning, turning the Garden into a hell which consumed the visitors. On a prior Lakers trip, someone had phoned in a fire alarm to their hotel so they found themselves out on the street at 3:00 A.M. Any time they saw a cleaning crew when they practiced in the Garden, Riley was sure the janitors were spies.

"He could get as paranoid as anyone," said Wohl. "I remember the last practice before Game 6. The Celtics go on and practice first. The media talks to them and we go on. There's a Gatorade container over there. So Pat sees it and he says, 'Gary, what's in that?' And Gary says,

'Just some leftover Gatorade.' And he literally told Gary to go change it because he thought the Celtics might have spiked it with something. Gary comes to me and says, 'Do I really have to change this?' And I go, 'Yeah, you better change it.'"

Nevertheless, the Lakers knew they had Game 7 at home to fall back on if they needed it, which took the pressure off. It was the Celtics who were up against it and wilted in the second half of Game 6, which was decided long before the historic final score was recorded: Lakers 110, Celtics 100.

Rabid Celtics fans began leaving early, as if they were the Lakers fans they sneered at. Johnson and Abdul-Jabbar embraced in front of the bench. Fans who stayed offered the Lakers polite applause. The Lakers poured champagne all over each other and soaked the tiny dressing room they hated so much. Abdul-Jabbar, who had averaged 28 points since Game 1, called it the highlight of his career.

Cooper said it was "the happiest I've ever seen coach Riley." For his part, Riley's primary feeling wasn't jubilation, but relief.

"Everything is purged," he said. "Now they can't mock us and humiliate us. . . . Let somebody else feel that pain for 10 months."

■　■　■

They were Riley's team now.

A lot had changed since he arrived on their doorstep like an infant in a basket in 1981. He was an accidental tourist that first season but soon discovered he had a knack for this. Influenced by his wife, Chris, a psychologist, he developed a style and language of his own, suggesting a sensitivity to feelings that was very eighties.

Riley had issues of his own, which he brought to the workplace. The son who had suffered the silence of a distant father and had turned to his coaches as father surrogates as a player, now wanted to make his team into the nurturing family he missed, whose members protected each other.

There were regular parties. The Rileys hosted one at Christmas, the Coopers had the one after the Celtics' game. When Abdul-Jabbar didn't come once, Riley made such a big thing about all the trouble the wives were going to that everyone understood these things weren't really optional.

In his own way, Riley was as haunted and as driven as West. He just didn't suffer publicly, as West did. Riley had always been dedicated and hardnosed, but it didn't count for much because he was only the number 8–12 man on the team. Now his hunger and his toughness became part of the Lakers' makeup.

The job was becoming his life, and his life was becoming the job. Chris was as much into it as he was. It was the quest he'd waited all his life to make, and the affirmation of their dreams.

"If you go back to the Crusades, he would be King Richard or somebody," said Wohl. "I think the job focuses his attention almost completely. He'll have a few words to say to you, he's always cordial, he's always polite, but he's kind of a man on a mission." Wohl remembers one incident in particular:

I'll never forget the toughness of the people. One day we were there and [Mitch] Kupchak, Rambis, and McAdoo all went up for an offensive rebound at the end of practice and they split Mitch's eye open. It takes 41 stitches. He's sitting under the basket with a compress on it, bleeding and everything.

Pat begrudgingly stops practice and brings it to a halt—we've been going about two hours—and everybody walks by Kupchak and looks at him. And Rambis goes, 'We're lifting weights now, don't be late.' Kupchak's bleeding. I mean, there was a toughness about that crew that went from the coaches through the players.

There was one more change. Riley was becoming a star.

He was great with the press, so he was always being quoted in that newspeak jargon of his—*toxic envy, the disease of me*, etc. He was a clotheshorse and as elegant as could be, having grown into his looks along with a little corrective surgery on his nose. He said it was to repair a deviated septum, but as a friend who ran a casting company noted, everyone who got his nose fixed said it was because of a deviated septum.

Now CEOs paid Riley $20,000 to address their employees, and women thought he was hot.

"It came out of nowhere," said Johnson. "We won the championship, and he always handled everything well, and all of a sudden, he was the most marketable coach. He didn't let himself become bigger than the team, but it just happened. Boom, success! It was just there. You talk about camera presence, it's Riley."

Riley was still their Riles. They would lose him somewhere in the ensuing years, when he didn't seem to have any time for anyone anymore, when he was so remote, he'd pass by people in the hall without speaking, his eyes going past them in a thousand-yard stare, his impatience something to be feared if he didn't get what he wanted when he wanted it.

But now, the trip was just getting interesting.

■ ■ ■

Once Riley needed the Lakers more than they needed him, but no longer.

The spring after their Boston triumph, they were unceremoniously toppled off their pedestal by a young underdog Houston team with a two-center tandem of Hakeem Olajuwon and Ralph Sampson. In the West finals, Houston beat the Lakers in a one-sided series, 4–1, before falling to the Celtics themselves in the Finals.

The Lakers took a look at themselves and discovered they were small. Suddenly everyone wanted two centers to combat the new menace, but all the Lakers had up front were Abdul-Jabbar, now 39, and two undersized power forwards, Rambis and A. C. Green.

Determined to add a giant, they worked out a deal to send Worthy to Dallas for 6'11" Roy Tarpley and Johnson's pal, Aguirre. Magic loved the idea, and Buss said yes. However, West was so upset, Buss wound up calling Mavericks owner Don Carter and asking to be released from the agreement, lest he lose his GM. Carter said OK. Within two years, the troubled Tarpley was in a detox program and the moody Aguirre was in a steep decline.

Riley wanted the retooling as much as anyone, speaking of a "core burnout," talking about the day when Abdul-Jabbar would retire, when "after all the years of success, we may not be a championship team any more." Even as camp opened in Palm Springs, the coaches kept hoping

West could get them a seven-footer (by now they were down to big nobodies like Chicago's Juwan Oldham). Finally, West told them to figure on going with what they had.

So Riley came up with the Career Best Effort. Everyone on the team had to figure out what he had to do to have his best season, and that way, they could catch the Rockets.

Of course, some of them were already trying to have their best seasons every season, and the ones who didn't, didn't care. On the other hand, at least it sounded like a plan.

Riley actually did have something tangible in mind, a reaffirmation of their philosophy. They weren't going to worry about Houston's size, they would make the Rockets deal with their speed by going back to their old fast-break style. The difference now was that instead of waiting for Abdul-Jabbar to set up, Johnson would become the number-one option in a quicker-hitting offense, and Abdul-Jabbar would be more of a last option they saved until they needed it. This would only work if Abdul-Jabbar accepted it. Riley held his breath, but Kareem did. Forbidding though he was, he was a team guy.

It worked spectacularly. The Lakers weren't going on the junk heap of history, after all, but back to their accustomed place atop the league.

Johnson's scoring average went from 18.8 to 23.9, and he became the first guard since Oscar Robertson in 1964 to win the MVP. The Lakers went 65–17, their best record in the eighties, finishing six games ahead of the second-best Celtics and 23 ahead of the Rockets, who turned into a fad, like hula hoops, and were never heard from again at the elite level in the eighties.

And who should be waiting for them but the Celtics for one final let's-see-who's-best Finals?

That was simple: it was the Lakers, who were so far out ahead, the Celtics now had all they could do just to keep it close. Like the Lakers, the Celtics had won three titles in the eighties, including the season before with Bill Walton making his last stand as a backup center, giving them four future Hall of Famers on their front line.

But the Celtics weren't kids, either. Walton's feet failed him now; he played 10 games all season and was no factor in the Finals. Parish was

34 and DJ, 33. Bird and McHale, gamers that they were, had serious mileage on them. Bird, McHale, Parish, and DJ had all finished among the top 21 players in minutes played.

Worse, the Celtics had to deal with the rising Bad Boy Pistons in the East finals, surviving a furious seven-game series only after Bird's famous steal of Isiah Thomas' in-bounds pass stole back Game 5.

Meanwhile, the Lakers stormed through the Western draw 11–1, winning by an average of 17 points a game. Except for a record 29-point fourth quarter by Golden State's Sleepy Floyd, the Lakers might have been unbeaten.

The first two Lakers-Celtics finals had been classics, but this one was just this side of a mismatch. The Lakers won Games 1 and 2 in the Forum by 13 and 19, respectively, scoring 119 and 141 points. The Celtics gathered themselves back in the Garden to win Game 3, but the Lakers won the pivotal Game 4 on Magic's oft-replayed "junior, junior skyhook" that put them up by one with :02 left.

This left time for one last dramatic moment, Bird taking the in-bounds pass in the corner and launching a 20-footer that was dead-on but just a little too long, slamming off the back rim.

There was also time for one more moment of Auerbachian fury as Red chased referee Earl Strom to the officials' dressing room, where Strom ducked back out and told him, "Arnold, you're showing the same class you always have."

In the next day's *Boston Globe*, Bob Ryan, poet laureate of the Celtics dynasty, called it "the single most devastating loss in Celtics playoff history." Had he been clairvoyant, or pessimistic, he might have also said it was the end of their glory years because it was their Finals farewell for the duration.

The Lakers lost Game 5 but went back home for two, needing but one, and got it in routine fashion with a 13-point victory in Game 6, ending the great Lakers-Celtics wars.

Riley wasn't done. He had one last trick up his sleeve, his "guarantee" they would repeat next season, too. In Riley fashion, he'd been working on the wording for weeks and now announced, "We will repeat. I guarantee it."

It wasn't anything you could guarantee, but it gave everyone something to "ooh" and "ahh" about. More to the point, as Riley's players realized immediately, it served notice they hadn't done nothing yet.

No one had repeated in 18 years, since 1969, when the Celtics punctured Jack Kent Cooke's balloon. Riley's players weren't enchanted at having their victory celebration shortened from months to minutes.

"I thought it was a little premature," said Abdul-Jabbar.

"I didn't even get a chance to take a sip of champagne," said Scott.

"We didn't even have a chance to enjoy the one we'd won," said Johnson.

Nor would they have much fun on the way to the one they were about to win, either.

■   ■   ■

Riley was big-time now.

That was the summer he turned down Robert Towne for *Tequila Sunrise* and wrote *Show Time*, which became a bestseller, spelling out his damn-the-torpedoes philosophy in the first two sentences:

There are two states of being in the NBA, winning and misery. Winning also breaks down into two categories, savoring victory or being too damn tired to savor victory.

Tellingly, the book revealed little of his background, noting his father had "scuffled to keep his ambitions alive" after baseball and "wasn't always an open and talkative guy, but he always seemed to be there when it counted."

In real life, Lee Riley was lost after baseball, finally becoming a janitor. He had a drinking problem and once went out on the floor at one of Pat's high school games.

When he died in Schenectady, Pat, then playing in San Diego, found out by phone. The last time he'd seen his father, Lee, who'd been visiting, looked out the car window and told him about making that stand, which had become Pat's watchword. Forever after, Pat would tell sons to have that talk with their fathers while there was time.

If Lee could see him now. That was the saddest part of the whole thing.

That old tape Riley was always talking about was still running, Lee telling him to kick ass. As hard as Pat was on players and staff, he was harder on himself. Nothing was good enough. The more Pat achieved, the more he expected

Sometimes it got hard to take. That summer, Riley sat in the empty Forum, doing an interview with a radio reporter named Joe McDonnell, who went way back with him. Now Pat was complaining about the press, which was never going to let them forget his guarantee.

Of course, this was just the way Riley had set it up.

"That," said McDonnell later, "was when I knew he had completely lost perspective."

Riley was now past being good old Riles, the piece of furniture. He was a taskmaster, and to redeem his guarantee, he'd have to go to the whip early and often.

They started 8–0, running off the previous season's momentum, but there were signs the engine was overheating. They lost six of nine as the 40-year-old Abdul-Jabbar's nine-season streak of double-figure games ended. With no streak to protect, Kareem kicked back, getting single figures 12 more times that season.

The playoffs, a romp the year before, were an odyssey. A young, physical Jazz team with Karl Malone and 7'4" Mark Eaton zoning off the middle, took them seven games in the second round, with Riley publicly questioning his stars' effort, then telling the players the press was writing them off.

They had to go seven more games against a young Dallas team in the West Finals. Then they went seven with Detroit's Bad Boys, who led the Finals, 3–2, going back to the Forum for the last two.

In Game 6, Isiah Thomas tried to close it out with a memorable show, scoring 43 points despite spraining his right ankle so badly, he was hopping around on one leg. Trailing 101–98 in the last minute and facing elimination, the Lakers came from behind on a Scott jumper and Abdul-Jabbar's two free throws after a ticky-tack call against Bill Laimbeer.

With Saturday off before Sunday's Game 7, Thomas took advantage of an invitation by a L.A. Raiders official, Mike Ornstein, to get treatment at the team's El Segundo facility.

Not that the Rileys were strung out, but before the next day's Game 7 when Ornstein wished Chris good luck, he said she replied, "F*** you," and accused him of undermining Pat's chances.

Nevertheless, Thomas only went 28 minutes, shot 4–12, and the Lakers collapsed just over the finish line. In the dressing room, Abdul-Jabbar pretended to stuff a towel in Riley's mouth to keep him from guaranteeing anything else.

Riley liked it so much, he reprised the moment at the parade, going to the podium wearing a gag. He sent pictures of that to friends, including the Dodger manager, Tommy Lasorda, who had played with Lee in the minor leagues.

Pat inscribed it, "To Tommy, My dad would never have let me guarantee anything, but he would have been just as proud of you, too."

Riley had now won four titles in seven seasons and had been in the Finals six times, but that luckiest-man-on-earth thing would never die. He had the fame, but the players got the credit. Even in a *GQ* cover story that summer (now *there* was a natural), Diane Shah, a *Herald-Examiner* columnist, quoted "someone close to the team" as saying, "In no way does the Lakers' success reflect on Riley. Moe from the Three Stooges could coach this team, Xs and Os–wise."

It wasn't true. The 1987 and 1988 titles gave them five titles in the eighties to the Celtics' three and made it a Lakers decade. As Johnson would note, the difference between the teams was Riley.

"I thought, 'Shoot, you're playing for a legend,'" said Cooper. "You have your Johnny Woodens, Ray Meyers, Red Auerbachs, Bill Sharmans. I think coach Riley can be considered in a group with those guys."

■　■　■

It ended as fast as it took a hamstring to tear.

The locomotive never slowed down, although Johnson did more and more (he won his second MVP in 1988–1989) and Abdul-Jabbar did less and less (at 41, he played 23 minutes a game, averaging 10 points).

They were best in the West and heating up at the right time, sweeping the Blazers, Sonics, and Suns in the playoffs by a combined 10–0 to reach the Finals against the Pistons, who had won 63 games to their 57, again.

Riley couldn't have been more focused on a third title if God, Himself, was going to come down and present the trophy. He even had a word for it—"threepeat"—coined by Scott but trademarked by Riley, although Riley got mad at the *Los Angeles Times'* Scott Ostler for writing about it.

The Finals loomed as a duel of giants, right up to the moment Scott pulled a hamstring in a rebounding drill the day before the opener, putting him out for the duration.

The Lakers lost Game 1. Early in Game 2, Johnson pulled his hamstring. Knowing what it meant, Magic almost wept on the floor. He tried to play in Game 3 but could only hop about woodenly. It was over in four.

No Laker ever complained that Riley had them practicing too hard before the Finals. It was what he always did. Right or wrong, good or bad, having lived by the ordeal for so long, they understood they would have to accept dying by the ordeal.

Of course, it was hard enough to endure Riley's intensity and gloom when they were winning. Losing, even if it wasn't their fault, multiplied the misery.

"I saw it building up for years," said trainer Gary Vitti of Riley. "I mean, his intensity grew more and more and more so that he was intolerant of mistakes or letdowns or human error as time went on. Almost to the point where it was intolerable.

"I think the pressure Pat put on himself manifested itself in that way. You know, it's hard for people to like someone who forces them to be the best they can be every, every, every second."

The two states were no longer "winning" and "misery." Now "winning" meant a title and the rest was misery. They kept getting older. He kept getting hungrier.

As Kurt Rambis, a Riley loyalist, noted, "You can only whip the mule so much before the mule turns around and says, 'I've had it.'"

■　■　■

It wasn't just a season that had ended, but an era, as Abdul-Jabbar finally said good-bye at 42. He had been easy to respect but all but impossible to know. He disdained the press and was aloof and intimidating to teammates, as well.

He had a human side, too, it just wasn't on display often. Every once in a while, Rambis once said, Kareem would open up and begin to talk to you, animatedly and at length, "so you thought he was your best friend.

"The next time you'd see him in the hall," Rambis said, "you'd go, 'Hey, Cap!'

"And he'd say, 'You got it,' and keep walking."

In Abdul-Jabbar's later seasons, when he did lighten up, he even made fun of his reputation for coasting in the movie *Airplane*, but he was always a man apart, as suggested by his third-person nickname: The Big Fella.

Abdul-Jabbar's game was no more exuberant than his personality. Nevertheless, his professionalism, constancy, and artistry were remarkable. There had been and would be more dominating centers and even his career scoring record—38,387 points, 6,968 points ahead of number two Chamberlain—would one day be threatened by Karl Malone, but Kareem would always be the ultimate low-post weapon. Bill Walton, fellow Bruin and NBA competitor, remembers playing against Abdul-Jabbar:

> You worked your tail off to get him to take the worst shot in the world, an 18-foot fadeaway hook shot, and he'd swish it every time. Much like Hakeem [Olajuwon], you get him behind the backboard, he's falling backward, he throws it up, swishes in.
>
> I had to play my absolute best against him. He was always the guy, every operation, every physical therapy, every training session, I'm just telling myself, "Jabbar! Jabbbar! I'm going to get that guy!"
>
> And I knew I had to play my best every time I went down court. And I did play my best against him. And he just killed me every time.
>
> He would throw 50 on me. He would throw 50 on anybody's face at any time he wanted to, particularly the new guys. Whenever a new guy would come up, he would never say a thing about them. Just walk out there and get 50 and walk out of there and say, "Yep, OK, welcome to my league."

Now for the first time in Johnson's pro career and Riley's coaching career, they were on their own.

■　■　■

The RPMs were at the red line now.

Johnson, like Riley, lived to show 'em. Like Riley, Johnson had always been aware there were people who said he wouldn't have won as much, or anything, without Abdul-Jabbar.

For Riles and Magic, 1 and 1A in the pecking order, the 1989–1990 season was a crusade. They went 63–19, not only best in the West—for the ninth time in Riley's nine seasons—but best in the league, four games ahead of the defending champion Pistons. Johnson won his third MVP in four seasons.

Nevertheless, the machine was making funny sounds. They had a rookie center from Yugoslavia named Vlade Divac, who had it all except American-playground toughness, which Johnson seemed dedicated to instilling in him on a nightly basis. West finally suggested to Magic he back off before Vlade got on a plane back to Belgrade.

If you could get Johnson to let up, Riley was a harder case. His old open door was down to a sliver; even his assistants knew better than to push a point he didn't like. As far as the players went, Johnson had entrée, but everybody else had better do it the way he said.

Riley didn't lose the team, but he was wearing on key players like Cooper, who was 34 and fading; on Scott, whom Pat was always pushing; and even the good soldier, James Worthy, who worried about the toll their hard practices were taking on his slender body.

In the front office, where staffers called him Norman Bates, Riley wasn't just obeyed but feared. There was actually a meeting in which the brass told the PR people they weren't working for Chris Riley and that her suggestions didn't have the weight of Pat's requests.

Pat's requests were going beyond controlling into comic. When they began chartering aboard the luxurious MGM Grand jet with its individual staterooms, he wanted everyone to sit in seats he designated, although no one went for that.

Riley would later say privately that the problem had been one player—Cooper—who went upstairs to complain to West, who overreacted. Cooper said he only went to see West as one of the tri-captains, with Johnson and Worthy, at West's invitation.

The bottom line was there were signs of distress. West had never let players get around Riley by coming to him, but now West asked to meet with the players. Riley hated the idea but had no choice but to accept it.

West and Riley had been pals in their playing days. If they were no longer running buddies, they remained friends, even if insiders suggested Riley had become the administrator West would have liked to be, as Jerry had been the player Pat wanted to be.

But before this, there had never been an issue that separated them, and now there was.

"I think the personalities finally clashed," Johnson said. "When things didn't go well that season, players took their complaints to Jerry. Now for the first time, Jerry West's got to confront Riley."

For his part, West felt caught between two forces, the team and the coach, that were pulling away from each other, and he had no choice but to try to mediate.

"I did it for him," West said. "The team was so fragmented. . . . It was something to try to right the ship, instead of having players bitch and complain."

The meeting, itself, was the usual thing in which West acknowledged the players' pain and told them they had to pull together, and they said they would. And they did, right up until the second round of the playoffs when the Suns, the number-five seed, KO'd them, 4–1.

The Suns surprised them with a 104–102 win in Game 1 in the Forum. The Lakers won Game 2 by 24, and the series moved to Phoenix for 3 and 4, which would be back-to-back for TV on Saturday and Sunday, which was bad for an older team like the Lakers.

Led by the fast-emerging Kevin Johnson, the Suns shot 60 percent and won Game 3 by 17. That evening, Riley called a meeting back at the hotel and, redrawing the line he'd drawn in 1985 in Boston, and in 1987 in Salt Lake City, scorched them to a crisp. This time, however, he exempted Johnson, who'd been getting big numbers, which tore it with everyone else. Johnson described the impact that had on the team:

Riley always felt he had to hop on me to get to the other guys, but that time he didn't. Here I am putting up 40-something a night, so wasn't too much he could hop on me about.

He jumped Orlando [Woolridge] pretty good, and he wasn't used to getting it. He hit Byron real hard 'cause he wasn't making his shot. He singled me out the other way, and that kinda killed everything—*"Only one guy's playing good, and that's Buck!"*

I was saying, "Oh, man." It was over. We were through after the meeting. *"He got on me! I can't believe it!"* No way we could beat them.

We started the next game, went to Byron three straight times—missed. Couldn't get him into it. He complained he wasn't getting enough shots, so we went to him.

And [Riley] just said, *"OK, Buck, forget it! If they're not going to play, I'm going to run this same play every time!"* And I changed the play one time and he got mad at me! *"I told you to shoot!"*

Johnson scored 43 points, but the Lakers lost by 13 and fell behind 3–1.

In a crowning irony, before Game 5, the league announced Riley had been voted coach of the year for the first time. The salutatory press conference was more like a wake with Riley playing the role of the departed, or black-humor night at the Improv, as when he joked, "I'm ready now to see if I can coach."

When West said how proud he was of Riley's record, Riley asked, "What, 533 wins or 1–3?"

"I know there's something you always hear about that they're tired of hearing the same old song," Riley mused, as if answering the doubts. "As long as you keep staying truthful and keep dealing with the present moment—I know I get accused of conjuring up all these motivational ploys and all this stuff—you can stay connected."

The truth was, his team was split and his connection to it had frayed down to the last wire in the cable. The next day at shootaround, Cooper, upset at Johnson for chiding teammates in the press, almost came to blows with Magic, who was like his blood brother. That night they took a quick, 15-point lead, but the Suns brushed them aside from there on in, winning, 106–103. It was game, series, and season.

As for the era, they would have to wait 27 anxious days for Riley to make up his mind.

He was at a crossroads. The league's TV contract was switching from CBS to NBC, so a new stable of announcers would be required, and he was the obvious number-one choice with his glamorous persona and broadcasting experience.

Nevertheless, when the exhaustion wore off, Riley found himself looking for a way to stay, and would have, if anyone had only asked him to. No one did, not the players, not West, not even Buss. Riley pondered his options for almost a month, going to the owner's home for lunch to talk it over. Buss was pointedly neutral, even saying he'd take care of Riley financially in either case, stay or go.

Buss, who was farther away from the situation, was the last loyalist, but West had told him the situation was untenable. As Paul Westhead had noted, Buss wasn't confrontational, he preferred to suggest his preferences and hope you got the hint. Now he told Riley, who had two years left on his contract worth $1.3 million, he was willing to give him a $2-million going-away gift as a way of thanking him.

Buss later compared it to his relationship with one of his sons, who asked why he hadn't driven him harder; Buss said his way was to let people find their own path, and if he didn't tell his own son what to do, he wasn't going to tell Riley what to do.

"There are certain people that I feel have converted the Lakers from another basketball franchise to, in my estimation, *the* basketball franchise," Buss said. "And I've tried to say thank you in monetary terms. I know Magic's aware of that. I know Kareem's aware of that. . . . And Pat Riley is aware of it as well."

Riley finally came to grips with the reality: insisting on returning might lead to greater horrors. With only one graceful way out, Riley went over to Johnson's house to tell him first.

"It was already a sad day because it had just rained," Johnson said. "It was dark. I said, 'Do you want to sit inside?'

"He said, 'No, let's go outside.' We went out there and he started talking. We started thinking about the season and what had happened in the playoffs. He just said it—'Buck, I'm going to retire.' He started crying. It was just wild. It was like I was losing my best friend. He started, and I think we were both doing it."

On June 11, Riley announced his resignation. The organization gave him a farewell press conference worthy of a slain Viking. Everyone dwelled on their accomplishments over the years with no mention of the unpleasantness at the end. Riley's successor, Mike Dunleavy, was introduced, and they wished each other well.

The next day in the papers, the blunt-spoken Scott called it "a resurrection . . . like a raising from the dead," but everyone else was discreet. Only later would the story of the last days get out, dismaying Riley, who wanted the entire experience remembered the way he remembered it.

Riley's first rule was they would protect each other vis-à-vis the press, but it was broken as soon as he left. Two years later—it was so painful to Riley, it took that long to address it—he told NBC's Bob Costas, "I regretted the fact that the team would not embrace protecting the eighties. . . . That's what I wanted most out of that thing and I don't feel like it was that way."

Stung, he even went as far as to tell *Vanity Fair*'s Ken Auletta, "They changed, I never changed."

But the reality sank in over the years. It was great, even if they had problems at the end. Everyone went on with their lives. Cooper applied for (but didn't get) a job on Riley's Knicks staff. When Scott became a coach, he said he had modeled himself after Riley. Pat went on to greater fame, made much more money, and drove everyone just as hard in New York and Miami.

"What happened was, he made more money, commercials, and things than players," said Johnson. "He became a national figure, bigger than some of the players. And then with the complaints—he just had to go. It wasn't any two ways about it. It was one way. He had to go. Not because he wasn't a good coach. . . . He could never come back to the team and coach those guys."

The mule had had it.

Chapter 5

SLOWTIME

I think somewhere out there, there's a young little kid who'll be as great as Magic Johnson as a player. But he won't be as great as a leader.

—Jerry West, on Johnson's 1991 retirement

■ ■ ■

WELL, IT WAS FUN WHILE IT LASTED.

Even with Pat Riley and Kareem Abdul-Jabbar gone, something that looked like Showtime showed up for the 1990–1991 season. Mike Dunleavy was a sharp young coach, and his low-key style was a vacation after the latter-day Riles. They still had Magic Johnson on the floor, movie stars in the stands. In the spring, they gave everyone one last thrill by making the Finals for the eighth time in 10 years.

But it was a brief thrill. They drew Michael Jordan's hungry young Bulls, delighting Johnson, who was eager to begin a rivalry with Jordan like the one with Larry Bird, but this was a little shorter-lived. The Lakers stole Game 1 in Chicago on Sam Perkins' last-second 20-footer, but the Bulls won the next four as their mystic coach, Phil Jackson, an ace at defensive game-planning in his Earthly incarnation, hounded Johnson with the tag team of Jordan and Scottie Pippen.

Showtime ended the day of the Lakers' Game 5 loss—June 12, 1991—although nobody knew it. The result became official the next fall—on November 7, 1991—when Johnson shocked Lakerdom and the world with the news he was retiring because he had become HIV-positive.

That's how quickly the stars that had twinkled so brightly went out and the party ended.

. . .

Johnson had just turned 31 that fall and was finally putting away child-ish things. If there was always a boy's delight in his game and his smile, there was a child who still held sway in his head, too. He was like a kid in the greatest candy store of them all. He was on the A-list for parties and ceremonies, on the sideline for Raiders games. There seemed to be come-ons in every woman's eyes. Social as he was, as he noted in *My Life*, he loved women as a species. He didn't do drugs, alcohol, or tobacco, but he did do them.

It all fit.

In his way, he was just as driven as West and Riley, although without West's guilt or Riley's yearning to recreate a happier past. When Johnson won, he enjoyed it, unlike West; and Magic's past was like *Leave It to Beaver* compared to Riley's. Johnson was just an action/attention junkie with a lifestyle that didn't encompass serious relationships.

Women had to understand, he would tell them, the game came first and he had to take care of himself. They couldn't stay the night. It seemed all right with them. There was always a tug-of-war going on inside that head. Johnson's parents were God-fearing, hard-working people who had raised him and six brothers and sisters strictly. He was careful never to lose touch with East Lansing, which, in his mind, stood for everything wholesome about him.

They were like distinct personas he carried in his head. Earvin was East Lansing. Magic was loose in L.A.

By then, the Magic persona had already seen it all. In the fall of 1991, two weeks before training camp opened, Johnson told his longtime fiancée, Cookie Kelly, who'd been waiting for him since their college sweetheart days, he was ready to get *m-m-m-married*.

The September ceremony in East Lansing was small and intimate with old pals Isiah Thomas and Mark Aguirre there, but mostly family. Earvin was in charge now.

. . .

Like Johnson's adolescence, Showtime seemed to be running out too.

The Bulls were better and younger, and the Trail Blazers were better, too, even if the Lakers always thought they could outsmart them in crunch time. The Lakers still had high hopes for the 1991–1992 season, having finally found a capable point guard, Sedale Threatt, so they could cut Johnson's minutes. They were still the Lakers, after all, and they would always be the Lakers while Johnson was there.

It was a long preseason, featuring a trip to Paris for the McDonald's Open, which was a marketing vehicle for the league but a pain in the butt for players, who weren't into museums, churches, and extra jet lag. The Lakers were so uninspired, they almost lost to a Spanish team, Joventut Badalona, except for a call by their friendly NBA ref, Eddie Rush.

Back in the U.S.A., they set about finishing off the drudgery of the preseason. Johnson got the flu and came home from a trip to Salt Lake City. They played the rest of the exhibition season and the first three games of the season without him.

Then on the morning of November 7, the Lakers called a press conference for that afternoon. Publicist John Black told the reporters he talked to personally what it was about, stunning them: "Earvin's retiring because he's HIV-positive."

Johnson had never had the flu. He'd been brought back from Salt Lake City by his agent, Lon Rosen, at the direction of the team internist, Dr. Mickey Mellman. Buss had been in the process of giving Johnson a low-interest $3.6-million loan, which required Magic to take a life insurance physical. The blood test revealed the presence of the HIV virus.

Rosen called Magic in Utah. Only a handful of others were told over the next 11 days, while Johnson saw his doctors and was informed of his options. It was simple. He had no options. Playing would put too much strain on his immune system. As far as medical science knew, he was under a death sentence. It was just a matter of how long he could draw it out.

Johnson had Rosen call his closest friends: Thomas, Aguirre, Riley, Bird, and Jordan. Now Johnson was up in front of the world in the Forum press lounge, with a battery of camera crews against the back wall, trained on him and CNN going live all over the world.

He had just come from telling his hastily assembled teammates in an emotional meeting in the dressing room. Having dried his eyes, he was now composed again, handsome in a tailored blue suit with a white shirt and a dark tie as he made the announcement that, after all those great moments, would become his defining moment:

> Good afternoon. Because of the HIV virus I have attained, I will have to retire from the Lakers today.

Despite the gravity of the situation he was revealing, Johnson was buoyant ("I plan to go on living for a long time, bugging you guys like I always have") and purposeful, if ungrammatical ("I will now become a spokesman for the HIV virus"). Dunleavy, standing nearby, was amazed at Johnson's poise. Even in these most dire of circumstances, he was still Magic.

Despite appearances, it had been humiliating. Johnson's first inclination had been to keep his infection secret, but he quickly realized it would take a lot of lying. When push came to shove, he was going out the front door, head held high. It was a heroic decision that would be credited with saving lives in the future, and a remarkable performance.

Nevertheless, the numbness dissolved into grief. In the organization, which prided itself on being a family, it was as if everyone had lost a brother. Players, staffers, and fans wept. Press people wept. On the other side of the country, at that night's exhibition game in Madison Square Garden, Riley, now coaching the Knicks, asked fans to offer prayers during a moment of silence.

For weeks afterward, it didn't seem right to even think about what would happen to the Lakers without Johnson. Everyone's thoughts were with him. Of course, who needed to think about it? Everyone knew what the Lakers' situation was now.

They were screwed.

■ ■ ■

It wasn't that they were horrible; it was worse than that. Horrible teams got top draft picks that could turn things around. The Lakers were just ordinary.

Whatever their future was, one thing was certain: they didn't have many players on the lot who'd be part of it. Vlade Divac was 23, but the other starters—Perkins, Threatt, James Worthy, Sam Perkins, and Byron Scott—were all 30 or older. The only other prospect was 6'11" Elden Campbell, the 1990 No. 1 pick, who was talented but unfocused. He was once spotted eating Pringles chips in the dressing room an hour before a game, with a pamphlet about nutrition sitting under his stool.

Worthy, their biggest remaining star, was fading. Without Johnson there to play off of, his scoring average dropped from 21.4 to 19.9, and his shooting percentage fell to a career-worst 44.7 percent. Two seasons later, he would be done at 33, his fears about the toll the hard-driving eighties had taken on his body realized.

Bad times were here. They weren't really the Lakers anymore, but it still said LAKERS on their jerseys. They would take some awful poundings on the road, before jubilant fans who couldn't have been happier if the home team had a foot on the prone figures of Johnson, Riley, and Abdul-Jabbar. What had gone around was coming back around, ready or not.

Remarkably, Dunleavy got them back into the 1992 playoffs as number-eight seeds, but they weren't even top dogs in town now. They finished two games behind the Clippers under Larry Brown. Celebrating the new pecking order, the once-bedraggled Clippers commissioned a new ad campaign, "It's Hip to Clip."

The Lakers were quickly eliminated by Portland in the first round. Then they lost the promising Dunleavy, who was allowed to leave to take a big offer running the Milwaukee Bucks' entire operation.

Assistant Randy Pfund became the new coach, but events undid him from day one. Johnson tried to come back but changed his mind during the exhibition season. Worthy's average dropped another five points to 14.9 as they fell to 39–43 in 1992–1993, although that was still good enough for the number-eight seed.

They even threw a scare into the number-one Suns in the first round, taking a 2–0 lead in the best-of-five series. For all his problems, Campbell had great length and quick feet and a knack for guarding Charles

Barkley, which threw a kink into the Phoenix offense, before the Suns regrouped and won the last three.

A year later, Worthy was down to 10.2 points per game and 40.6 percent from the field in his swan song, and Jerry West, who understood the theory of "the trap of the middle," pulled the plug.

In a move that would be little noted nor long remembered, West traded Perkins, their best player, at the All-Star break. In return, the Lakers got Seattle's unsigned No. 1 pick, Doug Christie, and the infamous Benoit Benjamin, who had already proved hopeless with two teams. West was turning his back on mere "respectability," in the sure knowledge it meant nothing to jaded Lakers fans, who wouldn't be satisfied by anything but titles.

The deal, itself, didn't help the Lakers. Christie lasted only that season and the next, and Benjamin was gone before that. What it did, however, was commit the Lakers to rebuilding. Whatever happened, there could be no turning back.

If this doesn't seem significant, other teams, like the nineties Knicks, would find themselves at a similar crossroads and choose the less painful option of trying to patch on the fly, insisting they had to maintain profits, or their fans wouldn't stand for it.

Meanwhile, the Lakers would be back in the Finals by 2000, although no one would have been too confident about that in 1993, not even West.

Unfortunately, trading Perkins kicked the last strut out from under Pfund. They were 15–20 when Perkins left, and 12–17 after that when Buss decided to try something else—bringing back Johnson as a coach. Johnson was cool to the idea but felt he owed Buss enough to try it for the last 16 games.

By the end of the 1993–1994 season, the Lakers were a collection of prospects and suspects as West grabbed the most talented players he could find, whatever their reputations.

First among head cases was Nick Van Exel, a cocky, left-handed point guard who'd lasted 37 picks, halfway down the second round, in 1993. He'd lasted that long, despite being considered a first-round talent, because he had bugged so many coaches and GMs in individual workouts. Christie had become persona non grata in Seattle by refusing to sign. Anthony Peeler, a young guard from Missouri, had been involved in a domestic beef on the eve of the draft, in which he pointed a pistol at a former girlfriend.

They had talent, but they were a long way away. They were also tired of hearing about the old Lakers and Showtime. They wanted a new name: The Lake Show.

Nevertheless, even from the sideline, Johnson's galvanizing personality still worked. The Lakers won five of his first seven games and the fans, who had fled in droves, streamed back into the Forum as if someone had switched the lights back on in Lakerdom.

However, it wasn't long before Johnson, who didn't really want to be there, was noticing how little they resembled the Lakers of his time. Being Magic Johnson, of course, he spoke his mind, right down to the last thought.

After a loss at Phoenix, he announced, "We've quit already," noting, "Elden, Vlade, all them, if they don't want to play, fine, they won't play." Not that Johnson's plans were much of a mystery after that. His record was down to 5–6 with five games left when he announced he wouldn't return and ripped everyone anew.

"It's changed a lot," Johnson said. "Back when I was playing, I used to love it. If you were late, those other 11 guys would just rag you until you couldn't be late anymore. We understood how to help each other. If you had a baby, we all had a baby. Every guy was there. If you had a tragedy, every guy had a tragedy. It was just that family.

"Now you've got a lot of individuals. Everybody cares about me, I, I, I. 'Where's my minutes, where's my shots? What's wrong with my game? Why can't I get my game off?' So it's a lot of that now, and I don't like that."

The Lakers lost their last five games, dropping Johnson to 5–11 for his coaching career, which would never be resumed. He wasn't sure what he was going to do but, like West, he knew it wouldn't be that.

■　■　■

It was just the way things were going all around. In retirement, Johnson was no longer teflon-coated.

If all athletes who leave have a difficult time adjusting, it was particularly hard for Johnson. He had retired, thinking he was facing a death sentence, but day after day passed, and he didn't even feel sick. He began wondering if leaving had really been medically necessary, after all, because if it wasn't, he was only 31, with a lot of basketball left in him.

He had left to worldwide sympathy, but within months, a backlash set in, as his admissions of promiscuity inspired a new perspective: he was no hero. Suggestions he'd been infected in a homosexual act made it into print, not in some tabloid but in a *Sporting News* column by the respected Dave Kindred. Critics thought his descriptions of his sex life in his book, *My Life*, were aimed at proving he wasn't gay and inappropriately gleeful in any case. Some of his TV appearances, like the one on Oprah Winfrey's show in which he acknowledged engaging in group sex, were worse.

Nevertheless, Johnson, who was nothing if not strong-willed, went about living his life on his own terms. There was still enough pro-Magic sentiment among fans to get him on the All-Star team in 1992, his name having already been put on the preprinted computer ballots. When players like Cleveland's Mark Price and Utah's Karl Malone worried aloud about getting infected, doctors discounted the notion of the virus being transmitted in a game and Commissioner David Stern ruled Johnson could play.

It was a wild weekend in Orlando. *Sentinel* columnist Larry Guest wrote a piece, questioning Johnson's participation and heroism. There was speculation about the players' response. However, when Johnson was introduced, Isiah Thomas led the East players over, and, daring contact, hugged him, after which most of the others hugged him.

Johnson then proceeded to have one of those performances he saved for the biggest moments when he was most psyched, scoring 25 points with 9 assists, hitting a high, arching three-pointer in his last shot, and winning the MVP, to turn it into the usual personal triumph.

That summer, he played on the first Dream Team at the Barcelona Olympics with Jordan, Bird, Malone, Barkley, Clyde Drexler, David Robinson, and Patrick Ewing, the greatest team ever assembled. This was the first Olympic appearance for NBA players; fans and fellow athletes treated them as gods come down from Mt. Olympus, and Johnson as Zeus himself. Once, the Cuban boxing great, Teofilo Stevenson, shouldered past an armed guard to get to Johnson.

The first L.A. Lakers superstar was the one few got to see in his prime, the great Elgin Baylor.

Mr. Laker, Jerry West (No. 44) arrived in the NBA in 1960, the same year the team moved west. Wilt Chamberlain (No. 13) came nine years later, and in 1972, they finally won their first title in Los Angeles.

Suddenly the destination of choice for superstar centers, the Lakers got Kareem Abdul-Jabbar, who towered over rivals, two years after Wilt Chamberlain left.

Magic Johnson, his parents, and Commissioner Larry O'Brien celebrate Johnson's selection as top pick in the 1979 draft, starting the party known as Showtime.

Less than 11 months later Magic Johnson celebrates his first of five titles at the first of his five parades with teammates (from left) Norm Nixon, Brad Holland, and Kareem Abdul-Jabbar.

New owner Jerry Buss and Magic Johnson drink champagne after winning the 1980 title. The favoritism the boss showed for his young star was difficult for other Lakers.

The coaching carousel whirled in the early eighties until Paul Westhead's lowly assistant, Pat Riley (above), landed the job of a lifetime.

The greatest team rivalry in NBA history, the one between the Celtics and the Lakers, is heightened by the individual one between Magic Johnson and Larry Bird and culminates in the first of their three meetings in the NBA Finals in 1984.

Magic Johnson makes the shocking announcement that he's retiring because he's HIV positive before a hushed press conference televised around the world on November 7, 1991.

Still upbeat in the face of what seems like a death sentence, Magic Johnson says he plans "to go on living for a long time, bugging you guys like I always have"—and he does, coming out of retirement three times, twice as a player and once as a coach.

Jerry West, who takes everything hard, on an especially sad day, talks to the press about Wilt Chamberlain's death. Wilt's untimely passing at age 63 was one more thing that persuaded West to get out while he could.

Johnson had been hinting for months about returning to the Lakers and, shortly after getting back from Barcelona, still feeling the glow, he made it official. But the comeback didn't even make it out of the preseason. Johnson re-retired after more expressions of concern from players and a controversy when he was scratched in an exhibition in Chapel Hill, North Carolina, where trainer Gary Vitti was photographed treating him without rubber gloves.

Johnson would be back again—and again—as coach in 1994 and a player in 1996, but neither of those comebacks would work out, either. If they were ever going to be great again, it would have to be by moving forward, not backward.

■ ■ ■

From out of the mist, the outlines of a plan began to emerge.

In their first three seasons without Johnson on the floor, they fell from 57 wins to 43, 39, and 33, but despite appearances, the talent level was increasing. In the spring of 1994, with the only lottery pick West would make in the nineties, he took Eddie Jones. For a future No. 1, West snared forward Cedric Ceballos off the Phoenix bench. When Johnson's coaching experiment ended in the spring of 1994, West replaced him with white-haired, 57-year-old Del Harris, a native of Plainfield, Indiana, who looked more like a schoolteacher than someone who would be "relevant" to Van Exel and the young Lakers.

What Harris lacked in cool, he made up for in competence. He quickly reorganized the team, which jumped from 33–49 to 48–34. They reached the second round of the playoffs for the first time since Showtime, and Harris was named coach of the year.

Ceballos was a revelation, averaging 21.7 points and shooting 49.7 percent, with the added benefit of requiring few plays run for him. He just moved off the ball and got open underneath, or scored on offensive rebounds, although he was a slender 6'6".

They were respectable again. More important, their best players were on long-term contracts at reasonable prices. In another season, when a big free agent class would hit the market, they would be able to create about $10 million worth of cap space.

In the meantime, they had a problem or two.

Van Exel, whom they'd gotten just because he was so prickly, had a problem with authority figures, especially white-haired ones.

Ceballos had been nudged out of Phoenix because he ran with Barkley and didn't pencil out as well as Charles did on a risk-reward basis. Cedric had been arrested for carrying a gun in a Tempe club and once hosted a party so wild, Oliver Miller was traded for his part in it.

Now Ceballos, a smallish, overlooked late bloomer, thought he saw an opportunity to go from role player to star and cash in, perhaps even be the Lakers' Sir Charles. Ced blossomed all over the landscape, appearing on TV, trying his hand as a rapper. He called himself 'Chise, short for Franchise.

That was when Johnson began thinking about his latest comeback. Michael Jordan was back from his first retirement, and the Bulls, reinforced by Dennis Rodman, were stomping all comers in the East. With no one dominating the West, Johnson thought he saw a chance to boot the Lakers into the Finals for a last tango with Jordan.

Of course, it was also possible to imagine many noses getting out of joint if Johnson returned, starting with Van Exel, who would have to give up minutes and the ball.

Van Exel, however, gave his assent, manfully. Harris designed a scheme which would keep Van Exel at the point, bringing Johnson off the bench and using him at forward, so both could play at the same time.

After which, everything went up in flames. Johnson joined a 24–18 team in January, and they went on to finish 53–29 (29–11 with Magic), but with intermittent horrors.

Johnson's time at forward was coming out of Ceballos' minutes, and Ced had mixed feelings about it. On one hand, he was thrilled to play alongside Johnson; on the other hand, he didn't want to go back to second banana.

"I think I've benefited a lot because I've been in his ear the whole time," Ceballos said. "I say, 'Magic, what would you do in this situation?' . . . He always says, 'Well, I got these five rings on my fingers and I don't know what to do, my hands are getting heavy.' I'm trying to get there where he was, but if I can learn as much as I can from him, I'll be satisfied."

Apparently, Ced forgot to ask Johnson what to do about the situation on March 24, the day he jumped the team. Ceballos was still their leading scorer, but he had scored a season-low 12 the night before in a victory over the Sonics. When the Lakers met the next day to fly to Seattle for a rematch, co-captain Ced was nowhere in sight. Nor had he called in. Instead, he took his family to Lake Havasu City, Arizona, checked in at the London Bridge Inn and Resort, and rented a houseboat. The team was still frantically calling around to see if he was OK when the press, tipped as to his whereabouts, located the man who rented Ceballos the boat. "He's on the lake having a good time," said the boatman. "He's got his family with him, and he's just out having a good time."

As the *Los Angeles Times'* Scott Cooper noted, "He had better be. It's a $30,000 trip so far."

That was what Ceballos had given up, based on his $2.4-million salary. The tab would climb above $50,000, but that was nothing compared to the consequences. The trip would tear things between Ceballos and teammates, terminate his usefulness to the Lakers, and mark the turning point in a career that was now headed down the drain. As a disbelieving Magic put it, "The Lakers don't have problems. They have a problem."

Ceballos missed two games, and his agent didn't even get in touch with the organization for four days. Ceballos reappeared, looking contrite, at a press conference at which he said he'd had family problems. The organization couldn't argue with that in public and would have been happy to go along if the other players had bought it, or if Ceballos had squared it with them.

Instead, feeling their resentment, Ceballos withdrew. His teammates had already voted to take away his starting job when Harris sought their advice. They barely acknowledged Ceballos' presence on a cross-country flight to Orlando. Harris stripped him of his co-captaincy.

"Once he apologizes, it should be OK," said Van Exel, the surviving co-captain. "Right now, it seems like some guys are still distant from him. He hasn't said 'I'm sorry,' or he hasn't even said 'Hi.'"

It was never OK. Ceballos eventually regained his job but was never the same player for the Lakers. By January of the following season, he wasn't even a Laker, going back to Phoenix in a deal for Robert Horry.

Coming off back-to-back 20-point seasons, Ceballos would play minor roles for four teams in the next four seasons and be through by 32.

If Ceballos was the only one who would actually stomp out, there would be enough strange behavior to suggest lots of people were feeling the strains of integrating Johnson, including Johnson.

Three weeks after Ceballos sailed into the sunrise, the fiery Van Exel, in one of his periodic slumps and frustrated over losing time in fourth quarters to Threatt, got into an argument with referee Ronnie Garretson in Denver. Led away by teammates, Van Exel tore away from them and headed back to get in a last word, only to encounter Garretson, who was only a few steps away, knocking him backwards onto the press table.

This was serious, the league taking a dim view of contact with refs, even those who weren't sons of the officials' supervisor, Darrell Garretson. Let's just say it's a bad idea to bump one whose report starts, "Dear Dad."

Van Exel was suspended for seven games and lost more than that. If he had grown up tough and emerged rebellious, he tried to do the right thing, had an endearing side, and was overrated as a thug. Now, however, *Sports Illustrated* put an investigative team in the field, and the ensuing story made him look like Al Capone.

In true Nick style, the chastened dead-end kid managed to hold on to a corner of his defiance, apologizing to everyone in sight—teammates, fans, the league—except Ronnie Garretson.

"I think sometimes authority uses its authority too much," said Van Exel, sticking to his guns at a press conference at which he was supposed to set things right. "I think officials, they go overboard sometimes. Sometimes they don't respect players, and I don't think that's right."

Of course, in his role as elder statesman, Johnson noted that this wasn't a wise thing to do but he said it in a nice way, and no one took any umbrage.

Imagine everyone's surprise, then, when *Johnson bumped a referee, too!*

Johnson had always been such an avid debater of calls, opponents said he should get his own whistle so he could call the fouls. However, he'd never come close to bumping a referee before he made contact with Scott Foster five days later, in a nationally televised win over Phoenix in the Forum.

Johnson had only been in for eight minutes and had eight points and two assists when he argued a call, got a technical from Foster, tried to step in front of him, bumped him, and was ejected.

Fans littered the floor with pretzels, cups, and ice. Johnson said Foster caused the contact by stopping short, but after seeing a replay, he sent for NBC's sideline reporter, Jim Gray, and apologized to everyone he could think of, from Foster, to the rest of the referees, to Van Exel, who wasn't even there, sitting the game out as part of his suspension.

"I'm taking it harder than anybody," said Johnson. "I feel I let my team down. I let Nick down. If I'm going to come down hard and strong on Nick, then I've got to set an example."

Johnson only got a three-game suspension. As NBA VP Rod Thorn noted, he hadn't actually knocked Foster onto a press table with a forearm shiver.

Suggesting his mounting disgust, which was now about 11 on a scale of 10, West announced, "As with Nick Van Exel's suspension last week, we agree with the league's decision 100 percent."

Now they had to finish the season without their first team and their momentum wasn't what it had been. Nor did they get the weak first-round opponent they were hoping for. Instead, they would play Houston, the twice-defending champions who had struggled all season but still had Hakeem Olajuwon, whom the Lakers couldn't guard.

Nevertheless, none of the Lakers was prepared for the disaster that ensued.

As number-four seeds to the Rockets' number five, they had home-court advantage but surrendered it by losing Game 1 as the streaky Van Exel went 1-for-11. Fans fled up the aisles as if their Lexuses were on fire in the parking lot.

The worst was yet to come. Afterward, Johnson blamed his own sub-par performance on not knowing what Harris wanted him to do.

"In the first half, he didn't want me to post at all," Johnson said. "In the second half, he said, 'OK, now post.' Now, wait a minute. I'm used to posting. Now he doesn't want me to post. I'm wavering. I'm going back and forth. It's a real weird role for me to play when I'm used to something different. Then I tried to turn it on, and then it wasn't there."

Now there was a shocker. The other players had been complaining for months about Harris, but they were clueless kids who had gone through four coaches in three seasons—including Johnson—without falling in love with any of them.

For his part, Johnson had never made excuses, much less lame ones like not knowing his role. He had always been the organization's loose cannon, but if his candor was uncomfortable for the hierarchy, no one could object if he could go out on the floor and back it up.

In those days, he had been the sun and everyone else was just a planet whirling around him. Now he was a good player who could still run a team and put up numbers but no longer had his old ability to take over games at will.

It soon became obvious this wasn't just a bad moment but the tip of an iceberg of discontent. Asked the next day if he missed the days when everything radiated from him, Johnson answered, "Yeah," looking unenthusiastic and venturing nothing more.

OK, how did he feel about it?

"I'm not going to even touch that," he said laughing. "You know how I am, too. You all have known me too long. You know I can't sit back. I'm not good at it, I'll say that. Is that an answer for you?"

He was now admitting he wanted to start but insisting he was OK with Harris and OK with coming off the bench. However, by Game 4 in Houston, with the Lakers down, 2–1, and on the verge of elimination in the best-of-five series, Johnson was noting Van Exel's problems, too. When Van Exel said they had to get the ball to Eddie Jones, Johnson noted that Nick was the point guard so he should just run Eddie's play. Van Exel, who'd gone out of his way to accommodate Johnson's return, now became so upset at questions about his temper and leadership, he broke down as he talked to the press at the shootaround the next day and began sobbing.

Mercifully, the Rockets eliminated them that night before they figured out more ways to embarrass themselves.

Van Exel and Threatt missed the break-up meeting at the Forum. Harris, who was ill, couldn't even make it. Johnson was still holding out hope about returning, but now he no longer fit. The Lakers were $10 million under the cap and every dollar they paid him would be $1 less they could offer free agents.

A massive free agent loomed on their horizon, and from then on, he would be their only priority. Showtime was finally over, the Lakers had learned.

Chapter 6

THE NEXT BIG THING

I'm a role model,
I'm a role figure,
I ask myself,
Can I get any bigger?

—From *Shaq Diesel* by Shaquille O'Neal

■ ■ ■

THE SHORT ANSWER WAS: YES.

His body would get bigger, literally. His fame would mushroom, too, and he was already famous enough to have cut his first CD and dictated his autobiography, *Shaq Attack*, which could have been titled "Shaq, the First 21 Years."

Shaquille O'Neal, rapper, actor, self-styled "cross between Bambi and the Terminator" and NBA star, was just coming off his rookie season. The world was already opening him up like a giant oyster to reveal a pearl the size of a basketball, and the fury of attention—indeed already as bewildering as his rap verse suggested—was only just starting.

He had been marked for greatness for years. When he was a freshman at LSU, Don Nelson, then coaching the Golden State Warriors, saw him and announced, "I'm in love."

Two years later, when O'Neal was preparing to enter the draft, Indiana Pacers president Donnie Walsh announced, "The NBA ain't ready for this kid. This is like Wilt coming into the league." O'Neal was a lot like Chamberlain, but the league was a lot bigger now and everyone was making more money, becoming more famous, and getting that much dizzier. At 21, O'Neal already had an inkling of what he might achieve. The surprise would be how it felt, as opposed to how he had imagined it would feel.

It's weird to be the biggest and it's weird to be the best but biggest and best is the weirdest of all.

Most of the superstar centers had been peculiar enough to suggest their own conflicts. Bill Russell was closed off. Chamberlain was grandiose, as if determined to act out everyone's fantasies, but also yearned for approval. Kareem Abdul-Jabbar was alienated but yearned for approval. Bill Walton was a revolutionary, who made millions playing a game, renounced the rest of the system, and considered the press lackeys of the imperialist masters.

O'Neal actually seemed the most comfortable of them in his role and his skin. He was down to earth, approachable, and had a sense of humor. He was respectful of elders, so even if rival centers like David Robinson were leery of him, the veterans liked him. Michael Jordan thought he was cool. Charles Barkley said O'Neal and Patrick Ewing were the two nicest guys in the NBA.

But as the years went by and O'Neal climbed ever higher until he was lord of all he surveyed, you could see the trip getting to him. He started putting the Superman logo everywhere: tattooed on one bicep, etched in the glass of the front door of his house, in the grillwork of his Escalade van.

Now it seemed the best of times were never good enough. There was always something to complain about, starting with coaches who called him to account and, worst of all, teammates who didn't kiss the ring, like, say, Kobe Bryant.

But we're getting ahead of ourselves. There were lots of highs and lows to traverse before he would come to L.A., where he would learn the true meaning of the thrill of victory, the agony of defeat, and the confusion of real life that underlay it all.

■　■　■

He was different, all right. He had that lyrical name—Sha-KEEL, O-NEEL—and that ready smile. And, appropriately enough, he arrived at the dawn of a new era in the NBA.

It was second phase of the NBA's commercial age, which would enrich everyone beyond anything anyone had ever imagined. It was a pregnant moment because Michael Jordan, who had started the whole thing, was fully booked, Magic Johnson and Larry Bird were on their way out, and advertisers were looking for The Next Big Thing.

The age was only eight years old, having started unofficially in 1984 when Nike's Sonny Vaccaro told Phil Knight to eschew the usual practice of signing up a bunch of college players who were turning pro and give all their money to Jordan and market him for all they were worth. As Vaccaro would note, this was not a slam dunk back at the home office in Beaverton, Oregon, and he had to withstand a blistering cross-examination from the company's influential and acerbic counsel, Howard Slusher, before Knight said yes.

Until then, athletes in general, and NBA players in particular, got bupkus from endorsements. Most of the basketball players were black, which was an additional problem, but the white guys weren't doing much better. You could be Johnson with your dazzling smile, or Bird, already credited with saving the NBA, and all you had was the same small-potatoes hookup with Converse.

Nike's revolutionary act demonstrated two things: 1) Jordan was divine, or as close as was available for hire, and 2) there was a huge teenage audience willing to pay incredible prices for high-end sneakers, which were now called "athletic shoes."

It wasn't just basketball players who'd been the target audience for the old-line companies, like Converse. It wasn't just athletes. It was everyone. They didn't just wear them in games, they wore them everywhere. Sneakers were now fashionable. Nike hired the hot Portland shop of Weiden and Kennedy, which produced hip, MTV-style spots with directors like Spike Lee. As Henry Louis Gates Jr. wrote in *The New Yorker*, "What Josef von Sternberg was to Marlene Dietrich or what Scorcese was to DeNiro, Weiden and Kenny has been to Jordan."

More markets emerged, and as fast as you could say *ka-ching!* Jordan could sell more things, like soft drinks, another market dominated by the teen demographic that NBA players now took over.

How about . . . fast food! Enter McDonald's, which also learned to "Love This Game."

A new reality emerged. As Jordan's agent, David Falk, noted, with enough exposure, the athlete was no longer just being exploited (at a price, of course) to sell a product, he was also selling himself. As a salesman, Jordan had it all; he was spectacular on the floor, at his best when the drama peaked and the audience was biggest, telegenic, and likable, too.

His fame would go beyond anything seen before in baseball, football, or any other sport. Race was suddenly no problem, or even relevant. As Falk noted, "Celebrities aren't black."

If Jordan didn't invent celebrity, he took it to the next level. His arrival in the NBA coincided with the rise of cable TV and the proliferation of channels, which produced the ravenous hunger for programming that made stars of anyone who was on regularly—Regis Philbin, Kato Kaelin, the Coors Light Twins, the Miller Lite Catfight Girls. Stars became superstars, and Jordan, the greatest superstar, became something bigger—a megastar.

With ever-greater media saturation, celebrity was a force unto itself, like wealth or beauty, and all prostrated themselves before it, no matter how mad, contrived, or nakedly attention-seeking its incarnation.

"When you see Barbara Walters sitting at the foot of a bed with Dennis Rodman and naming him one of her 10 most fascinating people of whatever year that was, you know that Barbara Walters has sold out because Barbara Walters doesn't remotely believe that Dennis Rodman is fascinating," said a disaffected Bob Costas. "What she thinks is fascinating is an 18.6 rating instead of a 16.4 rating, and if Dennis Rodman can help her get it, she's willing to do that. That's her version of Jerry Springer letting people throw chairs at one another."

Rodman, Jordan's teammate for three seasons in the Bulls' version of Greatest Show on Earth, was just a maverick with a lot of tricks—like tattoos, earrings, cross-dressing, and off-center behavior—to make the camera follow him.

Jordan was in another universe, bigger than Babe Ruth, Joe DiMaggio, and Muhammad Ali put together, bigger than presidents and rock stars. Chinese children named Jordan one of the two most recognizable men on Earth, along with Chou En-Lai. God comparisons became frequent, sacrilegious or not. Mike was credited with a faith healing in Nothern California. At the 1992 Olympics in Barcelona, a European reporter asked him, "Are you a god?"

"Well," Jordan said, "I live in Chicago."

If he was human, he was royalty, even if he had no formal title. Once, after a game in Washington, D.C., a Saudi crown prince asked to visit Jordan in the dressing room but was turned down.

Said Bulls publicist Tim Hallam: "There's a crown prince in every city."

Pulitzer Prize–winner David Halberstam devoted a season to following the team to write a book, *Playing for Keeps: Michael Jordan and the World He Made* (although Jordan would never once sit down with him.) Historian Walter LaFeber wrote a book titled *Michael Jordan and the New Global Capitalism*. The Gates piece in *The New Yorker* cited the *Journal of Personality and Social Psychology*, anthropologist and marketing theorist Grant McCracken, novelist Robert Coover, and economists Tyler Cowen and Mark Hertzendorf.

The NBA was a prime beneficiary and quickly became adept at marketing. If the eighties were a golden age, with the Lakers-Celtics rivalry as the centerpiece, it went hand-in-hand with the commercial boom. The league, so long derided as "bush" and "YMCA," rocketed into prominence, even threatening to overtake the old national pastime: baseball. In 1993, 1997, and 1998, the NBA Finals posted better ratings than the World Series.

It all happened at blinding speed. In 1984, Jordan, entering his rookie season, got that unheard-of $2.5-million deal with Nike, including his own line of apparel. Veterans were so upset when he turned up at his first All-Star Game in Indianapolis clad head to toe in his brand-name stuff, some of them conspired to freeze him out.

Isiah Thomas always denied he'd been part of it, but Jordan always believed he was. This had serious consequences for Thomas, like being left off the original Dream Team.

That year, Falk tried to get Jordan a regional deal for $50,000 or so from Chicago-area McDonald's and was turned down.

In 1993, O'Neal got a $10-million deal with Reebok.

In 1996, Allen Iverson, a tiny guard who played only one year at Georgetown and was known only to hard-core basketball fans, got a $20-million deal with Reebok.

In 2003, Nike, which had withdrawn from the hoop endorsement business to ride out the "brown shoe revolution" and the economic downturn, got back in by giving a high school kid named LeBron James a $90-million deal. Nike also signed Kobe Bryant for $40 million and another incoming rookie, Carmelo Anthony, for $18 million.

Whether the moguls running the sneaker companies and media conglomerates had lost it, or whether these were actually good economic decisions, it amounted to the same thing for NBA players, who were now arriving even younger. They awoke one day to find themselves demigods.

■ ■ ■

And the biggest of them was O'Neal.

He arrived in the NBA in 1992, a year before Jordan retired for the first time, with advertisers wondering whom they would get to replace Mike.

Jordan wasn't actually done yet, he would leave in 1993 but return in 1995 to extend his rule until Retirement II in 1998. (He would also stage Comeback II with the Wizards from 2001–2003, but that would be a mere postscript.)

Jordan represented a confluence of so many attributes, his mantle couldn't be passed to a single player, no matter how many the press nominated. There was a "Next Jordan" phenomenon with Grant Hill, Jerry Stackhouse, Penny Hardaway, and Vince Carter designated as successors. All were nice-looking, medium-sized players with spectacular games, like Jordan, but none was as good as he was, or lasted as long, or did as much, and none came close.

O'Neal couldn't be a Jordan either. Before Shaq, it was axiomatic that big men couldn't be big endorsers, since the public couldn't identify with them, but that was just one of the rules O'Neal changed.

He was a Wilt for the nineties. By the turn of the century, O'Neal was deemed to be in a league by himself, the most dominating player ever (or MDE as he called himself) by observers as venerable and detached as Pete Newell.

O'Neal was not only huge but remarkably well-proportioned, as if God had taken a normal person and blown him up. The Lakers doctors would notice it right away. There was an anatomical term—ectomorph—that described other tall players who had narrow trunks and thin limbs. Shaq was a mesomorph with a thick trunk, which would get thicker, big arms, and huge legs. He represented an evolutionary step, the first 300-pound seven-footer the NBA had ever seen who wasn't fat. As a rookie with Orlando in 1992, he had 7 percent body fat.

Like his fellow giant, Chamberlain, O'Neal couldn't shoot free throws but there wasn't anything else on the floor Shaq couldn't do. For all his bulk, he had amazing quickness. He was as nimble as the hippo ballerina in *Fantasia* and, over the years, he became one of the game's best-passing big men. He could even handle the ball; sometimes you saw him at practice in idle moments, dribbling the ball back and forth between his legs effortlessly.

There was one difference between Chamberlain and O'Neal. Wilt often seemed almost dainty on the floor, as if he wanted to show he was just as skilled as the other guys or was afraid of hurting them. When he did dunk, it was just like a layup that he tucked carefully inside the rim.

O'Neal was power incarnate, using his massive size to establish position as close to the basket as possible. He knocked opponents out of his way like tenpins, intent on dunking, and if someone remained upright to challenge him, so much the better. When O'Neal threw one down, it was with everything he had, often grabbing the rim two-handed and jackknifing himself up on it. He chose a silhouette of himself in the act as his logo.

Willis Reed, the 6'9" Knick center, a powerful man in his own right, competed at a dramatic disadvantage against Chamberlain, but years later, after seeing O'Neal, remarked on the difference.

"The first time I guarded Wilt, I had 32 [points], and he had 56," said Reed. "The year we won in 1970, Wilt was coming off a knee injury, and the league went from having a 12-foot lane to a 16-foot lane. . . .

"Now, Shaquille just stays in the middle of the lane when he gets the ball. He's so close to the basket. Wilt was a skilled player, a finesse player. He shot the ball well, he had the hook, had the finger roll and the fallaway jump shot. If Shaq gets the ball deep in the paint, he's going to get fouled or score."

On the plus side, O'Neal was less conflicted than Chamberlain, although he had had his own issues. His biological father, Joe Toney, didn't marry his mother, Lucille O'Neal, and after they broke up, Toney didn't try getting back into his son's life until he was an NBA star.

By then, Shaq couldn't have cared less. His father, as far as he was concerned, was his stepfather, a blustering career Army sergeant named Phillip Harrison. However, suggesting some hurt or embarrassment, Shaq didn't mention the fact that Sarge was his stepfather in his first book.

In his second book, *Shaq Talks Back*, written eight years later after the story was out, O'Neal told the story with an accompanying passage from his mother, Lucille:

He didn't take to my husband right away. Before it was all of us, it was me and Shaquille. And when Phil came around, Phil kind of invaded our space. Shaquille was just two years old. We had that bond, that special bond with mother and son. His attitude was, "This is my mother, what are you doing here?" I told my husband, "If you want me, you gonna have to take my son." And my son came before him.

It took a while, but Shaquille and Phil finally warmed up to each other.

As a kid, O'Neal was called everything—Sasquatch, Shaqueer, Shaquilla the Gorilla. He paid everyone back by pushing them around until puberty dawned and a kid he beat up because he "ratted me out" began thrashing around on the ground as if in an epileptic fit. After that, O'Neal said, it occurred to him that he could really hurt someone.

He did poorly in school. As he wrote in *Shaq Talks Back*:

I didn't get bad grades because I couldn't do the work, I was just a clown. I thought I was cool, wearing my pants off my ass. I had the suede Pumas with the thick shoe laces. I was 10 years old and I had all Fs on my report card. All Fs.

I think part of it was my size. I used to try to slouch down and be the size of everybody else. My father always told me, "Be proud. Be proud of being that size." He always used to say, "You'll see." But at the time I didn't care. I was a clown. . . .

So I was 10 years old, all Fs on my report card. I was afraid to go home. I dropped my books and my report card, ran as far as I could, all the way downtown.

I was in the local arcade. I wasn't playing video games. I was just sitting there because I was afraid to go home. Then the Sarge walked in.

"What are you doing?" Phil said.

"I ran away because I didn't want you to beat me no more."

He said, "You know why I beat you? Because you don't listen."

Then he had a talk with me. I started to change.

He and Sarge would have a few more talks over the years and there would be more beatings, with fists after O'Neal got too big for the belt to bother him. But Shaq did change.

He was 6'8" in his sophomore year at the base high school in Wildflecken, Germany—not even good enough to make the basketball team—when he attended a clinic given by a visiting college coach, LSU's fast-talking charmer, Dale Brown. Like everyone else, Brown thought O'Neal was a grown-up. When Brown learned he was 16, he asked to meet his father and told Sarge to start thinking scholarship.

The family moved to San Antonio, where O'Neal did make the Cole High School team, coming out of nowhere to become a McDonald's All-American by his senior season. He was 6'11", 265 when he accepted Brown's longstanding scholarship offer and went to LSU, where he spent three seasons with opposing teams circling him as if he were the Maypole.

NBA teams were salivating over O'Neal from the get-go, but Sarge wanted him to stay four years. O'Neal wanted to leave after his sophomore season, but bent to his stepfather's wishes. However, after LSU was eliminated in the NCAA Tournament in his junior year, he stopped going to class and presented Sarge with a fait accompli.

"[Sarge] went into his room and slammed the door," O'Neal wrote in *Shaq Talks Back*, "because he wanted me to get a degree. And he came back and he said, 'All right. But promise me you'll get that degree.' I made him that promise."

That spring, the Timberwolves had the worst record and the best chance of drawing the first pick in the lottery. O'Neal thought that was a little too close to the Arctic Circle, and his new Los Angeles–based agent, Leonard Armato, began putting out feelers, asking what would happen if Shaq said he'd refuse to report and demanded a trade to, say, the Lakers?

Shaq was then hanging out with Armato in Los Angeles as everyone's guest. He sat in Jerry Buss's box at Lakers games, played pick-up with Magic Johnson at Sports Club LA, hit the clubs at night, and fell in love with the place. From then on, he always kept one of his fleet of Mercedes Benzes there so he'd have his own ride when he was in town.

However, on lottery day, the top pick didn't go to the Timberwolves but the Magic, from Orlando in the sunny heart of Florida, a city that served as a big bedroom community for Disney World, Universal Studios, SeaWorld, etc.

This was no small attraction to O'Neal, who lavished all manner of toys on the 12-year-old that still resided within him. Theme parks were the Notre Dame and Sacre Couer of his world.

It was as if he wanted to give his inner child everything he couldn't have when he was 12. He built a $2.9-million mansion in if-you-have-to-ask-how-much-it-costs-to-live-here-you-can't-afford-it Isleworth. There was an eight-car garage, an indoor basketball court, and a special room for nine-foot-high (in other words, even bigger than he was), perfect-in-every-detail statues of his number one idol, Superman, and the monsters from *Alien* and *Predator*.

O'Neal had the Man of Steel's logo tattooed on one bicep and "TWISM" on the other, from *Scarface*'s Tony Montana's slogan, "The World Is Mine." Shaq loved his jet skis and paintball fights, and even went bungee jumping once, which scared Armato half to death.

There was no more talk of power plays. O'Neal got off the plane in Orlando wearing mouse ears and never looked back, for four years anyway.

■　■　■

Sure enough, the league wasn't ready for him.

O'Neal wasn't far along in technique when he arrived. His low-post repertoire was rudimentary, and when he was double-teamed, he was lost. On the other hand, with all that size, athleticism, and a good work ethic, there was only one way this was going to turn out.

Top picks habitually held off signing as their agents tried to pry more money out of their teams. O'Neal and Armato, however, were bent on making a haul in endorsements, too, and were controversy-averse. Shaq took a seven-year, $41-million deal and signed in July, the fastest a No. 1 pick in the draft had come in since Dallas' Mark Aguirre in 1981.

O'Neal also attended Pete Newell's big man's camp in Hawaii, where pro players gathered to learn new tricks. Not many rookies did that, either. In Honolulu, veterans like Sam Perkins, Stacey King, and Danny Ferry became the first to gaze at the new wonder and walk away shaking their heads.

One day a visiting ESPN crew asked Perkins what O'Neal was doing there.

"Hell if I know," said Perkins, laughing.

Newell, himself, would one day put O'Neal in a class of his own, but for the moment, he was merely impressed, as opposed to blown away.

"He's not a Wilt," Newell said, "but he's got some of the same stuff Wilt had, the overpowering physicality. He doesn't have all the moves yet, but for a kid his age, he's so much farther along than any kid I've seen in a long time.

"There are so damn many potholes out there with the money being what it is. You just don't know what's ahead."

By now, the competition was not only keener but bigger. When Chamberlain turned pro in 1959, there were only two other players over 6'10" in the league. By 1992, most teams had a seven-footer and some teams were almost half comprised of big men. The Bad Boy Pistons once had five: 7'0" James Edwards, 7'0" William Bedford, 7'0" Tree Rollins, 6'11" John Salley, and 6'11" Bill Laimbeer. By mid-decade when East teams were bringing in big men from everywhere to deal with the menace in Orlando, the Pacers had 7'4" Rik Smits, 6'11" Dale Davis, 6'10" Derrick McKey, 6'9" Antonio Davis, and 6'9" Sam Perkins.

But there were no other big men like *this*. Raw as he was, O'Neal wowed, or scared, all he came across in his first preseason. "He's 20 years old?" exclaimed Miami's 6'11" Rony Seikaly, who would be giving away 50 pounds to the new behemoth. "Give me a break."

The first time Seikaly put a move on O'Neal, Shaq blocked his shot into the stands. Yelled Orlando's Scott Skiles: "It's a whole new world, Rony!"

Skiles, a hard-nosed, reformed bad boy, made O'Neal his personal project. If everyone else was treating O'Neal like a prince, he was just another rookie to Skiles. More to the point, Shaq was a rookie with untold promise who had to be pointed in the right direction.

"He can start thinking about being one of the best players who ever played the game," said Skiles. "He can start thinking about doing all those things and then working very hard to get there. That's what your Magic Johnsons do, your Larry Birds, your Julius Ervings, Michael Jordans.

"And then there's your Darryl Dawkins." (Dawkins was a notorious screwup with a funny schtick, naming his dunks and claiming to be from the Planet Lovetron.)

O'Neal was a prodigy from a different planet. Raw as he was, he averaged 23 points and 14 rebounds as a rookie, and the Magic jumped from 21–61 to 41–41.

If Skiles sounded tough, that was just the polite version for the press. He would get right in O'Neal's face, or his stomach, anyway, as he did one day at practice when O'Neal had a problem with Larry Krystkowiak. Skiles came over and told them to fight or knock off the BS. A melee ensued in which O'Neal put a headlock on Skiles, who was happy to come out of it still wearing his head.

"My neck was sore for, like, six weeks," Skiles said years later when he was coaching the Bulls. "I don't think I'd go that route again." By then, he was also calling O'Neal "one of my all-time favorite teammates."

O'Neal's promotional push was just as impressive. He had chosen Armato because he had a tiny client list and because O'Neal liked his pitch about helping him make even more money off the floor.

(Of course, Armato also had to endure baptism by Sarge. As Harrison noted in *Shaq Talks Back*, he told the agent, "If you mess with my son, I'll kill you." When Armato looked at Lucille for some assurance Sarge was kidding, she told him, "He's not lying.")

Armato had a program. He gave O'Neal lessons in how to be gracious but noncontroversial with the press, with practice interviews conducted by Los Angeles TV reporter Randi Hall.

They got the Reebok deal, paying $2 million annually, in a bidding war with Nike. Within two seasons, O'Neal's off-court deals were reportedly worth $10 million a year. It had taken Jordan years to reach that level.

That was how fast things were changing. Jordan had to first demonstrate he was a spectacular player and a unique marketing vehicle before reaping his reward. O'Neal got his just by showing up. The result was a massive sense of entitlement. Where Jordan had to perform not only on the floor but with the press to show his winning personality, O'Neal started off with the riches in hand and considered the press a burden.

Actually, the beat guys were a small part of what O'Neal was called upon to do after all his commercial shoots, photo shoots, and one-on-one sit-downs with the biggies—NBC, the league's broadcaster, as well as other TV networks, national magazines, and big newspapers.

Nobody got a big piece of him. Alan Richman of *GQ* got 45 minutes of O'Neal's time, tagging along after him, for its coveted cover piece. Shaq was admirably candid about what he thought of the entire process. "I got four versions of the smile," he told Richman. "I got the $1 million, the $2 million, the $4.6 million, and, if you're real good, the $8.8 million."

The beat guys got what was left over, and that wasn't much, whether measured in time or attitude. From a cost/benefit perspective, they had little to offer O'Neal in terms of approval and opportunity that he didn't already have. They were also the ones who reported his bad games, which was a problem since he wasn't the thickest-skinned prodigy who'd ever come down the pike. So he "shammed" them. This was his own word, short for "short answer method." No one ever said he wasn't funny, but willing was another question.

O'Neal's normal voice was low enough, and when surrounded by a crowd of press people, he spoke even more softly to encourage them to leave. Once, during one of his usual nothing sessions at the 1995 Finals, a writer walking up asked, "Any new mumbles today?"

Even years later as a Laker, when O'Neal had cleaned up his act with the press (a little, anyway, since he still pulled the occasional month-long silence), he still murmured softly when he wasn't into it. Reporters at the back of the pack couldn't hear, pointed their tape recorders at him, and then played them back in the press room before writing their stories. The *Los Angeles Times'* Tim Brown called it "Shaq surprise."

■ ■ ■

And so it began.

The Magic missed the playoffs by a tie-breaker in O'Neal's rookie season, after which coach Matt Guokas was fired, to be replaced by his assistant, Brian Hill. Management insisted this wasn't a mutiny or anything out of line, but Jack McCallum, the *Sports Illustrated* writer who ghosted O'Neal's first book, later noted O'Neal kept telling him, "We've got to get Matty out and Brian in."

The Magic had been lucky to draw O'Neal's draft rights with less than a 30 percent chance, but what happened next was like having a lightning bolt come down to light your cigarette. Magic GM Pat Williams who had a 1-in-256 chance of drawing the No. 1 pick, drew the No. 1 pick. This was presumed to be Michigan's 6'10" Chris Webber, who would have given the Magic a front line to fear. However, Webber came off as spoiled in a visit, and team officials were also considering the theory that the most important position they had to fill was not power forward but point guard.

Meanwhile, who should call from the car phone in his West Coast Benz but O'Neal, who was in Los Angeles working on the movie *Blue Chips*. He'd been playing pickup with another player-turned-actor named Penny Hardaway, a highly regarded point guard from Memphis State, and had been dazzled. Hardaway had already worked out for Magic officials but hadn't been impressive. However, when they asked him to come back, he dazzled them, too. On draft night, Hardaway became theirs.

Hardaway had a reputation as fragile, physically and mentally, but he was a tremendous talent, as he proceeded to demonstrate, which left little doubt that the Magic was the team of the future.

In the interim, however, things were getting weird.

It was not uncommon for veterans to be jealous of young, hyped players. It had happened with Jordan in that All-Star freeze-out in Indianapolis in 1985 and it was happening again with O'Neal, who had gotten more than any young player ever had, even Mike.

It just so happened that by the time O'Neal's second All-Star game at Minneapolis came around in 1994, *Blue Chips* was coming out, and there were movie posters on billboards all over proclaiming his debut as an actor.

Then there were his TV commercials, which were like water torture for other players, like the one in which he was welcomed into the pantheon of greats by Chamberlain, Russell, Abdul-Jabbar, and Walton, with John Wooden there to suggest wisdom, or, perhaps, just because he was available that day. There was another commercial in which Shaq did a rap, roaring, "Do you want me to shoot? Do you want me to pass? Do you want me to slam?"

The veterans really wanted him to be quiet. Ironically, except for the commercials, which all the other players would have done if they could have, O'Neal showed older players nothing but respect. He never bragged at their expense, or told them to move over, or acted as if he was owed anything.

Nevertheless, in the All-Star Game, the West players spontaneously began ganging up on O'Neal whenever he touched the ball. This would have been routine in a game but not in this exhibition, in which they were all just supposed to be putting on a show. O'Neal wound up missing his first 10 shots, bricked seven of his 11 free throws, and scored eight points. Afterward, the West coach, George Karl, said it had been spontaneous, insisting he didn't tell his players to do that.

"I thought people were jumping out of the first row of the stands, trying to block his shots," said the West center, David Robinson, although he insisted he hadn't started it.

For his part, O'Neal didn't want to believe he had inspired a conspiracy, saying the press was making it up. Upon further reflection, he concluded there was something to it and after that, whenever he played one of the West All-Stars' teams, he began dropping huge numbers on them.

There was a full-fledged league-wide backlash arrayed against him now. It even got a name: Shaq-bashing. On a league conference call, the gentlemanly Robinson, whom O'Neal had singled out as his special rival, went off when asked about Shaq.

"It blows my mind, I get so many Shaq questions," Robinson said. "About his feelings, that he's upset about calls, that he doesn't like this or that.

"Who's Shaq? Why should I lose sleep that he's upset? It's funny to me everyone plays to him so much. He's a good player, no question. He's athletic, 300 pounds, a phenomenon. He gets credit for how good he is, but it blows my mind how people are concerned how he feels neglected."

In a *Sports Illustrated* poll that spring, 12 of 21 coaches picked someone other than O'Neal to start a franchise around. One coach who picked Alonzo Mourning called O'Neal "a part-time basketball player." This proved there were a lot of coaches in the wrong business. As ferocious as Mourning was, he was 6'9". It just wasn't the same thing.

Also, it was a little early to be writing off a giant who was en route to bumping his rookie averages of 23 points and 14 rebounds up to 29.3 and 13. O'Neal wound up missing the scoring title when Spurs coach John Lucas kept throwing the ball to Robinson so he could get 71 points against the Clippers in the last game, enabling him to tack another .5 to his 29.26 average and pass Shaq.

The Magic, which had improved from 21 wins to 41 the season before (while the Hornets were improving by 13), went to 50 and made the playoffs, although it didn't stay long. The Pacers' Byron Scott won Game 1, 89–88, with a late 20-footer, after which the young Magic players folded and were swept, 3–0.

The next season, 1994–1995 brought the missing piece, power forward Horace Grant, a mainstay on three Bulls championship teams, who bailed after Jordan's retirement.

Starting the 29-year-old Grant and four players 25 or younger, their win total went to 57. This time, they tore through the postseason, defeating the Bulls in Jordan's comeback in the second round, on their way to the title.

Almost.

■ ■ ■

Never, ever would what looked like a dynasty get so close and fall apart so quickly.

On June 7, 1995, Nick Anderson, the tough barrel-chested shooting guard who'd been the team's leading scorer before O'Neal arrived, went to the line, needing only one free throw to ice Game 1 of the Finals against the Houston Rockets.

It had already been a shootout at the O-rena, with the favored Magic going up by 20 in the first half, the Rockets rallying, and the Magic recovering their poise to take control at the end.

Anderson, a 70 percent free-throw shooter with a clutch reputation, missed the first one. Then he missed the second one, but got the ball back in the scramble for the rebound and was fouled again. So he went back to the line with :10 left . . . and missed again. Then he missed number 4.

With 1.6 seconds on the clock, Houston point guard Kenny Smith banged in a three-pointer to send the game into overtime, where the Rockets proceeded to win it. The Magic, which seemed destined to field the youngest starting lineup ever to win an NBA title, promptly folded, losing the next three games.

For the Magic, the future hadn't quite arrived. As it turned out, it never would.

Chapter 7

TWIN KILLING

He's kidding himself. Sure, he'd like to come out. I'd like to be a movie star. He's not ready.

—NBA scout Marty Blake, on Kobe Bryant's entry in the draft

■ ■ ■

ON APRIL 29, 1996, a senior at Lower Merion High School on Philadelphia's Main Line, dressed to kill in a suit and tie with his sunglasses pushed back atop his shaved head, announced at a specially called press conference that he would forego college to "take my talents to the NBA."

Local press people rolled their eyes, and no one else much cared. If one day Kobe Bryant would inspire awe, now he was just a 17-year-old kid who seemed to have gotten a long way ahead of himself. Not that anyone thought this had anything to do with the Lakers, including the Lakers. All their attention was focused on signing a big free agent, whose initials were S O'N.

It all came down in the week of July 11, the biggest caper the game had ever seen. Jerry West landed O'Neal and Bryant, compared by then–Phoenix coach Danny Ainge to a latter-day Wilt Chamberlain playing with a latter-day Michael Jordan.

After that, nothing would be the same.

■ ■ ■

Of course, first, the Lakers had to find out if O'Neal wanted them as much as they (drool) wanted him, and the answer was . . . uh, possibly.

And before that, O'Neal had to decide if he really wanted to leave and the answer was . . . uh, maybe.

If everything had gone spectacularly in his first three seasons in Orlando, right up until Nick Anderson missed those free throws in the 1995 Finals, O'Neal's last season had been a confused mess. He missed the first 22 games after Miami's Matt Geiger delivered a two-handed karate chop to his thumb in an exhibition. In what would turn out to be a mixed blessing, the Magic went 17–5 with Penny Hardaway playing brilliantly, averaging 29 points, even winning a shootout with Jordan in a nationally televised game.

On one hand, Hardaway was becoming a star in his own right. On the other, O'Neal didn't like it. This wouldn't be anything like the Shaq-Kobe feud with the Lakers because Hardaway was deferential where Bryant was not. O'Neal and Hardaway would never be anything other than cordial as teammates, but there was an intense rivalry between their agents, Armato and the Poston brothers.

Shaq hadn't turned out to be a coup for Reebok, but Penny was one of Nike's biggest stars, appearing in commercials with a puppet alter ego named Li'l Penny, who was as sassy as Big Penny was soft-spoken. Suggesting O'Neal's view of Li'l Penny, Shaq cut a Reebok spot in which he brushed a talking puppet off his sofa.

Magic management now decided that Hardaway was as important as O'Neal and so informed O'Neal. An upcoming free agent—7'1", 320 pounds, and insecure—was told he couldn't get a bigger deal than Penny's.

However, if O'Neal left GM John Gabriel's office steaming that day, and if he dated his departure to that meeting, it was actually remarkable how hard Shaq would try to stay after that.

A lot more would have to go wrong to get him out of there, and it did.

■   ■   ■

By now, the Magic organization was fixed on O'Neal's upcoming free agency. Everyone knew the Lakers were interested. Everyone knew Armato wanted O'Neal near him in Los Angeles.

And stuff kept happening.

O'Neal had a child out of wedlock, and an Orlando talk show host took issue with that at length. Through the press, Hardaway begged the populace to get off O'Neal's back, noting, "A guy like Shaquille doesn't have to take anything from anybody, especially in Orlando. If they keep putting pressure on him, maybe that will drive him away to somewhere like Los Angeles or a bigger city where people don't make a big deal about anything like this."

The All-Star Game in San Antonio was the usual drag for O'Neal, who led all scorers in an East victory, only to see the MVP go to Jordan, who was a lot more cooperative with the press. O'Neal stomped out angry, as usual.

The capper came when O'Neal's maternal grandmother, Odessa, died. The Magic went to great lengths to accommodate O'Neal, putting a corporate jet at his disposal, sending two officials to the funeral in New Jersey and a third to the wake, telling Shaq not to come back until he was ready.

Five days and two games later, O'Neal still hadn't called them, and the *Orlando Sentinel* reported he'd been seen out late in a club in Atlanta.

The next game was a nationally televised one at home against the Bulls with expectations running high . . . and no Shaq. He did arrive—late—but only after his mother phoned him at home and told him to get over there.

NBC was all over the story, reporting the late arrival breathlessly, with Jim Gray reporting that coach Brian Hill didn't want to play O'Neal but had been overruled by management.

"NBC," said Hill by way of reply, "is a pain in the ass."

O'Neal played, and the Bulls won. Embarrassed, O'Neal denied all the reports and blamed the organization for everything.

"I just wish people would stick up for me more," he said. "It just doesn't make sense. Where the hell did they think I was? They saw me at the funeral. Did they think I was out water skiing with Cedric Ceballos?"

The organization had no comment.

■　■　■

On sheer talent, the Magic won 60 games, three more than the season before, but they weren't the kingpins anymore.

With Jordan back in Chicago for a full season and Dennis Rodman joining him, the Magic's picture window of opportunity was now shut. The Bulls had won 72 games, a record, and 12 more than the Magic.

The season before, the Magic had seemed to come of age in the Bulls Round 2 playoff series, in which Chicago's Phil Jackson went out of his way to challenge Grant, his old whipping boy. Horace responded by knocking down jump shot after jump shot and was carried off the floor by jubilant teammates after they ended it in Game 6 in the United Center.

This time, when the teams met in the East Finals, it was Bulls 4, Magic 0.

Jackson had no compunctions about fouling O'Neal intentionally. It was such a common tactic, it had a cute Shaq name, Hack-a-Shaq. Journeymen like Luc Longley and Bill Wennington grabbed O'Neal whenever they felt like it and sent him to the line where he shot an embarrassing 12–33.

The Bulls took Game 1 in the United Center, came from 24 points behind to win Game 2, and after that it was a light-hearted frolic. Jordan, asked before Game 4 if he still considered the Magic a threat, answered, "This year or next?"

Meanwhile, well-intentioned Magic fans tried to help O'Neal with his free-throw shooting. Before Game 4, the pastor at the First Baptist Church of Orlando asked his congregation for a "love offering" to hire a free throw–shooting coach. A local radio station held a Beat Shaq free-throw contest; the *Orlando Sentinel* reported that among the kids who beat O'Neal's mark in this series—25 percent for the first three games—were nine-year-old twins from Daytona Beach.

Happily for Shaq, the Magic were eliminated in Game 4, saving him further humiliation, at least at the free-throw line.

Live TV was something else. Amid press reports that O'Neal wanted Chuck Daly to replace Hill, Armato went on the air during the Game 4 telecast. Asked about bringing in Daly, Armato said that was a "difficult call," adding that Daly "was one of the greatest coaches of all time."

Asked about Hill, Armato said the Magic coach was doing a good job—"this quarter."

Now, either Armato was down on Hill, personally—which would turn out to be Shaq's story—or this was coming from Shaq.

Elimination brought more speculation that the team was split, with Hardaway and Anderson backing Hill, and Shaq and Grant favoring Daly. After Game 4, Penny stayed on the floor congratulating the Bulls, while Shaq stormed into the dressing room and slammed a chair up against the wall.

However, if Hill was a problem for O'Neal, who was about to become a free agent, owner Rich DeVos frankly didn't give a damn. He had just given Hill a two-year, $3-million extension and now announced he had no intention whatsoever of firing him, noting, "We don't fire people on a knee-jerk basis. Brian Hill is a good coach and he's doing a good job."

DeVos might as well have added, "Around here, we don't let the hired hands run the rodeo."

Nevertheless, O'Neal was still with the program. The next day he went on NBC and pleaded ignorance on the Daly issue, declaring, "I don't know where that report came from, but I was raised to respect my elders."

Nevertheless, what had been the team of the future had issues, starting with O'Neal, whose free agency was six weeks away.

■   ■   ■

Amazingly enough, after all the frustrations, knowing the Lakers were waiting with open arms, O'Neal was still the Magic's to lose.

O'Neal had a problem with Hardaway and Penny's buddy, Anderson. He wanted Hardaway to throw him the ball more and was upset that Hill didn't crack down on the fragile Penny.

Nevertheless, he still liked it there. His $2.9-million Isleworth home with its eight-car garage was going up. He had just moved his mother, now separated from Sarge, there. His two sisters, his brother, and his best friend had all moved there.

For his part, DeVos wanted O'Neal back but in a seemly manner, which did not include a soulless auction in which they had to beat the highest offer Armato could solicit.

Catering to superstars was the NBA Way, but DeVos had only been in the league for five seasons. The Amway magnate was a Grand Rapids,

Michigan–based, American-heartland type of CEO, who'd bought the team in 1991, a year before it began drawing the top pick in the lottery annually. It was understandable if he'd been spoiled by the onrush of success and didn't understand how quickly it could go, or how hard it would be to duplicate.

DeVos put great store in principle. He had written a book called *The Compassionate Capitalist* and meant for the team to do more than win titles and make money. It was supposed to be a shining light in the community, as it announced in a mission statement embossed onto the team's expensive stationary.

DeVos put the word out through the *Sentinel's* influential columnist, Larry Guest, this wouldn't be about money and greed, and if it was, O'Neal could leave. DeVos wanted an expression of loyalty from Shaq; he told Guest he had advised Shaq, "I want your heart, not just your body."

More than DeVos would ever understand, he actually got an expression of loyalty from O'Neal, because Shaq's intention to stay didn't waver when the Magic opened the bidding with a four-year, $55-million bid. Seven-year deals were the standard, but Armato and O'Neal made no protest publicly, and negotiations continued.

It was a wild summer, with a huge class of free agents, some 165 players, more than half the league. The NBA had just begun a new collective bargaining agreement and, in order to get a rookie wage scale, had given the union a major concession. All the restricted free agents, whose teams had had the right of first refusal, were now unrestricted and on the open market.

O'Neal was among the restricted free agents who were freed. The Magic had given him an opt-out in the fourth year of his seven-year deal as a pro forma move to ensure that if his contract fell below the superstar pay scale, they'd make it up to him. Such moves were common and carried no risk, until the ground rules changed. In the stroke of a pen, the Magic lost its right of first refusal and would have to bid for O'Neal like anyone else.

O'Neal was the biggest star out there, but there was a long list of them. David Falk, the superagent for whom hubris was a way of life, even announced a price list for his clients: Jordan, $25 to $30 million (per annum, of course); Alonzo Mourning, $15 million; Dikembe Mutombo, $14 million; Juwan Howard, $13 million; Kenny Anderson, $7 million.

The numbers were astronomical, but teams would pay. Falk adroitly used one client to set the price for another, starting when he forced Charlotte to trade Mourning to Miami, having gotten Pat Riley's word he'd come up with the $15 mill for Zo.

Mourning's deal was for seven years and a total of $105 million, which meant one thing to O'Neal. He wasn't going anywhere for less than $105,000,001.

■ ■ ■

Meanwhile, Jerry West was having a cow.

Five years of rebuilding that began when Magic Johnson announced he was HIV positive had led to this moment when they might hit it big or go down swinging. West, a basket case under normal circumstances, was up to the challenge intellectually, but emotionally, he wasn't suited for competition with stakes this high.

Nevertheless, he now had the Lakers on the brink of something special. In two seasons, they had risen from 33–49 to 53–29, with their key players locked up in long-term deals that still left them with the ability to create cap space. They would be major players in the biggest free-agent bazaar the NBA had ever seen.

Doubling their cap space, on draft day West traded center Vlade Divac and his $4.5-million salary to Charlotte for the rights to Bryant. It would become one of the great steals in NBA history, on the level of Red Auerbach's Bill Russell–for–Ed Macauley deal in 1956, but at the moment it looked like it was just a convenient salary dump, moving the Lakers up in the O'Neal sweepstakes.

That was how little anyone knew about Bryant, except for the NBA people who had worked him out and had been dazzled.

At 6'6", 185 pounds, and 17 years of age on draft day, Bryant represented something new. He wasn't the first high school kid to dare the jump, although only a few—Moses Malone, Darryl Dawkins, Bill Willoughby, and Kevin Garnett—had preceded him.

But Bryant was the first prep guard to do it. Malone, Dawkins, and Garnett were all big men, and even Willoughby, who was 6'8", was a forward who might grow into a big man.

Instead, Willoughby became a bust. For all Dawkins' fame as a dunker and a comedian, the 6'11", 265-pound zany didn't amount to much, either. After they went in the 1975 draft, the NBA went 20 years before the next prep came out.

Garnett's entry in 1995 hadn't been overly controversial. He was a seven-footer with a lot of game; he was poor, and, although he had signed at Michigan, his SAT score wasn't good enough to let him play as a freshman. He had quickly proved he could function in a grown-up world.

A year later, along came Bryant, who wasn't a seven-footer, wasn't poor, and had a 1080 SAT, good enough to get him into Duke, which pursued him, or Harvard, if he'd been interested.

Skepticism was widespread.

"My people felt he was a great high school player," said Indiana president Donnie Walsh that spring. "We're not ready to say all these high school players are going to develop in the NBA. I think if you look at Kevin Garnett, he rose up to it. Maybe Bryant will too."

Nor were the Lakers interested. They already had three good guards, Nick Van Exel, Eddie Jones, and Anthony Peeler, who were 24, 24, and 26, respectively.

They had seen Bryant at the McDonald's All-Star game in Pittsburgh, which was now a stop on the predraft tour. There were a lot of hot young prospects in the game, like Jermaine O'Neal, Tim Thomas, and Mike Bibby, but the kids understood this wasn't about basketball but showing what they could do. It was a preening, highlight show in which everyone got out of everyone else's way and Bryant didn't stand out.

That was March 31. The Lakers didn't think about Bryant again for months until his agent, Arn Tellem, asked West to work him out as a favor. Tellem was Santa Monica–based, and his family and West's were friends; their kids played together. West said yes.

"In the beginning, after Kobe announced, before he worked out with any team, a lot of teams thought he'd go at the end of the first round," says Tellem. "He was a perimeter player, he wasn't Garnett, he wasn't

6'11". I really wanted to get a gauge so I brought him out to meet Jerry, have Jerry work him out."

The workout was in the Forum against a 6'8", 210-pound Mississippi State junior named Dontae Jones, who would go No. 21. It quickly went from a routine session to one you tell your grandchildren about. Bryant had a skill level that was off the charts. Even more remarkable, 17 or not, he had poise they couldn't believe.

"We interviewed Jermaine O'Neal when he came out," said Larry Drew, one of the Lakers assistants who ran the workout. "He was a high school kid. But Kobe, I saw him do some things I hadn't seen in a long time. I was surprised and shocked at his skill level, but I was more amazed at his level of a confidence, a kid coming out of high school. It was clear his skill level was much higher than Dontae's. It was pretty easy for Kobe.

"The thing that really struck me was, when I got to the gym before the workout, he hadn't come out yet. And he had kind of a slink walk about him. I could just kind of look at him and tell this kid was confident about his skills. . . .

"He did look like a high school kid. He was skinny. Still had the real babyish look. His body wasn't real developed—but he had a basketball body. When he did come out and stepped on the floor and got a ball, he knew exactly how to warm up. He didn't just come out and start taking shots all over the place. He went to a particular spot and stayed in that spot and shot one particular shot. He was shooting, like, 10 or 15 shots one way and then he'd go to the same spot and shoot 10 or 15 shots the other way."

Tellem, anxiously awaiting West's call in Santa Monica, picked up the phone and learned he was sitting on the mother lode.

"After the workout—I'll never forget it—when Jerry called up, he said it was the best workout he'd ever seen in his life," Tellem said. "At the end of the conversation, he said, 'We've got to figure out a way to get him here.'"

If West's report to Tellem sounded like hyperbole, there would be a lot of hyperbole that spring as Bryant worked out for the Clippers, Suns, and Nets.

Clippers coach Bill Fitch, a hard man to impress, said Bryant did some things in their workout "that nobody had done," doing a routine called the George Mikan drill where he kept throwing the ball against the backboard to himself over and over. "He did it the hard way, he didn't even give himself a step," Fitch said. "He just kept going right up and kept going up. It was amazing, his body control."

The Suns' Ainge said Bryant's workout in Phoenix was "by far the best workout we ever had in my four years of coaching."

Nets coach John Calipari, who had the No. 8 pick, worked Bryant out late in the process and immediately scrapped all his other plans, intent on taking him. "You have to understand," Calipari said, "we're building for two or three years from now."

The secret was out and the race was on.

■   ■   ■

From the moment West laid eyes on Bryant in the Forum, he wanted him. Now West saw a way to make it part of their quest for O'Neal.

West's first plan had been to renounce Elden Campbell, a free agent that summer, for the cap space they needed for Shaq. Now he began thinking about trading Divac for a pick high enough to get Bryant. He found a taker in Charlotte, where the Hornets had been obliged to trade Mourning by Falk's power play.

Trading Divac was risky, since it would leave the Lakers without a center, but it would get his $4.5-million salary off their books, dialing their cap space up to about $9 million, making them players in the O'Neal derby. The Hornets were at No. 13, which looked like it would be high enough.

This was a big draft, with highly regarded Allen Iverson, Marcus Camby, Shareef Abdur-Rahim, Stephon Marbury, Ray Allen, and Antoine Walker assured of the top six slots.

The Clippers were at No. 7, but their center, Brian Williams, was a free agent which, according to their tradition, meant he was out of there. They were already focused on a replacement, Memphis' 6'10" Lorenzen Wright.

The Nets were at No. 8. That was a problem because Calipari was set to take Bryant.

Bryant by then was completely in the Lakers camp, mentally, anyway, and no longer cared about going high, as much as coming West.

Tellem called Nets GM John Nash and told him Kobe had decided he didn't want to go there because it was too close to home. This was transparent but carried with it a threat; since the rookie scale only tied players up for three years before they became free agents, a disgruntled Bryant might be counting the days before leaving.

Nash wanted to take Bryant, anyway, but Calipari, who was in charge of the basketball operation, decided it was too much of a risk and went for Villanova's Kerry Kittles.

Dallas at No. 9 and Indiana at No. 10 went for big men, Louisville's Samaki Walker and Mississippi State's Erick Dampier, respectively.

The Warriors were at No. 11, but the Suns were doing backflips trying to get their pick. Phoenix owner Jerry Colangelo didn't like the idea of drafting high school kids, but Ainge had persuaded him this one was different.

The Suns had been hoping to get lucky with their pick, No. 15, but when the Divac deal was announced without specifying what the Lakers were getting, everyone knew it was the No. 13 pick, with which West would take Bryant.

"That's a pretty big sacrifice, trading Vlade away for a 17-year-old kid," Ainge said later. "We tried everything we could that day to get No. 11 from Golden State. We were offering the 15th pick plus a future pick so it was a pretty good deal. I mean, for Golden State, you move down three picks in the draft and get next year's first draft pick." He laughed, "And they turned it down to draft Todd Fuller, OK?"

When the Hornets took Bryant at No. 13, the insiders knew it was for delivery to the Lakers. Ainge remembers saying to nobody in particular, "Oh my gosh, they've got Shaq and Kobe!"

■ ■ ■

Of course, the Lakers didn't actually have Shaq yet. Nor, despite what everyone thought, were they getting warmer.

Armato, who was pro-Lakers, kept telling them they were still in it. But now it was July, the start of the free agent signing period, so O'Neal could say whatever was on his mind and he was still insisting he wanted to stay in Orlando.

West worried as only he could. He railed at writers for what he took as suggestions the Lakers had tampered with O'Neal. More often, he ducked the press. West's secretary, Mary Lou Liebich, once suggested to the *Times'* Scott Cooper that this wasn't the best day to talk to Jerry and he might try calling back at a better time.

Like next summer.

■ ■ ■

On July 1, eight days before the start of the free-agent signing period, O'Neal amd Hardaway were off with the Olympic team. Camp was in Chicago, opening with a media day in which there were few questions asked about the Olympics.

Now O'Neal didn't seem to be merely leaning toward staying where he was, he sounded as if he'd already made up his mind.

"Orlando is my first option," O'Neal said. "I've been saying that the whole summer. I just want a fair deal. Money's not the main issue."

For his part, Hardaway was all but attached to O'Neal's ankle.

"I might run him off, as much as I'm going to talk to him," Hardaway said. "I'm going to be begging. I might be outside of his door. I'm just going to say, 'We need you and you know that. I mean, I know you're going to make the ultimate decision yourself but we really need you and I want to retire with Shaquille O'Neal on my team.'"

You wouldn't want to have been sitting next to West when he read those quotes in the newspaper. The *Los Angeles Times'* story started: "Dear Vlade, come back, all is forgiven."

While the other free agents spent their time with their cell phones glued to their ears, talking in hushed tones with their agents, O'Neal, as Hardaway would note, was remarkably relaxed, spending his time with his earphones on, listening to one gangsta or another. Shaq said he was "chillin'" and at peace with his decision to stay in Orlando.

"Because I played there first," he said in the Hoosierdome, where the Olympic team played an exhibition against Greece. "Got a big 50,000-square-foot house there. Own a couple buildings, couple restaurants there."

And his love for Southern California?

"How'd you come to that conclusion?" O'Neal asked a reporter. Movies? Records?

"Did my movies in Florida," O'Neal said. "Universal Studios. I was told it doesn't matter where I'm at. If people want to offer me movie deals, I mean, I can get movie deals wherever. You guys have to realize that I don't do movies during the season. Movies and rap music are summer jobs to me."

Was this real or a negotiating posture?

"Do I need a posture?" asked O'Neal. "No. OK. If I don't need it, then I wouldn't take advantage of it. Me, I'm the type of guy, if I'm going to do something, I'm going to do it. I have my family in Orlando. The game's been going pretty good. Orlando is the first option."

Everywhere else, there was suspicion of a "done deal" with the Lakers. If it was, no one told West, who was twisting slowly, slowly in the wind. Years later he could remember assistant coach Bill Bertka, an old confidant, telling him he'd been nuts to give up Divac without a commitment from O'Neal.

Things were moving fast, but not, it seemed, in the Lakers' direction. When they offered O'Neal $98 million and he turned it down, West told Jerry Buss it was time to go to Plan B.

The Lakers had Mutombo and Dale Davis lined up if O'Neal turned them down. On July 13, Davis' agent, Steve Kauffman, who lives in Malibu, said they were so close, he was about to jump in his car to drive to the Forum.

■ ■ ■

By now it was clear O'Neal was Orlando's to lose, and the Magic proceeded to lose him.

The author of *The Compassionate Capitalist* now seemed more focused on the capitalism than the compassion. DeVos had come off his four-year, $55-million offer but was plainly gearing his proposals to the Lakers. The Magic could go as high as it wanted to keep its own player, while the Lakers were limited by cap space. Now $9 million under, the Lakers could offer only that seven-year, $98-million deal, which Orlando promptly matched.

The problem was, that was still less than Mourning's $105 million. The money had as much symbolic as real significance to O'Neal. He'd be getting a $10 million–plus starting salary in a deal worth about $100 million in any case, to go with the $17 million a year he was reportedly getting off the floor. Nevertheless, he wanted Orlando to pay him enough to prove it cared, and "enough" was more than Mourning.

Similarly, he needed $105 million–plus from the Lakers so he turned down their $98 million.

On Sunday night, after the Olympians' exhibition against Greece in Indianapolis, the team flew to Orlando for the last phase of their preparations at Disney World, which had a new practice facility.

Now, with the Magic playing it cool and public sentiment in Orlando actually going against O'Neal, things began to change.

The *Orlando Sentinel* ran a poll, asking fans if they thought O'Neal was worth $115 million, reported to be the Magic's latest offer. Over 90 percent of respondents said no, which was all the more embarrassing since O'Neal's Dream Team buddies were in town to see it.

Of course, the paper could have phrased it another way—Would you pay Shaq the going rate to keep him?—and elicited a different response. Worse, as far as O'Neal knew, the Magic had only offered him $110 million, suggesting the Magic was telling the *Sentinel* what it would do, even before they told him.

Meanwhile, back on the West Coast . . .

Although Buss usually deferred to West, the owner had stepped up before. They were in an ambiguous and dangerous situation, but Buss was a gambler. With Armato assuring them they could still prevail if they could get their offer beyond Mourning's $105 million, Buss told West to do whatever it took.

It took another dump. West had to get rid of George Lynch's $2.5 million, but no one else wanted it, either. The only way to do it was package him with Peeler, whom West liked, to get the Vancouver Grizzlies to bite. The Lakers took back only a second-round draft pick, creating enough cap space to increase their $98 million offer to $120 million.

The Magic countered with its final bid, $115 million, front-loading it so it was actually worth more than the Lakers offer, since Florida had no state income tax.

DeVos still didn't like the thought that he was dancing on a string for O'Neal and Armato, all but daring O'Neal to leave when he told the *Sentinel*: "If they are trying to squeeze another million or two out of this, then the Lakers can pay it."

If anybody had asked Buss and West, their answer would have been "No problem."

■ ■ ■

By now, West could have delivered an elephant.

He flew into Atlanta with the Lakers lawyer, Jim Persik, to get O'Neal's answer. Together, they took a cab to the downtown hotel, where Armato had a suite awaiting O'Neal's arrival from Orlando.

Just to prolong the agony, the Dream Team had to go through the labyrinth of Olympic processing, and O'Neal didn't arrive until 2:30 A.M. While they were waiting for him, West joked if the answer was no, he would jump out of the window. O'Neal said afterward he thought West was actually shaking when he walked in.

Happily, at least for West and the Lakers, the answer was yes.

It was announced the next day at a press conference held at Reebok's Olympic headquarters. West was jubilant, comparing it to the birth of his children. O'Neal, in a phrase he would live to regret, noted he had already "won at every level except college and the pros."

In other words, he had won his only title as a San Antonio high school kid. When things went wrong for the Lakers in the ensuing years, the *SportsCenter* gang would trot that quote back out.

Responding to local muttering, the following season the Magic hired a Cleveland law firm to find out if the Lakers had tampered with O'Neal. The barristers came back with nothing more than rumors, and the organization didn't file a formal complaint.

In one of the most stunning talent grabs ever seen, much less within a week, the Lakers now had O'Neal and Bryant, according to West's dream and Ainge's nightmare.

What could go wrong now?

Chapter 8

WE HAVE MET THE ENEMY AND HE IS US

Nobody can touch them. Nobody can match Shaq. I mean, he's just
the most dominant thing, other than Michael, in the game. If the
Lakers had their mental stuff together, nobody could touch 'em. . . .
But thank God, you've got to have brains.

—Charles Barkley, Houston Rockets, fall 1997

■ ■ ■

A FUNNY THING HAPPENED on the way to their greatness.

It was funny everywhere else, at least. In Los Angeles, where they'd
done everything but order the parade floats, it was agonizing.

Adding Shaquille O'Neal to a team that had won 53 games was supposed to herald a new age. The *Los Angeles Times*, taking the plunge, ran
a box with every game story in Shaq's first season, comparing the team
to the great ones in Lakers history—not that this would turn out to be
one of them.

In all, the Lakers' shakedown cruise would last three seasons, and by
the time it was over, most of them would have been shaken out.

Gone would be not only coach Del Harris but his successor, Kurt
Rambis, who would set a record by starting 10–0 and couldn't even get
invited back. Gone, too, would be Nick Van Exel, Cedric Ceballos, Eddie
Jones, and Elden Campbell. With Vlade Divac, who'd been traded for
Kobe Bryant's draft rights, that made the entire starting five of the Lake
Show, plus half the coaching staff. By the time O'Neal and Bryant ever

won a title, even Jerry West, the charter Laker who'd brought them there, would be on his way out.

It was a brutal beginning, but they were young and it was axiomatic in the NBA that, as the Bulls' Phil Jackson liked to say, "You win with men." O'Neal's Magic had almost proved you could do it with a kiddie-corps lineup if you were good enough, but in the end, all the kids did was confirm the principle by folding after they blew Game 1 against the Rockets.

It had taken the Magic four years to build a team around O'Neal, with the right power forward, Horace Grant, the number two star, Penny Hardaway, and the shooters who complemented Shaq's post game, Dennis Scott and Nick Anderson.

The Lakers didn't have a bona fide number two star. They weren't used to pounding the ball into the middle, they weren't great outside shooters, and they had intrapersonal issues, too. There were tensions all over the dressing room. Van Exel had a problem with Harris. Jones was an old friend of Bryant's from their days in Philadelphia, but if you looked down the road, they were on a collision course for the two-guard position and the big contract that would go with it.

Of course, everyone knew who would be the two-guard to stay. Bryant wasn't just an ornament, a long-range project, or a mascot. At 18, he was in the rotation of a title contender, which was yet another problem for Harris, since Kobe ran around like a colt in a meadow.

The young Lakers would fold as soon as anyone put pressure on them. Harris was like a kitten in a basket in an ocean roiled by the highest expectations. West backed him for as long as he could, but the bottom line was that management was as taken in as the fans. The front office thought they were ready to start winning titles.

Imagine their surprise.

■ ■ ■

Of course, it *looked* pretty good from the get-go.

O'Neal treated Lakers fans to a new sensation, the thrill of domination as they had never known it—not even with Kareem Abdul-Jabbar, who was more of an artist, or Wilt Chamberlain, who was 32 when he became a Laker.

O'Neal was huge, he was athletic, and best of all he was *theirs*. Fans thrilled at his power, forgave his shortcomings, and felt his pain as if it were their own.

One night early in his first season, as he stood at the free throw line after hurling up several line drives that could have hurt someone, a hush fell over the crowd. Said one of the writers on press row, "Can you feel the love in this room?"

They were like a circus act. Off the bench would come Bryant and his highlight-reel game. He was the fans' darling from the moment they laid eyes on him, and Jerry Buss' and Jerry West's, too. Everyone knew who it was who made them great, but where Shaq was force and mayhem, Kobe was breathtaking.

Harris tried to bring him along slowly since he was supposed to be winning titles, not building toward some better day. A child had no place in the rotation of a team trying to win a title, and no NBA champion had ever played one so, so young.

It wasn't easy to deny this one, who was upset enough at merely being held back a little. Bryant never understood what Harris was doing, or forgave him for it. When Harris was fired in Bryant's third season, Kobe, speaking from experience, said, "Players tuned Del out from day one."

Bryant had already begun to show how peculiar he was, even apart from his stunning package of athleticism, skills, audacity, and industry. If he wasn't Michael Jordan, as everyone suggested—Kobe hadn't actually done anything yet—he was further along than Mike, who'd been a late bloomer at 18, only three years removed from failing to make the Wilmington High varsity as a sophomore.

Bryant looked like everyone's little brother, but he was calm and unruffled, expressing surprise at nothing and bemusement if anyone questioned his confidence. It wouldn't be long before Lakers staffers would be saying the fun-loving, goof-off O'Neal seemed like the teenager and the sober, driven Bryant, the grownup.

Bryant would always be described as *mature*, a word thrown around mindlessly on the sports pages. What he was really was poised, focused, and serene in his quest. He knew where he was going, and nothing could stop him; any misadventures along the way, he knew, were only temporary.

His first summer in town began, typically enough, with a stunt no other player would have pulled, going down to Venice Beach to play in the pick-up games, as if to announce there was a new sheriff in town. The players weren't close to his level, but there were no referees and no telling what could happen with a real NBA player in their midst. Sure, enough, Kobe suffered a broken wrist that limited him in his first training camp.

Not that that exactly humbled him. O'Neal, who had always looked after the little guys at the end of the bench, like Darrell Armstrong in Orlando, tried to take Bryant under his wing. It was as if Bryant deliberately picked that wing up and put it back where it had been. A bemused Shaq backed off and began kidding Bryant as if he were an older player, naming him "Showboat."

No one made much of it then, but they were laying down the ground rules of their relationship, bumpy as it would be.

For their first two seasons, they were OK. Bryant was a kid trying to grow up overnight, getting 16 minutes a game as a rookie and 26 in his second season, and posed no challenge to O'Neal.

It was still too early for Bryant to be the one who backed O'Neal up. This was a problem since no one else on the team could do it either.

■　■　■

Nevertheless, when they weren't under pressure, and no one's nose was too far out of joint, they were pretty good.

By the All-Star break, they were 35–13, which was remarkable for a team in the midst of a major reconfiguration. When they sent Ceballos back to Phoenix in midseason for Robert Horry, it gave them nine new players (O'Neal, Bryant, Horry, Rick Fox, the returning Byron Scott, Jerome Kersey, Sean Rooks, and rookies Derek Fisher and Travis Knight).

Horry was no Boy Scout, himself, having worn out his welcome by throwing a towel in coach Danny Ainge's face. An anomaly of a player, he was a 6'10", shot-blocking small forward with three-point range. His attitude was so casual, Rocket teammate Kenny Smith said it was like they got an extra player in the playoffs when Rob began taking an interest.

Horry arrived in the midst of an 18–4 run that carried them to 37–13 when O'Neal pulled a stomach muscle that would bother him the rest of the season. He missed 31 games in all, and the Lakers finished a modest 56–26, only three more wins than the previous season.

Of course, the postseason is the real story. In their case, it would be a short story.

They blew past the Trail Blazers, 3–1, in the first round, drawing Utah in the second. The Jazz was coming off its best season at 64–18, but everyone knew they were past it, with John Stockton now 35 and Karl Malone 33.

The Jazz was everything the marquee Lakers were not, a small-town team, long scorned despite a tradition of consistent achievement because they'd never won a title. Players around the league disliked them. Neither Malone nor Stockton hung out with the guys. No one liked Stockton, who dared to set cross-screens on opposing big guys to free Malone. Opponents like Barkley considered it an affront and tried to intimidate Stockton by bowling him over, but he always came back for more.

Malone had a weightlifter's sculpted body at 6'8", 260 pounds and lived to intimidate, but he could also out-smart. If he wasn't trying to knock you into next week, he was flopping. He also worked harder than anyone else and played with more attitude. Not only did he invariably outplay the opposing power forward, he often reduced him to a grease spot.

They'd been written off annually for years. Every new guard-forward combination, like Seattle's Gary Payton and Sean Kemp, was hailed as the new Stockton and Malone. All but unnoticed, the unassuming Jazz GM, Scott Layden, son of the colorful former coach, Frank, had done an admirable job of rebuilding the team, bringing in important pieces like Jeff Hornacek and Bryon Russell.

The Jazz was also one of the great home-court acts, playing its physical brand of ball before loud, often rowdy fans, going 38–3 in the Delta Center that season.

Of course, as far as the Lakers were concerned, the Jazz was just a bunch of geezers whose time was up, so they weren't worried when the Jazz pasted them by 16 in Game 1 in the Delta Center. The Lakers had had to make a fast turnaround for TV, finishing off the Blazers Friday in Portland, arriving in Salt Lake City in the early hours of Saturday morning, staggering through a meeting and a practice, and opening against the Jazz the next day.

O'Neal, who had torched Portland, was ineffectual as the Jazz double-teamed faster than the Blazers, holding him to 2–9 from the floor in the first half, 6–16 and 17 points overall.

"They were probably a little bit tired," said Jazz coach Jerry Sloan, who would have choked the first player of his who ever used fatigue or anything else as an excuse.

In the world the Jazz lived in, it was a crime to take a game, much less a playoff, lightly, because you never knew what might happen in the next one . . . like Van Exel taking a three-pointer at the end, Malone swiping at him and, as TV replays showed, getting him on the left arm as referee Jack Nies swallowed his whistle instead of giving Nick three free throws. The Jazz won 103–101. Ooooh, were the Lakers upset or what?

Van Exel posted a statement in his cubicle that said: "Nothing personal, just 'No comment.'" Referees generally erred on the side of letting the players decide the outcome at the end, but the Lakers decided this was really about the officials' dislike for Van Exel, who knocked one of them onto a press table and, more recently, suggested they were on the take, for which he was suspended once more.

Rather than get everyone's minds back on business, Harris played along with the Get-Nick Theory the next day, coyly noting, "I'm not going to address that." He was hoping to get an edge with the officials, but he had an easily distracted roster that was now burrowing deep into the old self-pity.

O'Neal even brought out the race card, noting, "If I'm a cop and I don't like white people and I arrest a white person, I'm going to be a little rougher on that person. I don't think I can do my job effectively."

O'Neal wasn't a cop, he didn't have a problem with white people, and obsessing on the referees was something else NBA players at the elite level didn't do. No one fought harder for calls than Malone and

Stockton, who harangued the officials for every call that went against them, but when the game ended, all they were concerned about was the next game.

To no one's surprise, the Lakers won Game 3 back in the Forum, 104–84, as Malone, looking every day of his 33 years, went 2–20 from the floor.

To everyone's surprise, the Lakers argued among each other in Game 4. Less than two minutes into it, Harris yelled at Van Exel to tell Campbell to make an adjustment. Van Exel, according to Harris, "waved me off."

Harris promptly lifted Van Exel, who came to the bench cursing and kicked a chair, whereupon Harris got in his face, all on national television. Van Exel went back in two minutes later, but the Jazz went up by as many as 18 in the third quarter behind Malone, who was on his way to a 42-point game. The Jazz won, 110–95.

Harris should have shrugged this one off, but his shoulders were getting tired. Van Exel had been a problem for three seasons, and things were coming to a head. Only two weeks before, O'Neal and his bodyguard, Jerome Crawford, had had to separate Harris and Van Exel during a practice.

For the first but not the last time in the Shaq-Kobe Era, the Lakers were Officially in Disarray. After telling the story of Van Exel's insubordination, Harris decided the press was making too much of it and huffed, "I'm done with that issue. You people just want to talk about who doesn't play and who doesn't score."

Meanwhile, Van Exel was already saying his good-byes.

"I told my boys that could have been my last game at the Forum," he said the next day. "The way I look at it is I'll just keep playing while I'm a Laker and see what happens."

Not that the immediate future looked too bright, trailing 3–1 in this series, going back to the Delta Center. Nevertheless, in a style that would become familiar, if the Lakers went out, it would be with a bang, not a whimper.

Game 5 went down to the wire. O'Neal had fouled out, and Jones had just had a driving layup blocked when they got the ball back in an 87–87 game with :14 left. Harris gave the last shot not to Jones or Van

Exel but to the 18-year-old Bryant, who proceeded to airball a 14-footer. In overtime, Bryant airballed three three-pointers, making four—count 'em, four—to conclude his rookie season.

"At the time that I made that decision," Harris said, "I thought, 'Well, we'll either win this game and it'll really make him more of a man to know that at 18 years old he had a coach who was willing to give him a winning shot in a huge game. Or he'll miss it and we'll go into overtime and he'll still know that, even if he didn't make it.' Either way, he's going to gain from this experience.

"He was disappointed he missed it, but he felt very comfortable in taking it. If we'd gone onto the court and they'd said, 'Well, we've had something happen, there's a scoring error, we have to go back and play the last minute of the game over,' he would have wanted it again."

The usual things got said, but nobody had to assure Bryant that everything would be all right. He didn't look despondent. He looked the same as ever. The next morning, Bryant was back in the gym at Pacific Palisades High near his home, getting ready for the day that was still to come.

■ ■ ■

Now the Lakers were all set, the Lakers thought.

Even with all the hype and the disappointment, they knew they were on the right track. West wrote this off as the price of integrating nine new players and brought them all back, even Van Exel.

Said West, following the Utah disaster: "We're very, very pleased with the group of players we have here. Very pleased."

It was one of the most surprising things about West: twitchy as he was, he didn't act on his impulses, erring on the side of moving too slowly rather than too hastily. It was one reason, coupled with an eye for talent and a far-flung network of friends, that he was such a good GM.

This, of course, didn't turn out to be the right call, but it was tricky any way West went. He couldn't have gotten a good point guard for Van Exel, and Derek Fisher, a second-year man, wasn't ready.

Harris had more challenges than Van Exel. If Bryant was wild and disinclined to share with the others, he was also their future, and with

Buss and West doting on him, the future was coming up fast. Needing to get Bryant ready and to reach a better rapport with him, Harris even coached the summer league team to work with him.

Bryant played erratically that summer, but he had his own agenda, as usual. He was on a weight-lifting program, determined to bulk his skinny bod up to NBA proportions. Bryant ran his own program with his own staff. That summer, he hired a personal shooting coach (he'd already brought his own strength coach, Joe Carbone, from Philadelphia) and came back with a bizarre stroke with a hitch in it that horrified the Lakers coaches. Kobe had actually been a good shooter for a rookie, making 38 percent of his three-pointers, but it would be six seasons before he got his shot straightened out enough to do that well again.

Nevertheless, in camp before Bryant's second season, he showed amazing progress. It was something the Lakers would become used to; every summer Bryant would take a quantum leap, coming back in fall as a better player than he'd been at any point in the preceding season. Still coming off the bench, Bryant's numbers almost doubled in his second season, from 15.5 minutes a game to 26, from 7.6 points a game to 15.4.

His fame grew even faster. Before a game in Chicago against Jordan's Bulls, TNT hyped the "matchup" as if it were The Thrilla in Manila. The network took out newspaper ads. Play-by-play announcer Dick Stockton noted that at Bryant's stage, Jordan hadn't been a star either. Actually, Jordan had just turned 19 when he hit the shot that won the 1982 NCAA title. Two years later, as an NBA rookie, he averaged 28 points with a better shooting percentage (51.5 percent) than Bryant would ever have in the NBA.

Bryant, being Bryant, was delighted. The night before the Bulls game, after a win in Minneapolis, assistant coach Larry Drew remembers a glowing Kobe telling him, "LD, this is what I've been waiting for my whole life."

Of course, Bryant couldn't actually match up with Jordan coming off the bench, so it was purely ceremonial, the more so since the Bulls smoked the Lakers by 20 points with Jordan going for 36. Bryant had a career-high 33, a lot of them in garbage time. Nevertheless, Jordan knew he was there. Jordan usually tried to torch so-called challengers to cinders, but he admired Bryant's pluck and his manners. Kobe was openly admiring and not shy; he even asked Jordan for tips on technique during the game.

Then, of course, there was Bryant's athleticism, which Jordan, now 34, could no longer match. Watching Bryant throw down a windmill jam late in the game, Jordan asked Scottie Pippen, sitting next to him on the bench, if they could jump like that in their youth. Pippen said he couldn't remember that far back.

■ ■ ■

As far as the hype went, they were just warming up.

The real deal was the All-Star Game, with Kobe voted into the starting lineup by the fans, even if he didn't even start for his own team.

The key stat was the age of the voters—there were no limits and ballots were circulated at McDonald's, one of the NBA's prime sponsors. Bryant surged into the lineup at the end, after his young supporters started pulling up in massed formations, on their bicycles, under the golden arches.

Of course, the youth demographic being as important as it is in advertising, the league had no problem with that.

The game in Madison Square Garden was billed as another Jordan-Bryant shootout. NBC ran full-page newspaper ads showing Jordan and Bryant advancing on each other, towering over the Manhattan skyline like King Kong and Godzilla. NBC sports boss Dick Ebersol got Kobe onto *Meet the Press*. The segment with Bryant and a couple of other young players aired right after those covering President Clinton's problems and international affairs.

"It was great to be on there," gushed Bryant, "because they were asking some terrific questions, not just about basketball but just about society in general and about our youth. Those are questions I really look forward to answering."

Yes, as soon as he conquered basketball, he would get to work on society in general.

If this was getting excessive, Ebersol wasn't the least bit apologetic. "Promoting Kobe is no different than what we were doing promoting Michael in 1990," he told the *Wall Street Journal*. "Business is business."

Business could mess a kid's head up. Unlike the Lakers' game against the Bulls, this was an actual shootout, and Kobe, being Kobe, came out shooting. In his first 11 touches, he took 10 shots.

Of course, as Lakers publicist Raymond Ridder, sitting on press row, noted, "That's one less than he took in the rookie game." That was during All-Star weekend the year before. A lot had changed in a year, even for Kobe.

The outrages kept happening. Bryant waved off Malone, who was trying to set a pick for him, which was a new one for the Mailman, who promptly asked to come out. Barkley, watching the NBC coronation of Bryant at home, said, "Jim Gray almost made me vomit last week, talking about passing torches and that sort of thing."

Bryant wound up with 18 points in 22 minutes (in which time he got up 16 shots). Jordan, in what was presumed to be his farewell perform-ance in the All-Star Game, scored 23. Nevertheless, for the cherry atop the whipped cream on the sundae of Bryant's weekend, Jordan paid him the ultimate compliment.

"I didn't expect myself to come out here and win the MVP," Jordan said. "I just wanted to make sure Kobe didn't dominate me."

For his part, Bryant told the postgame press conference he was just sad it was over and, getting up to leave, murmured, "God bless," another first.

Nevertheless, real life now beckoned and it was some kind of pissed off.

■ ■ ■

The Lakers had started the season 11–0 and, as had always happened, everyone climbed on their bandwagon. Suns coach Danny Ainge, always an admirer, called them "the scariest team in the league . . . for the next 10 years."

O'Neal hurt his stomach again, but they still had enough momentum and esprit to keep it going without him, climbing to 31–9 when Van Exel began reporting knee problems.

Then Bryant returned from the All-Star Game, emotionally spent with an even bigger attitude. The Lakers had become used to the fact that he separated himself from the group; it wasn't mentioned much, the presumption being it was generational since he was so much younger.

However, they were also used to Bryant holding up his own end, but now he couldn't. After averaging 22 points in the last eight games before the break, he averaged 12 for the month after, and his shooting percentage fell 10 points.

Still, he would not concede he was in a slump; he called it "my so-called slump." One day he acknowledged being a little tired but said he'd fight through it. That night, he went on Jay Leno's *Tonight Show*.

The hype was still happening. In the weeks following the All-Star Game, Bryant was profiled in a *New York Times* business story on Adidas' inroads on Nike, appeared on the first *ESPN Magazine* cover, and did three photo shoots for a *Sports Illustrated* cover (with his sisters, with Magic Johnson, and on the beach at Santa Monica). *Rolling Stone* profiled him. Barbara Walters interviewed him, meaning she had now gone from Andwar Sadat to Kobe.

Nevertheless, it was still early enough in Bryant's career that even if the sky fell, it fell on someone else. In this case, it dropped onto the white-haired head of Harris. A *New York Daily News* item alleged he was in trouble, followed by a full-scale media pile-on, in which Fox anchor Kevin Frazier went on a radio talk show and announced the Lakers had voted 12–0 to dump Harris.

Nothing of the sort had happened. The next day, Fox broadcast interviews of half the roster ridiculing the story but neglected to mention they had started it.

However, if Buss and West weren't ready to pull the plug, and if the players didn't take any votes, no one was happy. Harris was seen after a game against the Warriors in the Forum, sitting in the stands with Jerry Buss, who seemed to be lecturing him.

No player stepped up to say how much they loved Harris and insist this was their failure. O'Neal, whom Harris treated like a king, was noticeably cool in his comments.

It was West's job to deal with this stuff, but he no longer had any stomach for venturing into a feeding frenzy and getting microphones stuck in his face. Instead of standing by his man, West split for Las Vegas to scout the Big West Tournament.

He did express his disappointment to the players—in a letter that was put in each cubicle:

> Each of you are on the verge of letting this season slip right through your fingers. Only one team will be champion. That team will have worked their butts off to get there, that team will know each others' every move, every thought. That team will be a machine that's fueled with compassion, desire, determination, drive, devotion and pride.
>
> That team could and should be the Lakers.

Of course, it would have been more effective if West had showed them he cared enough to show up and kick their tails in person. Nevertheless, coincidentally or not, the Lakers went on a season-ending 22–3 run. The bandwagon could have tipped over from everyone scrambling back aboard. West's letter went down with the Gettysburg Address.

The postseason seemed further proof that their time had arrived, at least for a while. They eliminated the Blazers, 3–1, in the first round. Then they beat a Seattle team, 4–1, that had won as many games as they had (61), with O'Neal making a mockery of Sonics coach George Karl's defensive schemes.

"Mentally, I think we've awakened a great basketball team," Karl said. Gushing about O'Neal, he quoted one of his assistants, Bobby Weiss, who played with Chamberlain, as saying, "It's not even close. This guy's more dominating and better."

The Lakers cruised into the West Finals against their old nemesis, the Jazz. Just like in *Bad News Bears*, everyone knew what that meant: bad news for the Jazz.

Maybe in the next life.

■ ■ ■

This time, it was personal. O'Neal didn't like Greg Ostertag boasting about holding him down the preceding spring. Ostertag didn't say it, but he got a lot of press in the Salt Lake papers and Shaq didn't even like the inference. Before the season opener the next fall in the Forum, O'Neal and Ostertag got into an argument that concluded with Shaq slapping him in the face.

Nor did the Lakers like Utah backup center Greg Foster's throat-slashing gesture. Rick Fox, the Lakers' poet laureate, noted, "I hold grudges for a long time."

Harris, noodling for the usual coach's edge, trotted out the old one about the Jazz being dirty, declaring their style wasn't "good for the credibility of the game."

Implicit in this was the Lakers' confidence they were golden. They were younger, better, and on a roll, too. The celebrities were coming around as they only did deep in the playoffs. Leonardo DiCaprio, the young star of that year's blockbuster, *Titanic*, was there so much, Harris was calling him "Leo" and doing bits from the movie.

Of course, the Jazz had won 62 games to their 61, which meant Utah still had that extraordinary home-court advantage of theirs. Still, the opener was a surprise, all around: Jazz 112, Lakers 77.

If the Lakers were condescending, the Jazz players paid them the ultimate compliment of taking them seriously, understanding they'd have to play their best to have a chance. So the Jazz did, and the Lakers collapsed, taking the worst, not to mention most embarrassing, loss of their 37-year history in Los Angeles.

The Lakers missed 11 of their first 12 shots and 17 of 21 in the first quarter, by which time the game was all but over. O'Neal had an awful night, finishing with 19 points, eight rebounds, and seven turnovers.

"It was like the *Titanic*," said Fox after Harris made them sit through the videotape the next day. "Not the movie but the ship."

Horry said it reminded him of the *The Wizard of Oz*, because the Lakers played like a team with "no heart, no brain, no courage."

Added Harris: "And no wizard."

And no future, either.

Game 2 was one of those grind-it-out games they specialized in at the Delta Center, and the Jazz won that, too, 99–95. The Lakers went back to complaining about the referees; this time it was Steve Javie, a top-rated official, even if there were no big calls, as with Jack Nies the year before. With the Lakers, it was always something and never them.

Game 3 was back in the Forum, where the Lakers were—once more—expected to assert their superiority over their elders. That one got away, too, as the Jazz played one of its vintage games, shooting 52 percent, making 7 of 11 three-pointers, winning by 11, and leaving the Lakers with the life expectancy of an hors d'oeuvre.

It had been only 12 days since the Lakers had polished off the Sonics, convincing everyone their time was at hand. Now everyone was burying them as clueless kids again, and even they were out of excuses.

Jones acknowledged how tough it was to see "a couple of old guys kicking our butt."

Van Exel compared it to "project guys going to play against a bunch of guys who set the pick and rolls, who do the little things while the project guys always want to do the little fancy behind-the-back dribbles and do the spectacular plays. Maybe it's the age. We feel if we go out there and just lace up the shoes and run around and do the dunks and do all the little things that we can win. But it's not like that."

There's nothing like self-knowledge, however dearly won. Nevertheless, it was late in this phase of Van Exel's career because he said one more thing that wound up getting him a one-way ticket to Palookaville. At practice the day before Game 4, when the players put their hands in during a huddle, pulled them out, and yelled "Lakers!' Van Exel yelled, "Cancun!"

Van Exel was given to dark humor and had worse faults than that, but he was also a tough competitor. This time, however, he angered O'Neal, who wasn't in a good mood, anyway. O'Neal was desperate, tired of having his "I've won at every level except college and the pros" line thrown in his face. He now divided teammates and coaches into two groups: 1) He can help me win a title, or 2) I want him out of here.

In Game 4, the Jazz polished them off, and it was now officially recriminations season. O'Neal lashed out at unnamed teammates, noting, "If they don't want to play, then they need to ask for a trade."

Harris was hanging by a thread, but West wanted to bring him back. However, Van Exel was gone; West had held Nick and Del together as long as he could. O'Neal's anger was the cannonball that broke the camel's back. West shipped Van Exel to Denver for a second-year forward named Tony Battie and draft rights to the No. 23 pick, Tyronn Lue. It was a dump, plain and simple. With the Nuggets coming off an 11–71 season, it was like exiling Van Exel to Elba.

Of course, if the Lakers thought this season was bad—and they did—they hadn't seen anything yet.

Chapter 9

THE RODMAN COMETH

Dennis is Dennis. We're not about to tell Dennis how to be someone else.
We'd take him the way he is.

—Lakers owner Jerry Buss, February 5, 1999

■ ■ ■

BE CAREFUL WHAT YOU ask for, because it's on your doorstep, in all its tattooed, pierced, histrionic, life-will-never-be-the-same-around-here glory.

A lot of things had to go wrong to lead the Lakers, one of the sharpest organizations around, into an act of desperation as patent as signing the aging, declining, and dissolute-as-ever Dennis Rodman.

All those things went wrong and more, resulting in a wild farce of a season that seemed like a lark when it began, threatened to pull the entire organization down, and showed the decline of what had once been a model front office.

Rodman came and went so quickly, it's easy to forget he was even there, hurtling through like a cannonball that came in one window and went out another. Not that anyone who was there would ever forget it. No one who knew Rodman was a tiny bit surprised, even if Lakers management was.

Talent notwithstanding, they were a humbled team coming off their second successive humiliation at the hands of the Jazz in the spring of 1998. They had discovered they were definitely missing something, but they weren't sure what that was.

Nick Van Exel had been sent away, but all that left at the point was Derek Fisher, a second-year man who had yet to prove he could start on a contending team. Del Harris was back but without the extension usually given to a coach on the last year of his contract, making it obvious he was a lame duck who'd go at the first sign of trouble. The power forward position was a problem, manned by Elden Campbell, also known as Rip Van Campbell, and Robert Horry, a 6'10" willow they were trying to convert from small forward.

The front office, once a harmonious operation from the top down, with everyone comfortable in his role, was getting old and eccentric. Jerry Buss, now a 66-year-old playboy, had become detached and remote. He was beginning to worry about his playboy sons, who usually only had jobs when he employed them. Now he wanted Jim, the older, who had tried his hand as a horse trainer, to get hands-on experience in the Lakers front office and named him assistant GM. Jim didn't actually come around much, but he did sit in on meetings and wasn't shy about offering his opinion, even if it was no more sophisticated than a fan calling in on talk radio.

Meanwhile, Jerry West, who was high-maintenance and needed stroking, was getting none and constantly talking about leaving. At the end of the 1997–1998 season, he announced he was burned out and would retire.

The announcement sent vibrations through the organization. Shaquille O'Neal and Kobe Bryant both venerated West. O'Neal announced if West was ever allowed to leave, "I'll be upset to the highest of upsetivity."

Then there was the lockout imposed by NBA Commissioner David Stern, the league's first work stoppage, which cut the season down to 50 games, pushed the opener back to February, and came perilously close to canceling the season. This froze transactions, paralyzed planning, and pitted O'Neal and Bryant against each other in another context.

O'Neal and his agent, Leonard Armato, were the foremost doves. Bryant and his agent, Arn Tellem, were super-hawks. For that reason, and others that had been emerging, O'Neal and Bryant got into an actual fight at a voluntary workout in January after the lockout ended.

"Everybody was playing real physical," said Fisher, who was there, "and they had bumped into each other quite a few times and started jawing back and forth. 'Next time you hit me, I'm going to get you.'

"I think probably it also got heated so fast because of harbored feelings that they had for one another. They were talking back and forth and they approached each other. . . . They walked up on each other and Kobe didn't back down. And Shaq—it wasn't like a slap, it was more like a push. And Kobe went back at him and then we all tried to jump in and get some order back. . . .

"I think most of it was about the season before."

Bryant had irritated more than one teammate the year before, but this was something new, a problem with a specific teammate. The great Shaq-Kobe feud, which would be on and off again for the rest of their time together, had begun. Yet few paid much attention at the time. The story of the fight leaked out weeks later, but there was no furor.

The Lakers were soon enmeshed in other problems. Camp was in nearby Santa Barbara, rather than their normal Honolulu site, since it had to be arranged on short notice. It was there that West began calling around, looking for a power forward.

He wanted Minnesota's 6'10" Tom Gugliotta, a good all-around player who would fit with O'Neal. Gugliotta, a free agent, wanted out, and the Lakers had a good sign-and-trade proposal on the table: Eddie Jones and Campbell.

However, the Minnesota GM was Kevin McHale, the ex-Celtic who didn't like having terms dictated to him by Lakers. Jones was two seasons from the end of his contract and McHale wasn't high on Campbell, who had limited utility but a monster deal with five seasons left at $7 million each. Whether it was rational or emotional, as the Lakers suspected, McHale wasn't playing.

It wound up backfiring for the Timberwolves, who got nothing when Gugliotta signed with the Suns, but that did nothing for the Lakers. When publicist John Black relayed the word to UC–Santa Barbara that McHale had turned their offer down, a disgusted O'Neal hurled a basketball at the ball rack, scattering balls all over the floor.

O'Neal loved playing with Horace Grant in Orlando and wanted someone like him, rather than Sleepy and Twiggy, Campbell and Horry. O'Neal was always talking about the things he needed, his shooter and his thug. Entering his third season as a Laker, they still had neither.

■　■　■

That was when the Rodman talk began. Rodman, who hadn't been invited back by the Bulls, was home in Newport Beach. At 37, he had mixed feelings about playing, but he liked the idea of walking into another title opportunity. Everyone had mixed feelings about him, too, aware that he had a peculiar genius and was out of control. On the other hand, the Lakers really needed a power forward, and Buss was friendly with Rodman, whom he often bumped into in clubs late at night.

Rodman had three rings to show for his three seasons with the Bulls, but his game had declined dramatically, and his behavior was more erratic by the day. The young Lakers weren't like the focused Bulls, a veteran team with internal leadership that flowed from the commanding Jordan, which made them distraction-proof. The Lakers could be distracted by a passing breeze.

When Rodman entered the NBA, he had been a conditioning maniac who didn't drink. Now he was a party animal who bragged about his alcoholism in his book *Walk on the Wild Side.*

"How do I do it?" Rodman had written two years before. "How can a 35-year-old man drink his ass off, sleep very little, and play in the NBA and still be the best conditioned guy out there? To give you the God's honest truth, bro, I don't even know."

Buss didn't understand the peril he was inviting; as far as he knew, Rodman was just an eccentric who was also a valuable player. West knew more about what had happened in Chicago and was skeptical. Nevertheless, West went along, loath to oppose Buss and assuming nothing could go too wrong, seeing as how it would be a one-year deal in a shortened season.

Actually, this had *madness* written all over it, in neon letters three feet high, like a marquee on the Las Vegas strip.

Rodman gave off distress vibes a blind man could sense. An intensely shy, withdrawn late-bloomer, he had grown up poor in Dallas. His father, appropriately named Philander, abandoned the family and, by his own account, conceived 27 children in the Phillippines. Philander stayed out of touch for 30 years until Dennis was an NBA star and the tabloid TV show *Extra* paid his way to Chicago to see his son.

Dennis claimed his mother threw him out of the house when he left high school, although she said she didn't. He worked as a janitor at the Dallas–Fort Worth Airport, where he was caught stealing watches. He hadn't played high school basketball, but after leaving, he grew nine inches to 6'7", leading to a junior college gig and two years at Southwest Oklahoma State, where the Pistons discovered him.

He was a deer in the bright lights of the NBA's fast-lane world, but he had amazing legs, incredible strength, and a gift for defending. His Pistons teams won titles in his third and fourth seasons. In 1991–1992, his sixth season, he averaged 18.7 rebounds, the highest average in 19 years, a feat that compared with Wilt Chamberlain's gargantuan numbers in the days when teams missed many more shots.

In 1961–1962 when Chamberlain set the record of 27.2, he rebounded 36 percent of the missed shots in his games. In 1991–1992, Rodman got 42 percent.

Rodman could guard any power forward, even though they were all bigger than he. Bulls coach Phil Jackson would even use him on O'Neal, who was five inches taller and 100 pounds heavier.

"Shaq is nothing to Dennis," said John Salley, a teammate in Detroit and Chicago. "Let me tell you why. Our first year, we went to the All-Star break. I go back to Atlanta. You know, I'm a 22-year-old ladies' man. He goes to Oklahoma and castrates 300 cattle.

"I say, 'What do you mean?'

"He says, 'I hold 'em down while they castrate 'em and throw alcohol on 'em.' I'm looking at him like, yeah, OK, I'm waiting for the punch line. He was serious as hell. . . .

"So with Shaq—doesn't have horns—that's no problem."

Rodman helped the Pistons win their 1989 and 1990 titles and became a star after the rest of the Bad Boys aged and left. Not that he had a chance of settling into this. He married a wild woman from Sacramento named Annie Bakes, but they soon broke up. Grieving, Rodman began piercing his body from top to bottom and covering his skin with tattoos, in a style he had learned from Annie.

The worse he felt, the harder he partied, the more he turned himself into a walking billboard, the more famous he became. In two tumultuous seasons in San Antonio, he became an outlaw icon, this being a leisure society that didn't demand that its outlaws actually break any laws.

Rodman disappeared into his new larger-than-life persona. The man who would rarely even talk to teammates was now all over TV. His agent, Dwight Manley, would point out that Rodman always wore his sunglasses for TV appearances; Manley said he needed something to hide behind.

Whatever Rodman did, however destructive it was of his life or career, he kept doing it as the alter ego took over. He blew the Spurs up in both of his postseasons with them, convincing them to cut him loose.

That was the summer the Bulls decided they could somehow fit Rodman into their oft-trumpeted "good people" profile. Rodman went to Chicago and became a superstar, the anti-Jordan to go with the real thing on the ultimate marquee team.

Jordan was just back from his first retirement, but he and the Bulls had been rudely dumped by O'Neal's Magic in the second round the preceding spring. With Grant gone to Orlando, they needed a power forward, so they decided to take a look beneath Rodman's tattoos and dyed hair to see what he was really like and decided he was actually OK.

Rodman was now trying to clean up his act and make some real money, having thrown away most of what he had in gambling sprees in Las Vegas, another new pastime and symptom of his grief. To that end, he had hired Manley, who was trying to counterbalance all the other forces in Dennis' life, internal and external.

The Chicago experiment worked well in the first season and not as well in the next two, but the Bulls won three titles and posted the two best records in NBA history. By the end of their run, however, Rodman was once more spinning out of control, theirs, Manley's, and his own.

He was suspended for kicking a TV cameraman in the crotch. His numbers fell off sharply and his play became erratic. Where he had once been a kamikaze, he now might just go through the motions if he wasn't into it. He had always been late for everything, but sometimes now he didn't show up or call. When he missed a practice, the Bulls sent someone over to his apartment near their practice facility in Deerfield, a middle-class suburb of office parks. It was a modest place, with little furniture and nothing that suggested its occupant made $9 million a year. Dennis, eating a bowl of cereal, explained he'd lost his car keys and couldn't make it.

This prompted Jackson, by now one of Rodman's last backers, to go over to see him.

"He had some guys hanging out with him," said Jackson. "He sleeps on the floor on a thin mattress. His TV is as big as the wall, eight feet from him. It's almost too big for the wall. Next to the TV were probably 150 videotapes. He always has to have something to distract him. I would say he has attention deficit disorder and he's hyperactive."

Dr. Phil finally had to take away Rodman's starting job. Then, when he tried to send Rodman into the game, he found he wasn't on the bench. Dennis had gone back in the dressing room to ride a stationary bike, obliging Jackson to send someone to get him. They solved that one by putting a bike behind the bench so Dennis could be available while he exercised.

Now with Jordan, Jackson, and Pippen gone, the Bulls had no use for an aging bad boy. Miami's Pat Riley said he'd be interested if Rodman would agree to follow all the rules, but that was a little too much structure for Dennis. Rodman's old Detroit coach, Chuck Daly, was now in Orlando and willing to consider it, but the PR-oriented Magic organization was not.

Rodman's preferred option all along had been the Lakers, and now, throwing caution to the wind, they wanted him, too. Of course, he knew all along they were over the cap and could only offer a $1-million exception, prorated down over the shortened 50-game season to $610,000, but this would be augmented by a $3-million bonus from his sneaker company, Converse. Rodman said he was willing to make the sacrifice.

It was not going to be that easy.

■　■　■

Rodman was all over the lot now. After leaving the Bulls, he had dumped Manley in a dispute over his marriage to actress Carmen Electra—they were married in a dawn ceremony after a night at the Las Vegas Hard Rock Casino.

Now Rodman was represented by a young entertainment guy named Steve Chasman from the prestigious International Creative Management. Chasman was used to the entertainment industry, in which stars ruled, and had no idea what to do with an NBA player, especially one who was lost, didn't know what he really wanted, and, as a way of putting off deciding, kept demanding more.

In Santa Barbara, a week before the February 5 opener, the Lakers, who'd been foiled in attempts to get Gugliotta, Grant, and Charles Oakley, acknowledged their interest in Rodman. O'Neal said he was for it, even if Rodman once called him a "whore" on Jay Leno's show. (O'Neal had replied his grandmother would have five rings, too, if she'd played with Jordan and Isiah Thomas.)

Showing this was really happening, Harris signed on, too, as did Bryant. Showing this was only going to happen on Rodman's schedule, it took a month to consummate this done deal, while Rodman refused to meet with West or even take a call from him.

On February 5, the Lakers opened with a victory over the Houston Rockets in the Forum. Before the game, Buss called Rodman a friend and reiterated his interest, noting, "As far as I can read the public, they want to win as badly as I want to win. They're very hungry for a championship. It's been a while. . . . I think a lot of people would forgive him as long as he tried to act somewhat orderly."

West, looking stressed, said he hoped to get it settled in the next few days.

On February 12, the *Los Angeles Times* reported that Rodman had decided to play for the Lakers. On February 15, the Associated Press reported Rodman would be in uniform within a day or two. On February 16, the *Times* found the elusive Rodman at the Las Vegas Hilton, registered under his own name. A call to his room at midafternoon was answered by a man who said he would see if Dennis was awake.

A moment later, the man said, "He would like to know what you're calling about."

Told it was about Rodman joining the Lakers, the man relayed the question, then reported back: "Dennis has no comments about that right now."

On February 18, Rodman and his sister, Debra, finally agreed to meet with a Lakers official—Buss—but without Chasman.

On February 19 on ESPN's *Up Close*, Rodman said Buss had told him he was too visible to sneak any money under the table—suggesting that Rodman had asked for some. Indeed, Dennis was reported to have asked for $600,000 to pay off gambling debts in Las Vegas. Rodman also threw out the possibility of playing for Miami, a transparent ploy since the Heat had pulled out weeks before.

On February 23, Chasman arranged a press conference at Planet Hollywood in Beverly Hills, presumably for the long-awaited announcement that Rodman was joining the Lakers. The site was novel, but Chasman was more familiar with Beverly Hills than basketball. Dennis appeared with Electra, who was back at his side. They made ribald references to their sex life but no announcement about the Lakers was forthcoming.

Instead, Rodman went back to his Miami-or-Lakers ploy, which was old news and an obvious bluff, until reporters hectored him into declaring he would play for the Lakers. Rodman bristled at a question of whether he was selfish from KABC's Lisa Guerrero, asserting, "I've been a team player, honey." He capped the wild session by breaking down and crying, tears rolling down his cheeks behind his sunglasses.

"I'm not going to never going to win in this game of basketball, am I?" he said between sobs. "No matter what I do for this league and for the game of basketball, I'm going to never win. And in a situation like this, when I'm playing for a minimum wage—I'm getting what, $250,000?—and I got 10 charities I'm going to give $10,000 to each charity. That's $100,000. I'm getting paid $150,000 on top of that and even with this, doing this right here, I'm still not going to win."

His entourage gathered around to comfort him as an eccentric local radio guy named Vic Jacobs yelled, "One love! One love!" It was one of those scenes you had to see to believe, and even then it was difficult.

■ ■ ■

That night, the Lakers lost their third game in a row. The next day—a month after the start of negotiations—Rodman reported and Harris was fired. Harris and Rodman crossed paths that day in the Forum, Dennis inbound, Del outbound.

"He came down and said, 'Sorry I couldn't be here but good luck to you.'" Rodman said. "That's when I heard it."

Harris was already on borrowed time, and this had been one distraction too many. With little backing and a losing streak, people could say he had lost the team. Actually, with the long-running fiasco of the Rodman "negotiations" making everyone crazy, the organization blew the team up under Harris.

Harris said later he'd been contacted by two teams that summer, asking if was leaving. He had then talked to Buss, who still said nothing about an extension. Still, Harris couldn't walk away from such a talented team and told Buss he worked best under pressure. After Harris was fired, he recalled the conversation, realizing Buss had been trying to tell him something and he hadn't heard it.

Named to replace Harris in a popular move was his assistant, Kurt Rambis, the old fan favorite from Showtime with his Clark Kent glasses, in a return to the old Lakers Family approach. Rambis had been a Lakers stalwart, who also had stints in Charlotte, Phoenix, and Sacramento, where his leadership was praised. His wife, Linda, a former Lakers front office employee, was best friends with Buss' daughter, Jeannie. O'Neal, who always had an eye out for the next coach, the one he hoped would finally get him that first title, liked Rambis. The Lakers saw Kurt as a young, hard-working guy rising from within their ranks, like Pat Riley.

There was one difference. If Riley was the luckiest man alive to inherit great, highly motivated players, Rambis was the unluckiest. He was getting this dizzy crew and Rodman.

Even as Rambis embarked on a record-setting 10–0 start, West was in the process of further reconfiguring the roster, getting O'Neal his shooter, Glen Rice, from Charlotte for Jones and Campbell. The deal had been in the works for weeks, hanging fire until Rice, who had a sore elbow, was ready. It was all over the local papers, and certainly on the minds of Jones and Campbell, which had been one more distraction for Harris. Jones was a fine young player but he wasn't quite a star. He and Bryant played the same position, and everyone knew the Lakers shooting guard of the future was Kobe, not Eddie.

Rice seemed a perfect complement to O'Neal. This wasn't just any shooter, this was one of the game's great marksmen, having averaged 22 points over his nine-year career, while making more than 40 percent of his three-point shots.

However, Rice was out of shape, having forced the Hornets to trade him by holding out. This gave Rambis two starters who would have to play themselves into shape, since Rodman had just arrived, fresh from the party circuit.

Rodman arrived in the second game of their 10-game streak. Rice and J. R. Reid in the 10th, but opponents just kept dropping like tenpins. After a win at Phoenix, an exultant O'Neal proclaimed, "I'm glad I'm the general manager of this team. I've got this team just the way I want it."

It just didn't stay the way he wanted it for very long. The overwhelming problem would be Rodman, who wasn't sure he really wanted to play before he came back and still wasn't sure, now that he was back. He still partied hard, often with Buss, staying out late with him in clubs on the Sunset strip on Fridays, which was why he missed a disproportionate number of their Saturday practices.

Ten days after joining the team, in the middle of their winning streak, Rodman missed his first practice. Chasman called in for him, and the Lakers said it was an "excused absence," which would be the first in a series.

"Because it's Dennis, everybody's going to blow it all out of proportion," sniffed Rambis, striking a defensive posture that would become familiar. Actually, everyone was trying to play along as long as they could. The story ran on the ninth sports page in the *Times*.

■ ■ ■

After that, it was a thrill a minute, like a roller coaster ride with the operator asleep at the switch.

March 12—Rice makes his Lakers debut as the Lakers beat the Warriors for their 10th win in a row. Rodman asks not to go back into the second half because his right elbow is sore.

March 13—More than Rodman's elbow is bothering him. He's late for Saturday's practice and says he can't go on an upcoming six-game trip with the team because of personal problems. Everyone says sympathetic things about understanding that Dennis has to get his life together.

March 14—The 10-game winning streak ends at Sacramento.

March 16—The Lakers learn Rodman has gone to Las Vegas to get his life together. Rambis says he'll be fined. On TNT, studio analyst Kenny Smith says Rodman should be free to spend his leave wherever he wants.

March 17—Buss, headed for Europe, tells West he can handle the situation however he thinks best.

March 21—Rodman returns from his leave, although NBC's Doug Collins says it looks like Dennis' body is there but not his mind. The Lakers rally from 24 points behind in Orlando as Bryant scores 33 points in the second half.

Rodman assures everyone he's back to stay. "Oh, I'm here for the rest of the season," he says. "I've used up my hall pass."

It's not like the Lakers looked the other way. He says they fined him $100 a day during his one-week absence.

March 26—Rodman refuses to go back in the closing minutes against the Kings, telling Rambis his body has tightened up. Sacramento wins on a last-second tip-in by Chris Webber.

March 27—Rodman is one hour and 15 minutes late for this Saturday practice, arriving with Chasman, who requests a meeting with Rambis. After huddling for 30 minutes, Rambis tells the press he and Dennis are now on the same page.

"I think we have come to an understanding that he is an important part of this ballclub and we need him to make a more concerted effort to be a part of this team," Rambis says. "Be at practice, be on time, all of those things."

April 6—Rodman's Beverly Hills PR firm announces he and Electra "have mutually agreed to end their six-month-old marriage under amicable circumstances" but "are and will remain friends."

That night, Utah's Karl Malone goes 12-for-12 against Rodman as the Jazz brush the Lakers aside in the fourth quarter to win, 106–93.

Afterward, Rodman rips unnamed teammates—presumably Bryant, who had problems guarding Shandon Anderson—complaining, "If you're going to commit yourself to play basketball, then play basketball.

If you're not going to play, then you should sit down and don't play. Don't even bother coming."

Of course, that's easy for Rodman to say. When he doesn't feel like playing, he doesn't bother coming.

April 9—Another Friday night flight: Rodman refuses to go back in during a 96–89 victory over the Timberwolves.

April 10—Rodman is more than an hour late for the Saturday practice.

■　■　■

So much for the honeymoon.

To that point, Rodman had been with the team for six weeks, in which time he'd had one leave of absence, had refused to go into three games, and had been late for, or missed, four practices.

Management's primary technique was to pretend it wasn't happening. West had all but retired; he wasn't even showing up in the Forum for games now, watching them at home on TV, instead. Said a friend: "I couldn't talk to him long. It was too depressing."

Rambis, who wanted to instill a Riley-like sense of mission and a Riley-like defense, was left to manage chaos and try to make it look like nothing unusual was happening.

Who, us . . . crazy?

"I have not let that bother me and I think the players are feeding off me," Rambis said. "I know that players not being at practice, whether they're sick or injured or whatever, doesn't lend itself to building the chemistry and unity and timing aspects of playing defense, but we don't have a whole lot of practice time anyway.

"But I have not let it bother me and I don't think it's bothering the team. That would just be counterproductive."

It would also have been human nature. The Lakers discouraged press inquiries, or pooh-poohed them, all but singing in chorus, "That stuff doesn't distract me."

Nevertheless, nerves were fraying. They leveled off, going 9–9 after Rambis' 10–0 start. O'Neal started snapping rebounds out of Rodman's arms; before, teammates had always let Dennis have everything to pad his numbers.

155

"I don't know who's upset, who's not upset," said Bryant, in a rare acknowledgment someone wasn't happy. "As far as veterans, Derek Harper, who's been in this league for 15 years, obviously, he's not going to be happy about it. You have certain personalities on the team who are not happy with it. But on the whole, I think we deal with it."

On the whole, they were in turmoil. As the Lakers drifted, it became clear it was only a matter of who would step up in the front office, and on what pretext.

Rodman didn't do anything unusual to precipitate his firing. The Lakers had just lost four of six, capped by a 113–86 wipeout in Portland on April 13, where he said he'd hurt his elbow once more and sat out the second half. After the game, he changed his story and said he had the flu. That turned out to be the last drop in the Rodman Water Torture.

At Rambis' urging, West and GM Mitch Kupchak, monitoring developments from Phoenix where they were attending a predraft tournament, asked Buss if they could pull the plug. Signaling the end of this fiasco, when Rodman arrived one minute late for the next day's practice—which was actually early for him—Rambis sent him home.

"They should've done this weeks ago," a Lakers official told the *Times'* Tim Kawakami. "He was tearing apart the team. Everybody could see it. The players wanted it, everybody wanted it. It just came down to Jerry Buss agreeing."

Rodman was cut that night—51 days after he arrived—in the same indecisive, responsibility-ducking style that had launched the misbegotten adventure in the first place and had let it go that long. The announcement came in a press release with West unavailable for comment. Buss went to practice the next day to pose with the team for the annual picture but wouldn't talk to reporters; his spokesman told them that Buss said his front office had done "what they had to do."

In Rodman style, this was just another turn in his tabloid life. The agent who represented Joey Buttafuoco, Tonya Harding, and John Wayne Bobbitt announced she could get Dennis work.

O'Neal, who had sponsored Rodman, blamed everyone but Rodman, claiming the press had overreacted. The Lakers lost their first game without Rodman the next night in Utah.

"You want to know the truth?" said Utah coach Jerry Sloan, upset at even being asked about Rodman. "I was shocked when they put him on the team. That was my shock. . . . I won't have to talk about him anymore. For crying out loud, is that all anybody talks about anymore?"

No. From then on, Shaq and Kobe would be all anybody talked about anymore.

■　■　■

Unlike Rodman and Rice, who complemented O'Neal, Bryant didn't complement anyone and barely seemed to notice O'Neal was around. As a rookie, he had asked Del Harris why they couldn't post him up instead of Shaq.

And so it started. O'Neal began dropping hints about "stupid, idiotic play," then more pointed hints, as when he told reporters, "You guys know the real problem, you're just scared to write about it."

Finally O'Neal just laid it out there. He had a deal with CBS *Sportsline*, and on a trip to Oakland, he disclosed his doubts to Mike Kahn of the Web site, in what amounted to the first shot fired in a struggle that would run for years.

"What is this, an experiment?" O'Neal said. "Nobody waited for me when I came into the league. The pressure was there as soon as I started to play. That's my job. Why wait? I'm not going to be here that long that I want to wait years for him [Bryant] to figure it out."

For his part, Bryant was mystified. His belief in himself was such, he thought everyone approved of what he did as much as he did. Nor did he sense any problem with O'Neal, who, Bryant noted, never complained to him about anything.

It would always be like that between them. Bryant offended O'Neal in a long list of ways—he was withdrawn, stubborn, didn't always play the right way (i.e., throw the ball inside to Shaq), and was still everyone's darling, especially that of West and Buss.

O'Neal was right—the ball was supposed to go inside before Bryant jacked one up from 20 feet. Nevertheless, this was also self-serving, and O'Neal had had this kind of problem before, with Penny Hardaway, whose game was a lot more under control than Bryant's.

On the other hand, it wasn't just O'Neal, Bryant was hard to reach for everyone. He was distant from teammates in general. He buddied up with older players like Byron Scott and Derek Harper, but went his own way the rest of the time. When the guys were out on the town, Bryant was in his hotel room, watching ESPN and calling his family or his old high school friends in Philadelphia.

Rambis tried to heal the rift in a meeting, asking players to understand where Bryant was coming from and take his age into consideration. That irked Harper, who announced that was wrong, that Bryant should be the one to join them, not vice versa. Harper, the starting point guard, promptly became a nonentity and played little.

Assistant coach Larry Drew later described the meeting, and the ones that followed, to friends. Everyone would line up to tell Bryant he was shooting too much. By way of reply, Bryant would put up 20 shots the next game. The issue that would dominate the next five years was finally on the table.

■　■　■

The Lakers finished that season 31–19, No. 4 in the West, and drew the No. 5 seed, Houston, in the first round.

The Rockets, who had won titles in 1994 and 1995, still had Hakeem Olajuwon with Charles Barkley and Scottie Pippen, but they were 36, 36, and 34, respectively. The Rockets were kind of like the Lakers, but older. They didn't get along, with tensions rising between Barkley and Pippen. They had brought Pippen in at great cost, thinking they were prolonging their title run, but they had been as big a bust as the Lakers had.

The Lakers ran them over, 3–1, and their bandwagon filled up, as it always did. With all their problems, the Shaq-Kobe tandem was devastating and, if they were playing together, indefensible.

"You're in awe at what's going to happen as these guys get older," said Rockets coach Rudy Tomjanovich.

"I've been saying for three or four years, Shaquille O'Neal is the most dominating player in the game," said Barkley. "He's unstoppable. Dream [Hakeem Olajuwon] did the best he could. Antoine [Carr] did the best he could."

But those guys weren't quite old enough yet.

Next up was San Antonio, the No. 1 seed, a tough defensive team that could contain O'Neal with its seven-foot tandem of David Robinson and Tim Duncan. This was a real rivalry for O'Neal, who'd gone to high school in San Antonio and didn't like Robinson, claiming the gentlemanly Admiral had been rude or brusque when the teenaged Shaq was introduced to him.

In a physical Game 1, O'Neal went 6–19 from the floor as the Spurs held him to 21 points and won, 87–81. O'Neal followed referee Steve Javie off the floor afterward, obliging Rambis to jump between them. Shaq stomped back to the dressing room and overturned the cart holding the TV and VCR.

Before Game 2, Lakers video coordinator Chris Bodaken took the liberty of taping the new VCR to the TV, just in case. Said GM Mitch Kupchak, helping him: "Tape it good."

In a sign of things to come, Bryant was brilliant in Game 2, scoring 28 points, looking like he was going to carry them to a breakthrough win—until he missed two free throws with :18 left and the Lakers leading, 76–75.

With a last chance, the Spurs called time out, then ran a low-post play for Duncan, guarded by J. R. Reid, as the Lakers knew they would. Rice was supposed to drop down and double-team, and the Lakers could take the foul they had to give, too. On the other hand, Rambis had tried to do a lot of things—like making the Lakers into a solid defensive team—that hadn't happened, and nothing he told them this time did, either.

The ball went in to Mario Elie, who wasn't fouled. He threw it into Duncan, who wasn't fouled *or* double-teamed. In splendid isolation, Duncan went up over the shorter Reid and banked in a jump hook, easy as you please, that won the game.

"They didn't foul Mario and I thought, 'Wow!'" said the Spurs' Avery Johnson. "They didn't foul Tim and I thought, 'Wow, wow!' I just knew Tim was going to get bladed."

For the Lakers, it was like amateur hour. Games 3 and 4 in the Forum were Spur romps. The double-teams didn't show up there, either, as Duncan scored 70 points, making 20 of 33 shots. At the end of Game 4, derisive Lakers fans chanted "Eddie! Eddie!" for the departed Eddie Jones.

So much for the never-to-be-forgotten-no-matter-how-hard-the-Lakers-tried 1999 season.

"Talent doesn't win in this league," said Rick Fox, his voice a whisper. "It may win in the regular season. It doesn't win you championships. It didn't win in high school. It didn't win in college.

"My high school coach told me talent, attitude, and skill make a basketball player. And most people think the most important one is talent—when it isn't. It's having the right attitude and obviously developing the skills as you go along. Because, as you've seen, the most talented teams in this league aren't always the ones that win. I've watched that enough to know it."

Harris was gone so they couldn't pin this one on him. Rambis looked like he was in over his head when Rodman was there, as anyone would have been, and after Rodman left, too. They still didn't have that power forward they needed, but they did have a new problem poking up between Bryant and O'Neal and the rest of the guys.

In what amounted to a declaration he wasn't a ghost, West, who had ducked the press all season, and ducked the season, too, talked afterward, which meant at least he was still on the job.

"Hey, everything we did was from good intentions," said Magic Johnson. "It's just that some people disagreed for the first time. We didn't have this before, in terms of bringing Dennis in, other situations, trades. . . . It was the first time everybody wasn't on the same page, but one out of 20-some years isn't bad, you know what I'm saying?"

Of course, it made it worse when the one was the most recent one.

In three seasons, O'Neal had only been as far as the conference finals once and had seen his teams booted out by scores of 4–1, 4–0, and 4–0. He bailed on the breakup meeting, as usual, and flew back to his Orlando mansion. He was now only a year away from being able to opt out, and teammates were already worried. "He was crazy upset," said one.

Said Harper, lighter hearted since he knew he wasn't coming back: "Maybe he had an excused absence."

But as their mothers told them, it's always darkest before the dawn.

WE'RE OFF TO SEE
THE WIZARD

I don't know what I'm going to come up with for this Laker team. They've got
their own thing going on. The Crips and the Bloods? That's really L.A.

—New Lakers coach Phil Jackson, January 2000

■ ■ ■

IN RETROSPECT, THE LAKERS' ride to glory under Phil Jackson looked easy
or inevitable. At the time, it even surprised him.

His mere presence was beyond the Lakers experience. He was an
outsider in their Lakers family. His asking price was $6 million per
year, which was more than Jerry Buss had budgeted for the entire
front office.

Buss would pay whatever it took for star players but, aside from that,
ran a thrifty organization with low pay for most of the front office. That
included his coaches, who'd been mostly Lakers assistants who worked
their way up, á la Pat Riley. Jerry West had courted a few big-name outsiders like Rick Pitino and Roy Williams, but he also liked the idea of
hiring from within, which had worked brilliantly with Riley, if not with
Kurt Rambis.

Of course, the team Riley took over not only had talent, it had
already won a title and had internal leadership from Magic Johnson and
Kareem Abdul-Jabbar. Riley had the luxury of being able to learn to
coach on the job. Rambis was more like a lobster thrown into a boiling
pot. Even after Rodman left, Rambis was short with subordinates and
the press and couldn't get the players to do what he wanted.

West seemed to acknowledge they needed a change on the last day of the season, noting Rambis had done "a very credible job under adverse circumstances." He added pointedly, "One of the things we did, we left our options open with regard to our coaching staff."

However, West didn't think Buss would go for any $6 million, and he felt bad for Rambis, who was Laker family to the core. Two weeks later, the *Times*, quoting Lakers sources, reported Rambis was expected to return. There was no comment from the team—and no protest behind the scenes—tacitly confirming the story, as did more people around the league who talked to West.

So, it came like a thunderbolt from the sky when the story broke that the Lakers were now in negotiations with Jackson's agent, Todd Musburger.

Jackson, retired for a season after his six-title run with the Bulls and off on an Alaskan vacation with his son, was caught by surprise, himself, although he had been eyeing the opportunity for years. Even before he left Chicago, Jackson had wondered where else he might ever coach, and anticipated what everyone could see coming in Los Angeles. He was interested enough to explain in a diary he did for *ESPN Magazine* just how he would handle the Lakers, even asking if O'Neal was "smart enough yet to know what he can and can't do in this game to be a winner?"

"I see that as a challenge," Jackson continued. "But the challenge also would be to have him submit to the triangle offense. I believe in its principles. It's a center-in offense. Who's the perfect center for the triangle? Shaq."

Jackson had a habit of speaking off the record to confidants and assuming they'd know what to use and what not to use. However, since Del Harris still had the Lakers job at the time he had written his diary, this was such bad form that in the next installment of his diary, Jackson was obliged to note lamely he hadn't meant it that way. This infuriated West, who hated to see the Lakers' business discussed in the newspapers, much less by outsiders. This was yet another reason no one expected the Lakers to turn to Jackson.

And yet they did, in a 180-degree turn from their tradition. No one explained satisfactorily why until the following spring, when the Lakers were flying high under Jackson, and O'Neal said he had told West he wanted Phil.

"I sorta gave the organization an ultimatum," O'Neal said. "This is my eighth year. I'm tired of winning 50, 60 games and going home early. Get me somebody that can take us to the next level.

"I just told Jerry [West] and Jerry Buss that we need to get it done. You know, they're kind of patient—'Oh, we got time.' But I don't really believe in patience all the time. I'd rather get it done now. . . .

"I didn't really talk to them for a while but then after it came up— what are we going to do about Kurt and should we look for somebody new?—they asked my opinion."

O'Neal told them to hire Jackson or Chuck Daly, whom he had tried to get the Magic to hire in his days in Orlando. The Magic actually had hired Daly a year after O'Neal left, but Daly had just retired for the last time.

So it was Jackson or Rambis, with O'Neal in favor of the former and down on the latter.

It was Brian Hill redux. O'Neal had loved Hill when he was Matty Guokas' assistant in Orlando but, within three seasons, was maneuvering to have Hill replaced. O'Neal loved Rambis as an assistant, but when Kurt seemed to bend over backwards for Bryant, and when they went nowhere in the playoffs again, that took care of that. Rambis was off the list.

So it was Jackson, even at his full asking price, five seasons at $6 million, plus a bonus of $2 million for every title he won. The package was more than Buss had paid his other coaches in his 20 seasons, combined. If it seemed the inmates were now running the asylum, in retrospect it was the right choice. Jackson had something rare, as events soon showed, and he would need every bit of it.

■ ■ ■

Jackson wasn't just outside the Lakers' experience. He was outside the experience of the entire league.

In the urban hoops subculture, he was from as far out in the country as anyone could be. The West he hailed from had nothing to do with

California or the Sunbelt or places as hip as Denver or Salt Lake City, or, for that matter, Fargo.

Jackson was from the thinly settled High Plains, born September 17, 1945, in a place called Deer Lodge, Montana, the youngest of three sons of Charles Jackson, a Pentecostal minister, and his wife, Elizabeth, an evangelist. They lived in a church basement until Phil was four, when Charles got an offer to take over a congregation in Williston, North Dakota, a hamlet in the northwest corner of the state, just east of the Montana line and south of the Canadian border. Charles consulted the family. The kids said they preferred scenic Montana to the barren Dakota plains. Unfortunately for them, Charles concluded God was calling him to Williston.

Their faith was fundamentalist and pure. They had no TV, and the boys were discouraged from going to movies or listening to rock'n'roll. In his book *Sacred Hoops*, Jackson describes his father as a warm and compassionate man who meant what he said, punishing misdeeds with a razor strap in the parsonage basement. His father only took him down there once, Jackson wrote, and wept while hitting him.

Nor was corporal punishment the worst of it.

"The point was to be not just an average Christian but an exceptional one, so when the 'end of times' came, we would be selected," Jackson wrote. "We were taught to believe that the apocalyptic version in the Book of Revelations was about to be fulfilled any minute and if we weren't prepared, we'd be left out when Christ returned and gathered up his saints. As a little boy, I was terrified of being excluded from the 'rapture of the saints,' as it was called, and losing my parents. One day my mother wasn't home when I returned from school and I got so frightened the rapture had started without me that I ran all over town looking for her.

"I was shaking when I finally tracked her down at a local radio station, taping a religious program with my dad."

This heart-rending passage is tucked away, almost as an aside, in a book devoted primarily to his experiences with the Bulls. Nevertheless, it suggested how difficult Jackson's childhood must have been and how alienated he must have felt as he found his place among the fleshpots far, far away.

"My instinct is that the disciplines that he got from that very strenuous fundamentalist childhood, and then the search to get away from it, but to hold on to some of it, has created an incredibly strong psychological person," says David Halberstam, the Pulitzer Prize–winner who became friendly with Jackson while working on two books about the NBA.

"I think it's the combination of that fundamentalist background—I mean really tough, awful—and the rejection of it, while still searching for something to replace it without going to nihilism, and then the enormous natural intelligence."

Phil wasn't the family rebel. That was Joe, the middle son, who once razzed Charles while he was conducting services. Charles leaped off the pulpit and chased him all over the church before collaring him as the horrified congregation looked on.

Nevertheless, Phil had his own path, and it didn't lead to the ministry, as his parents intended, but into the wider world his athletic ability opened. He was a local star in all sports, good enough to attract the attention of the basketball coach at the University of North Dakota, Bill Fitch. When Fitch came to recruit him, Jackson impressed him with his wing span, showing he could sit in the front seat of a car and open both doors.

Jackson married his campus sweetheart, and they had a daughter, named Elizabeth, after his mother. The team twice made the NCAA College Division finals, giving him enough of a stage to become a dark-horse second-round draft choice of the Knicks in 1967. In an even bigger surprise, he stuck.

Now at the end of the psychedelic sixties, with his marriage over, Jackson's search took him into the Chelsea section of Manhattan, handy to Greenwich Village, the beating heart of bohemia. With long hair, an other-worldly calm, and an interest in Eastern philosophy, Jackson was tabbed as the Knicks' house hippie. He liked to tell of going to the 1968 Democratic Convention where teammate Cazzie Russell, who'd been called up by the National Guard, was on one side of the picket lines and Jackson was on the other with the protesters.

Nevertheless, there was nothing that suggested peace and love on the court. Jackson was awkward and limited but he was tough, with sharp elbows everyone knew about. Off the floor, he studied the game at the feet of coach Red Holzman as avidly as he studied William James, Carlos Castaneda, or Krishnamurti.

The Knicks, scorned for so long, captured Gotham, winning the franchise's first (and only) titles in 1970 and 1973. According to swept-away Madison Avenue, the NBA was now "the game of the seventies." All the Knicks were stars in New York, although by mid-decade, their run was ending.

Jackson played with the Knicks until 1978, spent two seasons with the Nets, and retired at 35. He moved to Woodstock, the upstate version of the Village, although he didn't turn out to be destined for a life in the counterculture.

Like Pat Riley laying on the beach in Santa Monica after his last waiver, or Don Nelson, who was going to try go get back in as a referee, Jackson missed the game keenly. Remembering an old suggestion by Holzman, he coached in a summer league in Puerto Rico. That led to a job with the Albany Patroons of the Continental Basketball Association, who played before crowds of, literally, hundreds.

Jackson had served as an unofficial assistant to Holzman while sitting out the 1969–1970 season, and had put in a half-season as an assistant with the Nets. For their part, the Patroons were beside themselves at the thought of having an actual Knick.

To their delight and his, they found Jackson had a flair for the job, winning a CBA title and a coach of the year award, opening a career path where none had been before.

Now he had to find someone in the big leagues to give him a shot, even if he wasn't conventionally networked. Jackson had gone his own way in a league that otherwise missed the Age of Aquarius. His assistant coach at Albany was his friend, Charley Rosen, a writer he'd met in the Village who wrote a book about him called *Maverick*, detailing adventures like the one in which Jackson and a famous actress, whose name wasn't revealed, took LSD on a beach in Los Angeles.

Jackson's salvation was Chicago Bulls GM Jerry Krause, a prickly, tough-minded little figure, who stood 5'3" and made frequent references to his lack of stature in a league largely run by tall, handsome former All-American types.

Krause's answer was an obsessive work ethic with countless days on the road—he loved his nickname, "Sleuth"—looking under rocks for an edge, a player no one knew about, or a coaching talent too far down to draw notice.

Krause was always looking for the protégé who would remember what he had done for him. It would be that way with Tex Winter and Doug Collins before Jackson, and Tim Floyd after him.

Jackson still had his hippie reputation and wasn't sure how far he wanted to go to renounce it. After four seasons in Albany, Krause brought him to Chicago to meet his new coach, Stan Albeck. Jackson showed up wearing a flashy panama hat with a big feather, and didn't get the job.

Happily—for Jackson, at least—Albeck lasted one season. A year later, in the spring of 1986, Krause got Jackson an interview with his newest coach, Collins. Jackson showed up without the hat or any other fashion statements and got the job.

The Bulls had the already incomparable—and headstrong—Michael Jordan and little else. Krause, who'd inherited Jordan when he took over in 1985, was busily building a roster around him. However, Scottie Pippen and Horace Grant wouldn't arrive until 1988, so if the Bulls made progress, it was slow going.

It was also tortuous. Jordan was impatient and not shy about letting teammates know what he expected of them, or telling the press, which adored him. Collins was whip-smart but volatile. There were better teams in the East, like the Celtics, still tough in their sunset years of the eighties, and the rising Bad Boys in Detroit.

Collins lasted four seasons, getting the Bulls as far as the 1989 East Finals, where they fell to the Pistons as Jordan fumed about the shortcomings of "my supporting cast."

Then, Collins, a downstate homeboy and fan favorite, was suddenly fired amid reports of behind-the-scenes lash-outs at players and rifts with management. Collins, at odds with Krause, suspected Jackson of being a pipeline to the GM and stopped talking to his assistant coach, except in timeout huddles.

Like Riley slipping into the job amid the hue and cry about Magic Johnson getting Paul Westhead fired, Jackson's hiring was overshadowed by Collins' firing and was welcomed by players and everyone else suffering from Doug fatigue. Jackson didn't have Collins' stature, but he was as calm as Collins had been excitable.

Jackson's serenity, seemingly unshakeable even in the darkest days, was his great gift, the one that separated him from his peers. It wasn't that Jackson didn't feel the heat. Right after games, he'd go off for two quick smokes, which he'd suck down in about two drags, and he often went home, walked in the door, said nothing to the wife and kids, and shut himself in his room.

But you couldn't see it. Jackson didn't worry out loud, or dwell on things that could go wrong, or snap out at the press. Whatever happened, he had it covered. The other coaches were more like Collins, prone to mood swings with post-victory highs and post-loss, we'll-never-win-another-game lows.

Jackson's first priority would be establishing a working relationship with Jordan, who wasn't easy to impress. Jackson was installing Winter's triangle offense in an attempt to make it harder for teams to gang up on Jordan, even as Jackson pointed out to Jordan that no NBA scoring champion had ever won a title, trying to persuade him to pass more.

Making no secret of his skepticism, Jordan called the triangle "an equal-opportunity offense," which wasn't a compliment. Jordan could never see the logic in a system that took shots away from him and gave them to someone else. He and the blunt-spoken Winter had an ongoing debate, with Winter noting there was no I in *team*, and Jordan responding there was one in *win*, though.

In the end, Jordan gave—enough—and they won six titles between 1991 and 1998, the greatest run since Red Auerbach's Celtics won 11 from 1957 to 1969. By then, Jordan was a demigod who publicly pledged his devotion to Jackson, who was a star in his own right, known as the "Zenmeister."

Jackson's new style was as idiosyncratic as he was. He believed in an inner circle that nurtured its own, comparing his team to a band of warriors, complete with Native American totems on the walls. Eastern and tribal influences notwithstanding, Jackson was more like Niccolò Machiavelli when it came to how to keep people inside the wigwam.

It was never more clearly illustrated than in the 1994 playoffs, while Jordan was off playing baseball. Even without him, the Bulls had won 55 games and were now giving Riley's Knicks all they wanted in the second round.

At the end of Game 3, a fuming Pippen took himself out of the last 1.8 seconds after Jackson drew up the last shot for Toni Kukoc. Kukoc proceeded to hit a game-winning 20-footer. Jackson proceeded to give Scottie away, announcing Pippen's desertion before the press asked about it.

Any other coach would have made up an excuse to protect Pippen and dealt with Scottie privately. Jackson's approach was to dangle Pippen above the prevailing hysteria that attended the Bulls in Chicago.

One of Jackson's favorite quotes was Rudyard Kipling's "the strength of the pack is the wolf and the strength of the wolf is the pack." Sure enough, Pippen felt obliged to square it with his teammates and returned to the fold, uniting the team once more.

It was daring, it was unorthodox, and it worked. Pippen took the floor to a hero's welcome two days later in Game 4 and scored 25 points as the Bulls won.

Nevertheless, even as the Bulls won six titles in the nineties, the strife never went away. It just changed form. Jordan had no use for Krause, who presided with a heavy hand. Jordan's idea of an administrator was one who asked him what they should do; like many of the closely knit North Carolina alumni, Jordan's solution was usually to bring in some Tar Heel.

Krause wasn't keen on surrendering the slightest bit of his authority to Jordan or anyone else. So the standoff endured, even if Krause adored Jordan as much as anyone else, with Jordan needling him pointedly with nicknames like "Crumbs," a reference to Krause's appetite.

By the end of the run, there was a full-fledged rift between management and the players, with Krause and owner Jerry Reinsdorf making no secret of their plans to dismantle their dynasty before it got too old.

"The run of this team will come to an end at some point," said Reinsdorf, two years ahead of the fact. "The challenge that we have in management is not to become the Boston Celtics. Our challenge is to get the next run started as soon as possible. So we are going to have to make some decisions and they might be some hard decisions as to when we say, 'OK, it's been great. See you at the Old Timers' Game.'"

Of course, as it turned out, the Bulls' "next run" after they dismantled their own dynasty in midreign would turn out to be a long way off, if there was to be one, but who knew?

With the split between players and the front office widening, Jackson made a nontraditional choice: he jumped into the boat with Jordan and the team. Once the coach had been part of management, but men like Riley and Jackson were making it something else, a third power center.

Reinsdorf, prizing loyalty above all, backed Krause. Amid reports that Jackson was now asking that Krause's access to the team be sharply curtailed, Reinsdorf stood by his GM, introducing Krause after they won their fifth title in 1997 to a jeering United Center crowd as the man "most responsible" for their success.

By then, things were beyond bizarre. Due to a loophole in his expiring contract, Jackson had already been negotiating with other teams during the 1997 playoffs, turning down a $6-million-a-year offer from Orlando.

Jackson decided to return for one more season, on a one-year deal, to win one more title with the gang and then assess his options. Krause, showing how small he could be, actually barred Jackson from draft workouts, since he was not yet signed for next season.

It was open war. Jackson designated their 1997–1998 season "the last waltz," noting publicly that Krause had already tried to break up the team by trading Pippen that summer. Jackson added that Krause was "pretty unskilled socially."

Krause was on a rampage, quelling the revolution. In training camp, he was quoted as saying, "Players don't win titles, organizations do." Asked about all the "backstabbing" among the Bulls during a game by TNT's Craig Sager, Krause railed, "First of all, there's no backstabbing going on here, OK? Understand me when I say that? I'm not surprised and I'm even amazed you would make a statement like that! This team is comprised of professionals, composed of guys who understand what they have to do and are winners, unlike the comment you made."

Krause then stomped off, perhaps to work on his social skills.

The Bulls won that sixth title, punctuated perfectly by Jordan's championship-winning shot in Game 6 in the Delta Center, freezing his right hand in mid-follow-through for a dramatic second, as if saying good-bye.

Jordan retired (again). Jackson retired, too, and went back to his Deer Lake, Montana, home to await further developments.

In other words, no matter how crazy the Lakers might be, Jackson had seen worse.

Or so he thought.

■   ■   ■

It was going to be a transition, all around.

Jackson drove from Deer Lake to Los Angeles, at a turning point. Taking the job had effectively ended his marriage to his second wife, June, who'd had enough of being a coach's consort. She stayed behind and ultimately went to work in Bill Bradley's campaign in the Democratic primaries.

Somewhere in the Sierra Nevadas, Jackson popped in a tape his teenage daughters had made for him, wishing him well, and was so moved, he pulled over to the side of the road and wept.

"It was about going out and living life again, going out and finding love again," Jackson later told the *New York Times'* Mike Wise. "They were trying to tell me, 'You've got to find this passion again about moving on.' I felt so fortunate that they were so supportive, I just crossed a little two-lane highway and went to this space. I just felt like, 'Man, I've been given this unbelievable opportunity.'"

There were few opportunities like it, a championship-caliber team just sitting there waiting to be molded. On the other hand, the championship-caliber team had already unseated two coaches.

Jackson was greeted like a conquering hero. Bryant came over to his hotel before Phil's first Lakers press conference to get him to sign a copy of *Sacred Hoops*. Bryant had an abiding hunger to be coached and was always casting around for knowledge, as when he called Winter, who was still a Bulls assistant, to ask about the triangle.

Nevertheless, Bryant was tough to handle for his own coach and didn't run the triangle long before deciding he hated it. As Rambis could have told Jackson, honeymoons were short around there.

O'Neal was on board. He had even stopped off at Jackson's Deer Lake home over the summer to visit, which turned out to be a valuable chance for them to get to know each other. Watching O'Neal, who was always in touch with his inner child, borrow a neighbor's jet ski so he could go out on the lake, and threatening to collapse Jackson's son's trampoline, Jackson discovered he was about to coach the world's biggest postadolescent.

The Lakers were new to him, but then he was new to them, too. Jackson represented a new philosophy and a new system. The triangle required different personnel, and Jackson had his own profile for players. Mostly he liked former Bulls and tried to acquire them at every opportunity. West had always prized athletes, whereas Jackson was much more into experience and attitude.

So a shakeup ensued. Ruben Patterson, a talented young forward who had waged fearsome practice battles with Bryant in his rookie season, was waived and quickly picked up by Seattle where he became a starting player. As a backup center, Jackson chose 35-year-old John Salley, making a comeback after a two-year retirement. Off the waiver wire came creaky, 35-year-old Ron Harper, who'd played for Jackson in Chicago and would now take Derek Fisher's point guard job. A. C. Green, the old Showtime Laker who'd been gone for six seasons, was back at 36 to take over for Robert Horry at power forward. Brian Shaw, who was thought to be washed up at 32 after sitting out all but one game the season before in Portland, was signed as a backup.

The Lakers, who'd been big and athletic, with the deepest roster in the league, now looked more like Shaq and Kobe attending an AARP meeting.

Not that Jackson was worried. It never occurred to him he could turn the Lakers around in one season. In camp, he joked that as far as his system was concerned, his players were "autistic" or in "remedial school." He said he wouldn't even know what they had until Christmas, nor did he expect it to be good enough.

"It will be a season," he said, "in which I'll probably be coming to Jerry West's office and say, 'Jerry, there are some guys here who cannot learn what we're trying to do. . . . We're going to have to change some personnel to meet the kind of things we have to do. We don't have a power forward. We don't have another power player to go along with Shaq.'"

Silver-tongued devil that Jackson was, this all went down without protest from the organization, the fans, or the press.

"Every year, they used to say Del Harris was in trouble if he didn't win a championship," grumbled Portland GM Bob Whitsitt. "Now Phil gets a $30-million contract, and no one cares if they win a championship?"

Jackson was different, all right. The top coaches customarily drove their players hard. Compared to someone like Riley, who piled the misery on his players when things went bad, playing for Jackson was like being on vacation.

■   ■   ■

Coaching the Lakers meant coaching O'Neal and Bryant. If Jackson could make it work with them, everything would be OK, since their potential, if it was ever realized, was awesome.

O'Neal was easy. He wasn't a great practice player or a conditioning maniac, but he was in his prime and hungry for the title that would get the cast of *SportsCenter* off his back. Having tabbed Jackson, he was fully with any program Phil had in mind, even sitting still for Jackson zinging him in the newspapers, which was Jackson's way of telling O'Neal what he expected. O'Neal noted that Sarge had raised him the same way and called Jackson "my white father."

For his part, Bryant was drawn to older mentors and eager for knowledge but he was also stubborn and hard to convince. Even among superstars, Bryant had an unusual confidence in his ability and destiny that made him all but bulletproof. It was his blessing and his curse.

He had no fear of—nor was he haunted by—failure, shrugging off that four-airball game at Utah his rookie season as if it had never happened. The way he figured it, anything that went wrong was just one more step before everything went right and he realized that golden destiny. His lack of fear also made him hard to reach, or coach. He didn't care what the group thought about him, or the coaching staff. Having grown up as the adored youngest child of a close-knit family, he cared only what his innermost circle thought. His isolation from teammates had passed without comment for two seasons, since everyone thought it was because he was so young, Now he was 21, not 18, and the same distance prevailed. It had become an issue, and Rambis, trying to heal the rift, had fallen into the chasm.

Jackson had had eight seasons of Jordan, who could be as aloof and headstrong as any living legend. On the other hand, Jordan had been reachable and a guy's guy who enjoyed being with his teammates. It didn't take Jackson long to see that Bryant was different. Jackson said at midseason:

Kobe's a distant person, and he's got a very different makeup and he has set himself apart. And we've had numbers of talks about how to become a good teammate.

I told Kobe, "I would guess you'd like to be the captain of this team some day as you get a little bit older—maybe like 25."

He says, "I want to be captain tomorrow."

I said, "Well, you can't be captain if nobody follows you."

I was coming in here pretty much blind. I didn't know them. People told me Kobe was a person, if you raised the bar, he would still try and clear it. No matter what height you put it, he was still going to attempt to clear the bar.

And the other thing was, he was the kind of person, if you coached him, he would say, "Uh-huh, uh-huh," go back out onto the court and do the same thing, repeat his mistakes. And I found out a lot of that's true. You have to get through to Kobe more than once or twice. He's a hard-headed learner. He doesn't just learn by absorbing things. He's got to have it experientially happen to him and fail, or something happen, and then he makes the *aha*, the discovery.

Jackson was actually being diplomatic. He would have to get through to Bryant a lot more than once or twice.

■ ■ ■

The exhibition season did not offer promise of a fast turnaround, with the team going 2–5 and Bryant breaking a bone in his right hand, putting him out for the first 15 games. So everyone was surprised when the Lakers went to their old house of horrors, the Delta Center on opening night and held the Jazz to 84 points in an upset victory.

They were 11–4 when Bryant got back. Even Jackson began to wonder what was going on when they won 20 of their next 21. At Christmas, when Jackson had said he'd be giving West a list of all their hopeless players, they were 23–5, so that talk was put off.

Not that Bryant was exactly where Jackson wanted him, or close. Bryant had always been on the wild side but now he was frantic, trying to catch up.

"Getting hurt messed up his head," said Black, the Lakers publicist, who was close to Bryant. "He was driving everybody crazy. You know what time he got to the game the other day? Guys who come early come at 5:00. The other day he came at 3:00."

Even West, who doted on Bryant, worried about Kobe's progress, which came in giant leaps, often followed by major regressions, with one principle standing above all others: he would always err on the wild side.

"There's nights," West said that season, "I would go home and say to myself, 'My God, is he ever going to learn how to use his teammates better? Is he ever going to learn situations in games? Is he ever going to learn how important time is in a ball game? Is he ever going to learn to value the basketball?' It used to bother me a lot. . . .

"Obviously, there was a player in that locker room that a lot of our players had a difficult time playing with. They had a hard time playing with Kobe, I don't think there's any question about that.

"You sit there and think, 'How in the world can this kid do this?' But also the other factor was, the kid was 20 years old."

At 31–5, they finally leveled off and the Shaq-Kobe issues emerged. After Bryant turned the ball over six times in a January 19 win over the Cavaliers, they had a snarl-off in the dressing room, exchanging *f**** *you*'s, according to a member of the staff.

Teammates generally avoided choosing sides in the hope their superstars could learn to work together, but O'Neal wasn't the only one exasperated by Bryant. Fisher, who would always be Bryant's liason to the group, said:

That's how everybody felt. Nobody wanted to talk about it, though. Guys felt like it was somebody else's job, whether it was Coach or Jerry West. . . .

OK, guys know how the star system works in the league. Now, if you want to say something, you can but your job is not as secure as Shaquille's. So if you start beefing and talking about what's going on with Kobe, I mean, you're taking your chances, basically. But it was something that I think the entire group felt, that even though he had been with us a couple of years, he still was separating himself from the group. . . .

There were a few times that year when, as a group, we still felt just like we felt in the past, that Kobe wasn't coming on board with everybody so that we all could learn the system and we all could get used to working with one another so that we could reach the potential that we've always had.

Maybe after that Cleveland game and a couple of other times, guys that have been here and have been with Kobe, we didn't see him getting over that hump. And we were thinking, "OK, if Kobe's not willing to do it, he's going to be forced to do it, 'cause we had a coach come in that's going to make him do it, he's worked with the best."

And there would be times when were scared because he didn't think he was going to conform to the group—again. And once again, we would win a lot of games and make it to the play-offs and not do well.

And even our coaching staff didn't understand how deep-seated our frustrations were for wanting Kobe to be with us so we could win the championship. That's what it's always been about. It's never been about, "Kobe, come be with us because the way you're doing it is wrong." It's about, "Kobe, come be with us because you can't do it by yourself. We can't do it without you, so let's join together and let's win."

Jackson's suggestions to Bryant became pointed: pass the ball and if you have a problem with that, Jackson would try to work out a trade to another team.

It was the kind of thing Harris could never have said because Bryant would have recognized it for the empty threat it was. Even Jackson might have had a hard time getting Buss and West to trade their darling, had Bryant called his bluff.

It never came to that. Bryant reined himself in, although it didn't happen overnight. His assists went up to a career-high 4.9 a game. The Lakers finished 67–15, first in the West.

If Bryant thrashed about before accepting his place in Jackson's pecking order, the season was a triumph for O'Neal, who posted huge numbers (29.7 points, 13.6 rebounds, 3.8 assists) and missed by a single vote (CNN's Fred Hickman, who voted for Allen Iverson) of becoming the first unanimous MVP.

In true Shaq fashion, he expressed disappointment at the one vote he missed, seeming to overlook the 120 he got, but the best was yet to come.

■　　■　　■

With Jackson yet to be convinced this could happen this soon, and with the memory of their playoff pratfalls, the Lakers approached this post-season with something resembling humility. But they were an older, more experienced, more professional team now with O'Neal and Bryant in line and all the veterans they had brought in. They no longer fell apart at the first hint of trouble, which was good because there was trouble out there.

They had to win a Game 5 to eliminate the Kings, 3–2, in the first round. They waxed the Suns, 4–1, in the second, and advanced to the West Finals against Portland, a 59-game winner, considered their fore-most challenger.

The Lakers took a 3–1 lead, but the Blazers came back to tie it, 3–3 . . . and surged into a 15-point lead in the fourth quarter of the seventh game.

The Portland coach was Mike Dunleavy, the former Laker who knew his defense and had a roster loaded with rangy athletic players like Scottie Pippen and Rasheed Wallace, who could cover vast distances and disrupt offenses. Dunleavy had decided O'Neal wasn't going to beat them and double-teamed him hard, leaving Harper open, challenging him to do his worst.

Visions of debacles past danced in Laker heads: the 1997 embarrassment at the hands of the Jazz, the 1998 humiliation at the hands of the Jazz, the 1999 sweep by the Spurs. Now they were about to blow a 3–1 lead in the West Finals. It wasn't a new day after all. They were cursed. They were flawed. They were . . .

Then the most amazing thing happened. In the first of what would become a years-long series of amazing things—improbable comebacks, memorable shots, theater of every kind—the Lakers rallied.

Before June 4, 2000, no NBA team had ever blown a lead that big in the fourth quarter of a Game 7, even if Robert Horry said later he wasn't worried.

"Nah," said Horry. "I've been in situations like that before."

In a 15–0 run, Horry hit the first of his string of famous three-pointers, taking an offensive rebound, dribbling out to the arc, turning around, noticing no one had come with him and knocking down the shot. The Blazers went 0–13 from the field, and Shaw hit the three that tied it, 75–75, with 4:00 left.

With 1:34 left, Bryant drove the lane and double-clutched on a runner, drawing a foul on Wallace, who rolled on the floor to protest the call. Bryant made both free throws and the Lakers would never trail again.

At the other end, Wallace was fouled but missed both free throws.

Bryant hit a 17-footer with 1:09 left to make it 83–79, Lakers.

Pippen missed a three.

The Lakers spread the floor. Bryant crossed over and blew by Pippen, spotted O'Neal and threw him a high lob, which Shaq . . . just . . . barely . . . tip dunked.

Bedlam ensued. O'Neal came away from the hoop with his eyes bulging, his mouth in a wide O, and his arms out ahead of him, looking crazed. The Blazers hadn't even called time out yet when he ran into the Lakers reserves, who were streaming off the bench, and gave Fisher a chest bump.

That summer, Dunleavy called Black, the Lakers publicist and a friend from their days together, and told him that was Dunleavy's bleeping ring Black was wearing, mother. In a turnaround, it was now someone else's turn to suffer.

■　■　■

Of course, there was one more obstacle, the actual title, which would have to be won in the Finals.

The Lakers were heavily favored over the East champion, Indiana, for good reason. In one corner were the Lakers and O'Neal, with his Superman tattoos and persona. In the other corner, was 180-pound Reggie Miller, who'd started wearing an "S" T-shirt under his warmups that spring, although the effect wasn't the same. As teammate Sam Perkins noted, the only thing big about Reggie, besides his heart, were his ears.

Since O'Neal had become a Laker in 1996, the league had begun to tilt with big man after big man winding up in the West: Tim Duncan, Chris Webber, Rasheed Wallace, Dirk Nowitzki, Vlade Divac. Meanwhile, the best of the East, like Patrick Ewing, Alonzo Mourning, and Rik Smits aged on the vine.

East teams were ill-equipped to deal with someone like O'Neal in the post, even the Pacers, whose defense was designed by Larry Bird's respected assistant coach, Dick Harter. Harter taught tough, knife-between-the-teeth defense with few gimmicks, like double-teaming and rotating. This was fine against everyone else but had no chance against O'Neal, at the peak of his powers at 28 and as he closed in on the title that had eluded him.

Pacers president Donnie Walsh said he began to get a bad feeling before the opening tip in Game 1 when he couldn't see Dale Davis, who was standing behind O'Neal. Shaq went for 43 and Bird decided they'd better come up with a new defensive scheme fast.

After three games, it was O'Neal 116, Smits 22, and Bird was being asked if he'd stay with his big Dutch Boy.

"Who we going to change to?" Bird replied, ending the discussion.

The Lakers won the first two games in Staples but lost Game 3, 100–91, in Conseco Fieldhouse, with Bryant sitting out with a badly sprained ankle. The Pacers were within a game of tying the series, and the Lakers seemed to be considering flipping back out. Rice's wife, Christina, blasted Jackson for short-timing her husband, telling the *Los Angeles Times'* Bill Plaschke, "If it was me, I would have already been

Latrell Sprewell II." (Latrell Sprewell I had choked his coach, P. J. Carlesimo, so she probably didn't mean it as a compliment.)

The series turned on Game 4, which went into overtime . . . when O'Neal fouled out, with the Lakers trailing, 115–112. Showing That Day had arrived, Bryant took over, scoring eight of his 28 points, leading the Lakers to a 120–118 victory and a commanding 3–1 lead. The year before, he had missed the two free throws at the end of his brilliant Game 2 in San Antonio. At 21, he was finally the star O'Neal needed to get over the top.

The Lakers donated Game 5 to the Pacers in Conseco but held them off, 116–111, in Game 6 back in Staples and the long-deferred party was on.

Bryant jumped into O'Neal's arms. The celebration turned into a riot outside Staples, where fans had been watching on a theater-screen–sized TV. A police car was burned.

The Shaq-Kobe Lakers had their first parade. O'Neal, the erstwhile rapper who knew what to do with a microphone in his hands, asked the crowd, "Can youuuuuuuu dig it?"

They were just getting started. They were young and strong and, just like the tattoo on O'Neal's arm said, the world was theirs.

Chapter 11

THE AGE OF KOBE, OR A CHILDHOOD IS A TERRIBLE THING TO WASTE

When I was 19, I was talking to every girl. I was buying every car. And when I got my first NBA money, I was buying the freshest Benz. I'm getting the rims, I got the system. I got the windows down, I got the gold chains, I'm back in the 'hood letting the boys know I made it. . . . Kobe? Stays in the house and reads.

—Shaquille O'Neal, *Shaq Talks Back*

You ask what Kobe was like as a kid. That's just it, he was never a kid.

—Del Harris

■ ■ ■

KOBE BRYANT WASN'T THE FIRST player to skip college and go to the pros. That was Moses Malone in 1974. Nor was it Bryant who launched the Children's Crusade that began to take over the game in the nineties. That was the Fab Five, starring Chris Webber in his two years at Michigan from 1991 to 1993. Bryant wasn't even the first in the nineties wave of high school players who turned pro, which got bigger and bigger until it overran the draft and changed the game forever. That was Kevin Garnett in 1995.

But it was Kobe who came out of Lower Merion High School in 1996, who went the farthest and showed what was possible, for better and worse.

If most of the kids had talent, he had the most. If many were successful, none was more successful. If some became rich, he became the

181

richest, with $14 million in salary and an estimated $20 million in off-court commercial deals by the 2003–2004 season.

If they were all young and had things to learn, Bryant was the most sheltered, which meant when he emerged from his cocoon, he'd have the most to learn. His lessons would turn out to be the most painful.

When he became engaged in 2000 to just-turned-18-year-old Vanessa Laine, who was fresh out of Marina High School in Huntington Beach, Bryant had just turned 22, himself. Friends and family counseled him to go slow, but he had a stock answer for that: "I do everything young."

It was true. He was 17 when he was drafted, 18 when he won the All-Star dunk contest, 19 when he started in his first All-Star Game, and 21 when he won his first NBA title.

It wasn't exactly easy, but he had gifts that went beyond his startling physical ability and the greatest skill level anyone had ever seen on a 17-year-old. Given his confidence, his toughness, his dedication, and his poise, it wasn't that hard. Jerry West saw it coming years away, as did Phoenix coach Danny Ainge, Clippers coach Bill Fitch, and Nets GM John Nash, just to name the people who tried to get Bryant. It was more like it was inevitable.

Bryant saw it coming way before they did. As far as he was concerned, he didn't have a future but a "destiny," and he realized his early.

"I think we all do," he said at 21. "I think some of us just figure out what it is, figure it out at an earlier age."

When had he figured out his?

"I knew it since I was five," he said.

In keeping with his youth motif, he was 24 when he fell from grace, charged with sexual assault in the celebrated case that would turn his life around and finally end his childhood.

How was he supposed to know life was so much harder than basketball?

■　■　■

If it seemed as if he was never a kid, he sure looked like one.

If everyone would quickly learn how deadly serious Bryant was, in the beginning he was the most adorable little thing you ever saw.

His father's contribution would always be exaggerated compared to his mother's, since Joe had been an NBA player. However, Kobe had his dad's elfin looks, with the slanted eyes, the little ears, the same ready grin, turned up at the corners of his mouth, and the same boyish face, so no matter how old he was, he always looked younger.

Kobe was born August 23, 1978, in Philadelphia, the youngest of the Bryants' three children but the first boy, two years younger than his big sister, Sharia, and one younger than Shaya. Joe had just completed his third season as a 76er, but the Bryants were already home, Philadelphia natives from solid families. Joe had been a star at LaSalle before leaving after his junior year. Pam Bryant (née Cox) had attended Villanova, where her brother, Chubby, a highly rated prep and a friend of Joe's, started at guard.

A *New York Times* profile would say Kobe was named after the Japanese cow which is raised to precise standards to ensure its meat is flavorful after it's slaughtered. This would have made it an ironic portent, indeed. Actually, he was named after the Kobe Steak House in suburban King of Prussia, because his parents liked the name.

His full name was Kobe Bean Bryant, an allusion to Joe's playground nickname, Jellybean which everyone still used. The name fit Joe, anyway; he was light-hearted, sweet-tempered, and easy-going, with a flashy game for a 6'9" player.

In looks and temperament, Kobe was like Joe, but at the core of his determined personality was Pam. Joe was flighty and carefree, but Pam was strong-willed and believed in doing things by the numbers. Both sisters went to college, and with his 1080 SAT, Kobe could have gone anywhere from the Pac-10 to the Ivy League.

Nevertheless, they weren't quite the Afro-American *Ozzie and Harriet*. In the summer of 1976, after Joe's rookie season, he was arrested for leading police on a high-speed, late-night chase through West Philadelphia before crashing into a wall, with a female companion and two vials of cocaine in his car.

Pam was in the courtroom with 10-week-old Sharia when Joe was found not guilty, after a parade of character witnesses, including 76ers coaches, players, and owner Irv Kosloff. At one point, the judge allowed himself enough whimsy to inquire whether any Boston Celtics would be testifying.

Years later, Pam and Joe would let Kobe make his own decision about turning pro, but one thing was clear: he was not going to run the streets with the guys, or as Pam characterized it in his prep days when his parents still talked to the press, "drugs, alcohol, and fast women."

Kobe said later he never actually decided to go pro, he always knew he would. By the same token, everyone assumed that wherever he went, the whole family was going, too. Kobe wouldn't have had it any other way.

■ ■ ■

You have your stars and your role players, and then you have your journeymen, like Joe.

He played four seasons with the loaded 76ers in the days of Julius Erving and George McGinnis. They traded him to the young San Diego Clippers, where he played enough to average 11.5 points in three seasons. He ended his NBA career in Houston under Del Harris, who would be Kobe's first coach.

An eight-year NBA career is nothing to sneer at, but most of Joe's dreams went unrealized. Coaches weren't interested in 6'9" small forwards, much less 6'9" guards, and Joe wasn't good enough to break the mold.

From his perspective, he was just ahead of his time. When Magic Johnson became a 6'9" point guard in Bryant's fifth year in the league, Joe ruefully noted, "When I did that, they called it playground."

That was when Harris first met Kobe, as a four-year-old, toddling around after his father. Harris remembered:

Oh yeah, he was a cute little kid.

Joe was a good guy, fun-loving type of a guy. He loved playing the game. He was not a disciplined player. He had a lot of flair, an exceptional ball-handler for a man his size. Kinda visualized himself as a guard in a power forward's body and he did have good skills with the ball.

Unfortunately for him, he was usually on bad teams, and our team was no exception. We had a truly bad team. Philadelphia had been able to lure our best player away, Moses Malone. Moses had been MVP twice for us, but we had a new owner come in who decided the best thing to do, since we were going to lose Moses, was just let some other players go, too. Five of our top eight players didn't play that year. Mike Dunleavy went to San Antonio, Robert Reid took a leave of absence.

The idea was, we'd join the Ralph Sampson sweepstakes. We were going to finish last, get Ralph Sampson. We owned Cleveland's draft pick, who figured to finish last in the East and we'd finish last in the West. We'd get picks one and two and we'd be right back on top.

So Joe's only year there was that year, 1982–1983. We did finish last. We did get Ralph Sampson, but then they paid me off and brought in Bill Fitch, and he didn't keep Joe.

Joe stayed and sold cars for a time for the owner, Charlie Thomas, and then got the opportunity to go to Europe.

The opportunity was in Rieti, Italy, where Joe became a star, staying seven seasons. Kobe was six when the family first went over and 13 when they came home to stay. As far as Kobe was concerned, no one could have had a better childhood, going to the arena with his father, watching everyone cheer him, working out with the other players' kids, dreaming only of doing the same thing.

Kobe and his sisters went to local schools, picking up the language quickly, getting a lot of it watching American TV programs, like *The Cosby Show*, which were dubbed into Italian. Kobe says he encountered no racism, and they always went back to Philadelphia in the summer.

The expatriate experience drew the family closer, which was close, indeed. Joe was sweet-tempered, Pam was nice, and the kids were well-mannered. Even when he became an NBA star, if Kobe said he'd meet you at 4:00 P.M., he met you at 4:00 P.M. on the dot, making him the rarest of celebrities.

Kobe's upbringing produced a supremely confident young man who cared little what anyone outside his family thought. Knowing they'd always be behind him, he had no fear of failure, which he considered only temporary. As his father told him before he won the All-Star dunk contest as an 18-year-old rookie, "If you miss, don't worry about it, we love you, anyway.'"

However, if there was nothing childish about Kobe's dedication and his poise, in a real sense, he remained a child long after entering the NBA. All children dream, but then one day they awake to find out they're not going to be Hollywood stars or rock musicians.

Bryant's dream never faded. He lived it exactly as he dreamed it. He was on a mission, seemingly from birth. He remembers himself at eight or nine, refusing to write things down, training his mind to remember them, instead. When his uncles back in the States sent him videotapes of NBA players, he studied them for moves and hints, like an archaeologist poring over ancient texts. He wrote his name on scraps of paper and gave them to friends, advising them to save them since he'd be famous one day.

He was always playing against older kids, even grown-ups. When he played his cousins back home during the summers, he learned playground style, which was all about flash and macho—completely different than the fundamental style he learned in Rieti, but he picked that right up, too.

In 1992 when Kobe was 13, Joe brought the family home to stay, settling in suburban Ardmore, Pennsylvania. Kobe began playing in the Sonny Hill League downtown, where all the best young players came together. Counseling was part of the program. Since relatively few of them could go all the way, it was no longer considered OK to say you were going to be an NBA player. You were supposed to say you wanted to be a businessman or a coach, even if you didn't really mean it.

Bryant, of course, said he was going to be an NBA player.

"The guy said, 'NBA players are one in a million,'" Bryant said. "I said, 'Man, look, I'm going to be that one in a million.'"

A year later, he entered Lower Merion. The local basketball community was tight so it wasn't long before everyone knew Jellybean's son had big-time talent, maybe even greater than his father's.

John Lucas, who was then coaching the 76ers, had a daughter at Lower Merion and was in on it early. He was so impressed, he invited Kobe to come work out with the Sixers. He said:

I come in off a seven-day road trip, and my wife says, "I've seen the closest thing to you in high school."

I say, "What are you talking about?"

"Kobe Bean!" That's all she could say: "Kobe Bean!"

I go to see him play. I say, that's Jellybean's son! I saw Jellybean and his wife there and I went and talked to them. I was talking to Kobe. I asked him, "What's your goal?" I said, "Well, come on and work out with our guys in the summer."

I remember, Rick Mahorn took him out on a play. He got right up, didn't say a word. Every time I would come to the gym, he was there. He'd be one of the first guys there. So I saw the desire that he had.

Other kids played basketball. Kobe lived it. As a 16-year-old high school junior, he had no less confidence in his impending greatness than he claimed to have had at five. He treated the press people, who had begun coming around, as if they were Wise Men from the East and he was the Babe in Swaddling Clothes. A high school friend, Matt Matkov, told *Rolling Stone*'s Chris Mundy his mother kidded Kobe that he was never nicer than when he was talking to reporters.

"But that's just Kobe," Matkov said. "When he's talking to the reporters, it's proper grammar, telling them what they want to hear. Going into that famous mode is something he has to do because it's going to get him more fans."

Bryant was already as dedicated as the most dedicated of the professionals, driven men like Magic Johnson and Larry Bird. If he wasn't practicing with his high school team, he was at the St. Joseph's Field House where the 76ers practiced, working out with them, or lifting weights at the direction of the Sixers strength coach, Joe Carbone. Kobe liked the routine so much, he wound up hiring Carbone as his full-time personal trainer and bringing him along to Los Angeles.

Sometimes, it seemed that Bryant was either going to school, playing basketball, working out, studying basketball, or sleeping. He wasn't actually that monastic; he had girlfriends, but they knew the game came first. They would say he was nice but he didn't take them seriously. As he told Mundy, "Basketball was it. My girlfriend was basketball."

He was still a 6'5" stringbean weighing, he said, "a buck sixty," after his junior year in the spring of 1995, when his legend began to flower. In a Sixer workout, he went one-on-one with Jerry Stackhouse, a 6'6", 220-pound tank from North Carolina, in town to work out for the 76ers, who would subsequently take him No. 3 in the draft.

They didn't keep score and neither ever actually claimed he had won. Nevertheless, Bryant held his own, wowing everyone. Stackhouse immediately called Dean Smith and told him to get on this kid.

"The more he played, the more my guys kept saying, 'Luke, he's a pro,'" Lucas says of Bryant. "He fit. He belonged, right from the beginning."

That summer, Bryant took over Adidas' ABCD Camp at Fairleigh Dickinson University in Hackensack, New Jersey, a showcase for rising talent. Tim Thomas went in as the nation's top-rated player but didn't seem driven to prove it. Bryant, now known as "Grant Hill with a jump shot" among prep bird dogs, won the MVP.

Only weeks before, Garnett had become the first high school player to enter the draft in 20 years and the campers were giddy, as if Garnett was their emissary to the New World. Thomas had yet to sign with a college; as his cousin and summer-league coach, Jimmy Salmon, pointed out, there had been so many coaching changes, Tim was having trouble deciding.

"Let's face it," Salmon noted, "he's not going to be in college that long."

Even at this level, few of them could actually follow Garnett, but the best took it as a new standard; if you were really great, the pros wanted you straight out of high school.

Bryant had yet to choose his school, either, although, with Joe back at LaSalle as an assistant coach, everyone assumed he'd go there, or Duke. Meanwhile, Joe was getting a lot of feelers from colleges about a head coaching job. There was talk about Kobe going pro, too, but that was just gossip coming from the high school bird dogs, not the pros, who had barely heard of Bryant.

He was just a guard; the pros had plenty of those.

■　■　■

The storybook ending of Bryant's high school career at Lower Merion was appropriate to the birth of a new legend and to his opinion of himself.

The Bulldogs were en route to a 31–4 record and a state title, with Bryant averaging 31 points, 12 rebounds, seven assists, four steals, and four blocks. He broke the scoring record once held by Wilt Chamberlain, was named the prep player of the year by *USA Today* and *Parade*, and became a McDonald's All-American.

The pros were actually on the case now. Before Garnett, GMs didn't attend high school games, but when Lower Merion went to Myrtle Beach, South Carolina, over the Christmas break for the Beach Ball Classic, Miami's Dave Wohl and Orlando's John Gabriel, were spotted in the crowd. Gabriel later said Bryant had been "borderline sensational."

"You like to use basic scouting principles and he passes with flying colors," Gabriel said. "He's a once-in-a-blue-moon type athlete. He's way beyond his years in coordination, maturity. That alone makes him a prospect."

Gabriel, a former 76ers exec, was friendly with Joe, who confided his doubts about what college could do for Kobe. Joe had his own issues as to what LaSalle had done for him.

John Nash, the Net GM who had also come up through the Sixers organization, asked Joe how he saw his son's career. Joe said he thought Kobe would spend the first season adjusting . . . then become an all-star in his second. Nash said he kept a straight face, as if he'd just met someone at a cocktail party who claimed he'd seen a flying saucer.

Kobe would be tested frequently but always lived up to his billing. On January 14, the Bulldogs went downtown to the Palestra, a hallowed venue on the Penn campus, to meet the other area power, Coatesville, led by its star guard, Richard Hamilton.

The Coatesville players were tough kids from hardscrabble Chester County, as opposed to the young gentlemen from the Main Line, who were expected to get knocked around and sent home. Instead, Bryant led Lower Merion to an dramatic 78–77 victory, rebounding a missed free throw with :03 left, taking it downcourt, and launching a long, game-winning three-pointer at the buzzer.

"People here still talk about it," Jim Smith, the Coatesville assistant coach later told *USA Today*'s Greg Boeck. "I've never seen anyone get from the far foul line to midcourt as fast. He pulled up a step past midcourt and made the shot. All net. We still have a sour taste in our mouth."

Nine years later, when Bryant hit another big three over Hamilton in the NBA Finals, Kobe would still remember the first shot as the biggest in his career, the one that first showed the skeptics he was for real.

At the level he aspired to, there was no shortage of skeptics or advisers. If Bryant had already decided to turn pro, his fellow Philadelphians thought they had a voice in his decision. The city was a basketball hotbed and longed for its best players to attend one of the local schools in Philadelphia Big 5.

Unfortunately, none of the five was an NCAA powerhouse. Villanova, a member of the Big East, and Temple under John Chaney came closest, but the best local players went elsewhere, Wilt to Kansas, Andre McCarter to UCLA, Gene Banks to Duke, Rasheed Wallace to North Carolina.

Nevertheless, Philadelphia never stopped hoping. If the question became whether Bryant could skip college entirely, local fans were apoplectic; the issue burned up talk radio for months.

"There was a newspaper article that said: 'LaSalle or the NBA?" says Jeremy Treatman, the Lower Merion assistant coach. "Kobe was a trendsetter 'cause here was this kid with a 3.0, 1100 SATs, good neighborhood, wealthy family. What in the world was he doing this for? People were mad at him. Why are you giving up the chance to go to Duke or to LaSalle?

"People from Philadelphia didn't see him at Myrtle Beach. They didn't see him at ABCD. They didn't understand what they had here. They had a treasure here and they just didn't understand."

By then, the entire Bryant family was hunkered down. Joe stopped going to LaSalle. They changed their phone number to an unlisted one and no one got it, not even old Baker League friends like Sonny Hill, who had helped Joe find his team in Italy. Frozen out of the process, the old friends were exasperated, too.

On April 29, 1996, Bryant announced he would take "my talents to the NBA" at his press conference. For the perfect finale to this overheated teen saga suitable for Nickelodeon or the Disney Channel, he took Brandy, the pop singer and star of *Moesha*, to the senior prom. He had just met her while doing a TV awards show, gotten a friend to ask her, and waited while she checked with her mother. This, of course, sparked talk of a romance, but it was just a date, or a photo op. Pictures of the couple ran in *People* and *Jet*. Other students at the dance asked them for autographs, giving some school administrators the sense this had gone w-a-y too far.

So, you couldn't say Bryant was unaffected by the process. After sparking a controversy with his first act as a professional, he would always be highly protective of his privacy. After seeing what his fame could bring him, he was thrilled to be in the spotlight. That, of course, was a contradiction, but who ever knew?

■ ■ ■

The youth revolution was getting more insane by the moment, and it wasn't just in basketball, where it was considered controversial, since the teens were bypassing the college game, a powerful institution in its own right.

The NCAA Tournament, with its single-elimination format (and its 64-team field which made it perfect for office pools), was still the biggest thing in the game. As such it had network and corporate partners and commentators to defend it, like CBS' Billy Packer, who called the NBA "the enemy of basketball."

Nevertheless, this was a phenomenon that cut across sports, with parents allowing their children to enter, or pushing them into ever-more-specialized programs, effectively turning them into little professionals before puberty. Little girl gymnasts moved to Houston to study under Bela Karolyi. Little boys and girls moved to Florida to attend Nick Bolletieri's tennis academy. By 2004, 14-year-old Michelle Wie was playing in WPGA events and 15-year-old Freddy Adu was with with D.C. United in the MLS.

Entire books were devoted to the subject of professionalized children, including Joan Ryan's *Little Girls in Pretty Boxes* (gymnastics); Chris Brennan's *Inside Edge* (ice skating); Alex Wolf and Armen Keteyian's *Raw Recruits* (basketball).

Awareness, or shame, couldn't slow the process, which only sped up. As a 1999 *Time* magazine article noted: "The good news is that the cold war is over. The bad news is that the East Germans won."

In basketball, the process had begun more than 20 years before but had been put on pause when everyone found out how hard it was all around. Malone's jump in 1974 was followed by Darryl Dawkins and Bill Willoughby in 1975, but Dawkins was a disappointment and Willoughby a complete bust.

Nor did the pros have much appetite for long-term projects. In 1977, 76ers assistant coach Jack McMahon scouted Louisville Male High School's Darrell Griffith and reported back that he was more talented than any player who'd be in the draft. By then, however, coach Gene Shue was up to here in mistake-prone kids who were not shy about complaining to the press, like Dawkins, Lloyd (soon to become World) Free, and Joe Bryant.

However, change was already in the air before Garnett came out 18 years later.

Michigan's Fab Five, the first all-freshmen starting team led by Webber, Juwan Howard, and Jalen Rose, became youth icons, reaching the NCAA Finals in 1992 and 1993 and re-setting fashion with their oversize trunks that dropped below their knees and their black socks. Rebels that they were, they didn't even ask coach Steve Fisher if they could wear new stuff. They just ran out onto the floor, tore off their warm-ups, and coach Fish found out about it when the rest of the world did.

Garnett wanted to follow them to Michigan but his test scores wouldn't allow him to play as a freshman, and he was poor on top of it. His decision to go pro was hooted in the beginning, but when the pros saw him in predraft workouts, he shot up the ladder, going to Minnesota at number five.

He soon showed he belonged. In his rookie year, Sam Cassell, then in New Jersey, was asked what Garnett brought to the Timberwolves.

"Maturity," said Cassell.

The incoming preps became a trickle and then a flood. In the 2001 draft, three of the top four picks, Kwame Brown, Tyson Chandler, and Eddy Curry, were preps. In 2004, eight went in the first round.

The kids were sure they were old enough to turn pro, but a lot of them still didn't think they weren't old enough to leave home and brought their moms, dads, and/or homeboys with them. Bryant brought his entire family. Joe Smith, leaving Maryland after his freshman year, brought his mother to Oakland. Vince Carter's mother was so involved with his career, the Toronto PR office had to check all interview requests with her.

The kids weren't just famous but rich. Advertisers now saw their youth as a virtue and lavished million-dollar deals on them before they scored their first basket. If the kids would have been dizzy enough, now they were many times dizzier.

Generational conflict, always present, became dramatic. Allen Iverson, the walking embodiment of baggy-pants, tattooed, hip-hop culture, was dogged by referees, who didn't like the way he palmed the ball; by league officials, who didn't like the way his shorts sagged down his rear end; and by other players, who didn't think he was respectful enough after he talked trash to Michael Jordan in their first meeting.

The clash crystallized at the 1998 All-Star Game in Cleveland, where the all-time top 50 players were honored. The top 50 played a merry tune on Iverson, including noncredible spokesmen like Elvin Hayes, a career pariah, who announced, "If he doesn't show any respect for the guys in this room and for the top players of today, then maybe he should read up on them."

Showing what it was all about, Walt Frazier, the old Knick, slammed Jordan and Charles Barkley for skipping the media session, declaring, "All of the guys should be in this room, paying homage to us."

Not having kids, Frazier had missed a few trends, like: the homage thing was over.

"Nobody in this room waited their turn," said Webber, the most articulate of the young guns. "I remember when they were talking about older guys being mad at Jordan because he came into the league, scoring at such a pace. It's a cycle. We've gone through this many times.

"Allen Iverson, is he supposed to go kiss Jordan's feet when they play? Believe me, he respects Jordan. He respects the guy, but when you meet the monster, you're supposed to look him dead in the eye and try to defeat him."

The kids were still kids, with things to learn, except now they were rich and famous and got lots of bad publicity when they screwed up. There was a new phenomenon: promising young teams blowing sky high.

The Warriors were building a powerhouse around the 20-year-old Webber, but he didn't like Don Nelson, an old-school players coach who treated his rookies like galley slaves. No one to be yelled at, Webber held out before his second season, demanding a trade. No one to be dictated to, Nelson accommodated him, dealing him to Washington and shocking the other Warrior players. The team imploded and Nelson fled halfway through the season.

In Washington, Webber and Howard were supposed to be the building blocks of a new power. They managed one playoff appearance in four seasons (an 0–3 sweep at the hands of Michael Jordan's Bulls), presumably because they were too busy partying. After myriad arrests involving illegal substances and disturbances of the peace, Webber was packed off to Sacramento for Mitch Richmond, a 33-year-old guard.

Webber became a star with the Kings but his past kept following him. A claim by a Michigan booster that he'd given Webber $280,000 under the table led to a prosecution for obstruction of justice, in which Webber's father and his aunt were also charged before the case was dropped. Webber had to plead guilty to criminal contempt for lying to a grand jury. Michigan forfeited all his games; officially the Fab Five didn't even exist any more.

In Dallas, the Mavericks' Three Js, Jason Kidd, Jamal Mashburn, and Jim Jackson, lasted two seasons together and never got to .500. The highlight was the Kidd-Jackson feud, which started over pop singer Toni Braxton. Braxton was supposed to go out with Kidd on a trip to Atlanta but didn't show up. The next morning, she called to ask Kidd how he was feeling, explaining that Jackson had told her he was ill and had sent Jackson in his place.

"The Toni Braxton thing, I don't know where that came from, but I guess that's going to hang over our head for a while," Kidd said. "But we have to move on."

The only moving they did, it turned out, was out of town.

Stephon Marbury arrived in Minnesota at 19 in a draft-day trade after telling the Milwaukee Bucks, who were going to take him, he had his heart set on playing alongside Garnett, his buddy from their schoolboy days.

Marbury lasted two seasons with his pal. A new bargaining agreement that took effect after Garnett got a $117-million deal capped

Marbury at $80 million. Steph ripped Minnesota and demanded another trade, saying he couldn't play alongside Garnett at such a pay differential. The Timberwolves sent him to the Nets in 1998 . . . who traded him to the Suns in 2001 . . . who traded him to the Knicks in 2004.

Then, of course, there were the Lakers with Bryant and O'Neal, who were starting in on each other in earnest when Phil Jackson arrived in 1999. They were your modern dynasty; they narrowly avoided blowing up and rode to glory, fighting with each other every inch of the way.

Regrets, all the kids would have a few of those, too, starting with the trailblazer, Garnett, who arrived just in time to catch the end of the J. R. Rider era.

"It was hellfire," Garnett said. "Guys going after other guys, guys upset at coaches, all kinds of stuff. I said to myself, 'This is the league? This is where I dreamed of playing?' Grown men acting like this. Guys moping on the bench, one guy saying he's going to kick somebody's butt. Sometimes being in the middle of two guys who wanted to go at it. I started telling my boys, 'Go to school, man, stay in school.' The attitudes shocked me."

In 2002, the process produced the ultimate fiasco when the companies vying for the youth demographic began fastening on LeBron James, who appeared on *Sports Illustrated*'s cover as a high school junior.

James was amazingly level-headed, but no one could get out of this unaffected. He sometimes punctuated dunks, yelling "King James!" and told *ESPN Magazine*'s Tom Friend, "LeBron stays humble just by being LeBron."

That summer, James worked out with the Cavaliers at the invitation of their coach, Lucas—who was then suspended by the league. In a madhouse senior year, James' Akron (Ohio) St. Vincent–St. Mary High School team traveled the nation on what was billed as "The Scholastic Fantastic Tour." Home games were moved off campus, and several were televised nationally, with cable networks falling all over each other to add more when they got big ratings. A regional cable company showed games on pay-TV.

Then—shockingly—there was a scandal when LeBron was discovered to have accepted two retro jerseys worth $845. The $50,000 Hummer he drove to school, however, was deemed to be OK, since his unemployed mother had taken out a loan to pay for it. James was suspended by the Ohio State High School Athletic Association but was reinstated in time to lead SVSM to another state title.

The insanity was obvious even for veterans of the youth brigade, like Bryant, by then a five-year veteran who wistfully acknowledged for the first time missing what he had given up.

"It's being tired, wanting to sleep in," he said. "Running around, hanging out with your buddies, playing video games—you can't do that. You have to watch film. You have to go to practice every day. But I wanted to play against the best. So I was like, I'm just going to do this and whatever comes my way, I'll just deal with it, but this is my focus. . . .

"I remember when I first came into the NBA. I used to ride around the UCLA campus, just looking. Checking out some of the students, imagining what it would have been like if I'd have gone to school."

For his part, Webber said, "LeBron has my sympathy. I wouldn't want to be in his position and grow up in the public eye where you don't have the right to make a mistake."

That was the life they had chosen and the pitfalls that came with it. They just didn't know it at the time.

■ ■ ■

No one would give the kids a chance to grow up, including the kids. The grown-ups were supposed to know better, but the kids were just kids, and Bryant was the most brash of them all.

If Bryant ever felt daunted as a teenager in a man's world, he never showed it. The only thing he found surprising about playing pro ball was how surprised everyone was to see him do it.

"Wasn't it scary, thinking about jumping to the pros?" Bryant was asked in his second season.

"No," he said smiling.

"You never thought to yourself, 'I might get there and find out they're too good?'"

Bryant laughed out loud at that one.

Showing how comfortable he was, he was poised and gracious from the moment he got there. The Lakers, who knew something about the demands of celebrity, got more media requests for Bryant than they had for Magic Johnson, and Kobe handled it as well as Magic had.

Lakers publicist John Black used to joke that Eddie Jones had a love/hate relationship with the press, while with Nick Van Exel, it was strictly hate/hate. With Bryant, Black had only one request: don't ever change.

With teammates, however, there was another dynamic. Bryant didn't hang with them or even communicate much with most of them. His isolation made him look aloof, although it was more like self-obsession. He wasn't down on them; he didn't think much about them at all, and if he did, he assumed they regarded him the way he regarded himself.

If he had supreme confidence, he assumed they all had supreme confidence in him. If he already expected to take over in crunch time, he assumed they were OK with that, O'Neal included. If none of them matched his dedication or put in as many hours, he assumed they realized that, too. A princeling in his family, he assumed royal prerogatives in the world at large.

When they were on the road, he was in his hotel room, eating pizza, watching *SportsCenter,* or phoning high school friends, like Anthony Bannister. Bannister told *Rolling Stone* they made up verses for their "spiritual rap" group (Kobe was "Kobe One Kenobe the Eighth.") Bannister said that before they hung up, they would pray together.

If Bryant did reach out, it was to someone like Jerry West or Arn Tellem or a veteran like Byron Scott or Derek Harper. They were his surrogate fathers; he was their surrogate son.

"He's different," said Scott, a teammate in Bryant's rookie season. "He would have done well in the eighties with us. At least, he showed me a tremendous amount of respect back when we were working at practice and I would tell him things that we would try to work on, and I don't think he was doing it for show.

"He was very interested in hearing about our team in the eighties, and we would sit down and talk about that. He's totally different than a lot of the guys that are coming into the league with the big heads and the egos and things like that."

Of course, Bryant's father was his original mentor. If Kobe was headstrong, the Lakers inevitably thought Joe was the problem. Nevertheless,

Joe tried to stay out of the picture. Aware that people thought he was trying to cash in on his son, he rarely did interviews. In Kobe's first three seasons, when Joe and Pam could have gotten any seat in the Forum, they sat behind the corner opposite the Lakers bench, 25 rows up.

"We don't go to the Forum Club," Joe said. "We sit here and eat our nachos. This is Kobe's life. This is Kobe's time. He wants us, needs us, we're there, but there's a lot of things he has to figure out for himself. . . .

"It's the same at home. Mom has breakfast, lunch, and dinner ready. He goes, watches videotapes. Take out the trash. All those things. Just a normal life. It's nothing special."

Of course, this was a hard adventure to stay out of, with the world at their feet. Joe now worked for Adidas, the sneaker company Kobe had signed with. Kobe liked Adidas because it wasn't Nike, determined to show he could carve his own path to commercial greatness.

It was working, too. Jordan had showed basketball players could move product. Bryant now showed that if the target demographic was in its teens, so was the ideal spokesman.

"If you just look at the sale of Lakers jerseys, the little 8, the little kids' jersey, is probably the number one jersey, even over Shaq's," said Adidas creative director Peter Moore in Bryant's second season. "Kobe has a magical appeal to young people. I think they sort of see the kid in him.

"Most of our consumer base is, frankly, between 14 and 20. I mean, that's who's buying this stuff. The endorsement world is slightly different today than it was certainly five or six or ten years ago. Then it would have been the older guys who set the example. Now kids are emulating kids."

In this world, you got old fast. Tony Gervino, the editor of *Slam*, a basketball magazine aimed at teens, ran a piece on O'Neal, who was 24 in 1995 and was surprised to see how badly the readers received it. That did it for O'Neal in the pages of *Slam*.

"Our readers are 13 to 24," said Gervino. "What Kobe has is what Jordan has, the ability to be different things to different people. My mother loves Jordan, I love Jordan, my nephew's eight years old, loves Jordan. Jordan sort of spans generations.

"Kobe's the same way. He's handsome, friendly, polite, understands the media game, plays the media game well at a very young age. He's a hip-hop kid, listening to hip-hop. I mean that's the key. That's what binds all 18-, 19-year-old kids together. This is a hip-hop generation, and they grow up listening to rap, not the rock that we grew up listening to.

"He's also the kind of guy the NBA's been waiting for, a kind of guy they can put their marketing push on and are pretty confident there's not going to be a 4:00 A.M. drug arrest."

■　■　■

Of course, Bryant had to change. As a basketball player, he was a prodigy but in life, he was just 18. If the date with Brandy, which was little more than once around the dance floor before they parted, showed his head could be turned, he was still relatively grounded, Pam and Joe's well-mannered young son. Kobe was respectful, punctual, and dutiful. If he had a problem with something—like Del Harris holding him back— he kept it to himself, no matter how often he was asked.

Bryant was 21 in 2000 when he and his teammates won their first title. He was no longer living with his parents but had only gone down the street in Pacific Palisades. He was thinking about buying up all the lots in between and making it a Bryant complex.

He was still wholly a creature of his family, hanging out with his cousin, John Cox, his sisters, and Jerrod Washington, Sharia's husband.

"I roll by myself," he said. "If I don't have my cousin out here with me, I'll go by myself. I have no problem with that. Or I'll go with my sisters. I just don't believe in a big entourage. I believe in having people close to me that I know, that I can trust, feel comfortable with."

He loved his life so much, he wanted to replicate it, right down to the time overseas. He wanted to raise his children in Italy, too, and even began planning for his future there, buying 50 percent of a basketball team, Olimpia Milano. He put Joe in charge, noting, "When my NBA career is over, hopefully I'll be there."

How was he supposed to know?

He had planned his basketball career to a T and it had happened just the way he knew it would. Anyone who doubted him just didn't know him.

How was he supposed to know life was so much trickier than basketball?

That was the spring he met Vanessa.

Chapter 12

BIG DOG AND
THE GOLDEN CHILD

I was so good so young but no one gave me time to grow up. They wanted to criticize me ... There goes Shaq again, getting swept in the playoffs. People would write, Shaq ain't concentrating, he's making rap records. You wrote about me riding around L.A. in a 'Benz, not taking basketball seriously.

Then what happened? I got angry. Phil Jackson come to town. Uh-oh, I got a taste of a championship. Shaq comes in fat the next year, they still get a ring. We've got to come up with rules to help defenses guard him. Too late. The monster is here to stay. You can't put it back in the bottle.

—Shaquille O'Neal to *New York Times'* Mike Wise
before the 2001–2002 season

There was no miscommunication. I'm taking care of business. When it comes to family, I don't have to call anybody. I'm not calling him. And that fine? That motherf***er knows what he can do with that fine. You write that, too.

—O'Neal on Jackson, a month later

■ ■ ■

THERE WERE GOOD TIMES, there were bad times. With the Lakers, it was just hard to tell which was which.

With O'Neal at 28, Bryant at 22, and a title in hand, greatness surely awaited them. It just didn't turn out to be the kind they were thinking of. They aspired to dynasty but often produced comedy, or farce, instead. It was an open question if they would go down as one of the greatest teams or the wackiest, and they often looked like both.

Bryant's problems would one day overshadow all that had gone before, making it seem as if he'd been the issue all along, but he was just part of another Lakers triangle. Like Jerry West, Wilt Chamberlain, and Elgin Baylor in the sixties, the tensions between Bryant, Jackson, and O'Neal were ongoing, and alliances were shifting but there was a weird stability there, too. Shaq, Kobe, and Phil lasted five seasons and won three titles to two and none for Jerry, Elgin, and Wilt.

With the new Lakers dynasty, you didn't have to imagine the possibilities, which presented themselves in headlines daily. Jackson and O'Neal were at odds as much of the time as O'Neal and Bryant were at odds.

It wasn't Old School but it wasn't boring.

■　■　■

Proving this still wasn't an organization like any other, they were still celebrating the 2000 title when West quit. He still didn't like parades.

Having acquired O'Neal and Bryant in the greatest haul in NBA history and having finally found a coach who could handle them, with the heavy lifting done and little to do but kick back and enjoy the last three seasons on his $3.5-million-a-year contract, West decided he couldn't take it anymore.

He had been so strung out at the end, he had even stopped attending the Finals games at home. Before Game 6, as fans gathered inside and outside the Staples Center and in taverns and homes, West hopped in his car and fled. He said later:

> I was up past Santa Barbara, as a matter of fact. I had a friend of mine at the game. I said, "Call me when it's over."
>
> That made me realize this had become almost a sickness and that I just couldn't do this anymore. It was the last game. And I thought how happy the people were. I know how happy the players were, how happy the fans and the owner. And it was nothing to me.
>
> It's really hard to say that because I don't think unless you sort of lived all this stuff and was as close to watching this, that

you could even imagine feeling that way. And even to this day, it was like, if that series hadn't gotten over that night—you know, it's not even really funny.

At times, you almost feel ill in even thinking about them losing. That really convinced me that I didn't need to do this anymore. It was terrible for me. It was terrible for the people around me, my family, my friends. Everything ceased to become fun.

Word spread again that West was retiring, now, supposedly, in a power struggle with Jackson. Any struggle was only in West's mind because Jackson didn't want to do anything he did, like sit in an office, make trades, or talk to agents. In any case, West was still West, with more than enough cachet to withstand any challenge had Jackson actually posed one.

However, there was a new element. Jackson, now separated from his wife, June, and in the process of getting a divorce, had begun dating Buss' daughter, Jeannie, a Lakers marketing exec who was such a stunner she had even appeared naked in *Playboy*. (Her dad said it was the only issue he ever missed.)

West was horrified, privately predicting problems for the organization if they broke up, but there was more than that working. Buss' growing detachment had been a problem for West for years, and now there seemed to be a new favorite on the lot. Of course, West had been eyeing the door years before Jackson arrived, once complaining privately, "I'm taking pills I shouldn't be taking." He was worried about his heart and became even more distressed at the death that spring of his old friend, Chamberlain. Restless as West was, no one gave him a shot to stay retired longer than a week if he ever actually tried it. When rumors that he was leaving spread once more, Magic Johnson said he'd believe it when he saw Jerry standing on the podium.

In the end, there was no podium. In a style appropriate to West's career in the front office, he didn't even show up to accept the thanks of the grateful franchise he created in his own image. Publicist John Black read the announcement off a press release. Buss wasn't there, and only a handful of press people came. The greatest Laker of them all, Mr. Clutch, the Logo, the last link to the 1960 team, the beating heart and stressed soul of the franchise, was gone.

Now it was a Lakers trinity, Shaq, Kobe, and Phil, against the world and, of course, each other.

■　■　■

O'Neal used to joke that when he won a title, he'd come back looking like the Hindenburg. He turned out to be as good as his jest, coming in heavy for camp in what would become a rite of autumn.

Bryant had his own thoughts on how this season should go, telling friends he wanted to win the MVP. If Shaq's slow start created a vacuum, Kobe was just the young man to fill it. Bryant had gotten over the hump the season before when his assist average climbed to a career-high 4.9 but was now headed back across that hump at high speed. He opened the season at Portland with a midrange jumper that ricocheted off the backboard without hitting the rim, and turned the ball over 18 times in his first three games, against six assists. Bryant was like an Old West gunfighter looking for trouble and hoping to find some. In a December 6 overtime loss at Golden State, he and the Warriors' Antawn Jamison engaged each other in a shootout in which each scored 51 points while several of Kobe's teammates yelled from the bench to pass the ball.

"Can you feel the love tonight?" Rick Fox would say months later, after internal hostilities finally died down. "We couldn't feel it that night."

There was no doubt who was right and who was wrong. As Jackson noted, they had the ultimate weapon in the low post so the ball had to go into O'Neal before it could be hoisted from long range. Bryant was in one of his periodic regressions, trying to sort out his duties from his options from his ambitions anew. "Turn my game down?" he told *ESPN Magazine*'s Ric Bucher in early December. "I need to turn it up. I've improved. How are you going to bottle me up? I'd be better off playing someplace else." Asked if he trusted his teammates, Bryant replied: "I trust them. I trust myself more."

For once, Bryant actually regretted something he'd done, pulling back. He talked with Jackson, who told him if he didn't like the way things were, he'd help Kobe go somewhere else. Before the magazine came out, Bryant said that was just how he'd felt at the moment.

"At the time I was struggling and I was going through a moment where I was trying to find my game," he said. "It's human nature. There was some curiosity, wondering what it would be like to be in another situation. I think every player has been through that type of situation. When I first got here I wondered what it would be like to be on another team, but it was nothing serious. Really, it's nothing serious."

Unfortunately for the Lakers, it was something serious, all right. Bryant had pulled back too late. O'Neal got mad and stayed mad for months.

"I've never been one to get into whose team it is," O'Neal said. "But, clearly, when everything went through me, the outcome was 67–15, playing with enthusiasm. The city was jumping up and down, we had a parade. Now we're 23–11. So you figure it out. . . .

"I don't have to coexist with anybody. I've proven I'm here to do a job. I've always been an unselfish big man, play defensive, rebound, score when I get the ball in the paint. That's all I do. That's what we're used to doing. That's what we did last year. We got an extra gold ball for Jerry Buss. That's what we need to continue to do to form a dynasty. If not, we'll see what happens."

The Shaq-Kobe feud had moved into its public, headline-making phase, and the season got wilder by the day. After a loss in Phoenix, O'Neal told GM Mitch Kupchak he wanted to be traded. West, aghast at developments, was out of the loop but he still had the same wide circle of confidants, so lots of inside stuff began getting out via back channels. The beat guys would then have to ask Jackson to confirm or deny. It happened so often, Jackson wondered if the *Times'* Tim Brown was West's guy. Actually, Brown was new on the beat and hadn't even met West.

At the All-Star Game in Washington, D.C., O'Neal told the *Orlando Sentinel's* Brian Schmitz he'd love to return to the Magic. When Schmitz asked if he was serious, O'Neal replied, "Look in my eyes. I'm not lying. I love Tracy McGrady. I could play with him. He's the most unselfish player of all the young guys. He's the model for the next NBA stars."

O'Neal also liked Jason Kidd. On the way home from the All-Star Game, Armato reportedly asked Suns GM Bryan Colangelo about trading Jason for Bryant. In fact, everyone had a trade. Jackson's old CBA assistant coach, Charley Rosen, was now writing columns for *The Sporting News*, in which he unfailingly lambasted Bryant as selfish. Now Rosen began proposing various deals to move him. The content wasn't unusual, but since Rosen was still close to Jackson, everyone wondered if he was speaking for Phil.

Indeed. Jackson was so exasperated at Bryant, he told the *Chicago Sun-Times'* Rick Telander a story he'd heard about Bryant being so willful, he used to keep his high school games close so he could take over at the end. Jackson had no first-hand knowledge of this. It was just a story someone had told him, which was hotly denied by Lower Merion coach Gregg Downer. Jackson had a habit of talking freely with confidants, like Telander, assuming they'd know what to use and not to use. This added up to a big and costly misunderstanding.

Bryant would never get over it. Bryant said nothing but fumed in private. His agent, Arn Tellem, wrote the Lakers a letter on legal letterhead, demanding an apology, and when none was forthcoming, wrote another. This got into the press, too, as everything else did that season. *The Long Beach Press Telegraph's* Doug Krikorian, an old Lakers hand, even suggested that Bryant might sue Jackson for slander.

Feuds were nothing new in the NBA, but there had never been one like this. O'Neal and Bryant fired on each other whenever they felt like it. Jackson's presence kicked it up to another level as he spurned the usual denial and cover-up mechanisms. In Chicago, it had been Jackson's acknowledgment of behind-the-scenes strife that had put the player-management rift on the record, allowing the press to go big with it. Now his acknowledgment of the O'Neal-Bryant rift, and the one between him and Bryant, kept the story going.

Jackson's way was not to get between his superstars, even if everyone always wanted him to, including Armato and Tellem. Instead, Jackson would just turn up the heat by bringing it into the open, so the players had to deal with it. Unorthodox as Jackson's technique was, it worked. Of course, it also made for harrowing, adventure-filled seasons, and this was the most harrowing and adventurous to date. After all Jackson had gone through in Chicago, after all the hysteria surrounding Michael Jordan, after Jackson went job-hunting in the middle of the

Bulls' title run and was barred from the practice facility, after the hue and cry around Dennis Rodman, Jackson said this was his toughest season.

The story kept growing like the Blob. Since Lakers were in demand as celebrities everywhere, the feud got sucked right up by the networks. In February, asked by HBO's Bob Costas which star he would choose, Jackson said it would be O'Neal. By March, asked the same question by Jay Leno on *The Tonight Show*, Jackson said it would be like choosing between his sons. By April, with the team running number two in the West, the organization seemed to be splitting along the Shaq-Kobe fault, with O'Neal and Jackson on one side against Bryant, supported, tacitly at least, by West and Jerry Buss.

"I definitely think it has put a strain on the organization," said Magic Johnson in his role as minority owner. "You never want an organization or a team to seem like it's divided or guys jumping on sides and things like that.

"Our whole organization has been built on the fact that we've always taken care of our own. We've never aired our dirty laundry. We've taken care of it in-house. Because now it's more than Kobe and Shaq. It's much more than that. Now instead of focusing on basketball, we're focusing on issues outside of basketball. And I think that's taken a toll on the team, on the management."

■　■　■

The feud was what showed on the surface. Beneath it, Bryant had real problems. The preceding spring, in 2000, he had met Vanessa Laine, a 17-year-old high school student from Orange County, on a video shoot. By summer, they were engaged. By fall, there were rumors of trouble in the family with Joe, Pam, and Tellem urging Kobe to insist on a prenuptial agreement, if they couldn't talk him out of marrying so young, which they couldn't.

At midseason, Joe and Pam, who were visible at home games at Staples, now sitting in a box midway up the lower bowl behind the Lakers bench, dropped out of sight. They moved back to Philadelphia but weren't even seen there that June, when the Lakers played the 76ers in the Finals.

Only later would the details of the split come out, and it was bitter: Kobe sold the Pacific Palisades house, obliging his parents to leave. Sharia and her husband, Jerrod Washington, who had headed Kobe's production company, had to leave Kobe's West L.A. condo. Shaya had to give up her job in Tellem's office.

Once wholly a creature of his family, Bryant now switched families. When Vanessa's parents divorced, her father alleged Kobe gave them cash and gifts worth more than $500,000, paid off a $230,000 mortgage, and subsequently bought Vanessa's mother a $2.7-million house, a block away from theirs in a posh gated village in the hills above Newport Beach.

Kobe and Vanessa were married in the spring of 2001, in as small and as private a ceremony as he could arrange. There were 12 people there. Pam and Joe didn't attend. None of Kobe's teammates was invited. When the *Orange County Register* was subsequently tipped and Lakers beat writer Kevin Ding arrived to cover the event, Bryant, who was so unhappy at even this minimal coverage, snarled at Ding.

Outsiders weren't fond of Vanessa, or as one of Bryant's old friends put it, "She ruined his life." It wasn't surprising; once he'd been theirs to an extent; now he was wholly hers.

Despite Vanessa's youth, she was a formidable personality in her own right, and if she was even younger than Kobe, she was a choice he had made.

Two years later, in the spring of 2003, Joe, who hadn't seen his son in years, came back to town in a new role as spokesman for a short-lived league which played basketball on a trampoline. Asked about Kobe by the *Times'* Bill Plaschke, Joe acknowledged their rift, saying, "When Kobe made a decision to be with someone he cared about, Pam and I decided it was time to back off, that's all it was. It's his life, we've got nothing to do with it. We've done our job."

For his part, Kobe said he missed his father ("It's not about basketball. It's about having somebody to go to a ballgame with. It's about having somebody to hang out with. That's what I miss.") but attributed the split to his family's rejection of Vanessa. Kobe told Plaschke that Joe was uncomfortable with Vanessa because she was Latina. Joe denied it, saying he and Pam were concerned that Kobe was marrying too young.

"It's right there in the Bible," Kobe said. "When you get married, your mother and father and sisters are no longer the priority. Your wife and daughter are the priority. That's the way it has to be."

With Plaschke's column breaking the ice, Joe went to Kobe's house in Newport Beach for the first time and was introduced to his three-month old granddaughter, Natalia. Nevertheless, if the argument was over, the distance remained. The Bryants, once so close, were never the same.

■ ■ ■

The Lakers were aware this was going on in the spring of 2001 and that it had something to do with the attitude he was bringing to the workplace. There was nothing they could do about that but cross their fingers and try to get through it in one piece.

Somehow, they did.

In early April, Tellem took Bryant over to West's home for Karen's spaghetti and Jerry's counsel. Jerry talked about other tug-of-wars: the problems with Chamberlain and Baylor; the years of negotiation between Johnson and Kareem Abdul-Jabbar before they became friends. This wasn't new, only more visible.

"All I'll say is, he was a pretty angry guy," West said later. "If your teammates are talking about you and your coach is coming at you in the papers, you just can't be a great player in this league. You can't play better unless your teammates respect you."

That worked both ways. The Lakers were a dizzy, exasperated bunch. O'Neal still dreamed of shipping Bryant out, and Bryant still dreamed of going. He even called Jordan, who was running the Washington Wizards, to ask for advice or a rescue.

The operative word around the Lakers was dysfunction. After Portland's Rasheed Wallace threw a towel in the face of teammate Arvydas Sabonis in a game at Staples, Rick Fox announced, "This year we have the trophy for team dysfunction. We're not giving our trophy to them after one towel toss."

Meanwhile, Bryant read Friedrich Nietzsche's "That which doesn't kill me, makes me stronger," in the paper and started repeating it.

On April 1, they dropped to number four in the West, losing at home to the low-flying Knicks who were so banged up, they had to put 6'5" Larry Johnson on O'Neal. Bryant, who had tried to return after missing two games with a badly sprained ankle, lasted 11 minutes and went out for another week while they went on the road for four games, looking lost.

The trip started at Utah, where Horry, in one of his rare regular-season appearances, came off the bench to score 20 points with eight rebounds in a 96–88 upset of the Jazz. Horry then went a combined 0–4 on the rest of the trip, but the Lakers won those games anyway.

Returning home where Bryant was to rejoin them, Jackson stressed the need for a "seamless" transition. O'Neal stressed his need for the ball. ("When I'm not involved, then I'm not the player you're used to seeing. I'm somebody else and I can't be somebody else. When I'm somebody else, I get upset. Then I say what I feel like saying. . . . When I get these dog cookies, then the dog will walk, sit, bite, run, fetch, do whatever you want.")

Of course, they'd been through it before. When Bryant returned after an injury in March, they said the same things and he took 95 shots in the first three games. This time Bryant started looking for teammates from the moment he returned, in a 26-point rout of the Suns, and it just kept getting better from there.

"The first game Kobe came back, the first quarter, I might have made four baskets that were all from him," Fox said. "I mean, the times I sat out on the wing and watched my man, for lack of respect for me, go to him because they knew that he would try and score and Kobe would take the tough shot.

"I tell you the truth, I was feeling some emotion. I was, 'cause it was like day and night. I mean, he really, truly was making the rest of us better. To sit there and have had to discuss for 70 games what was wrong and to feel, honestly, through some of his statements that he didn't trust us. . . .

"It was kind of a thing where we weren't confident basketball players and for him all of a sudden to turn around and say, you know what, I was wrong, let me ask for forgiveness through my actions. . . . In the middle of the game I said, 'Man, I appreciate that, you've really turned the corner, you're showing us by your actions, not by just talking.'"

After that, no one had a chance.

With Bryant back, they won their last four games to finish the regular season on an 8–0 run, then went 15–1 in the playoffs, a new record, for a grand total of 23 wins in their final 24 games.

Portland, a 50-win team, looked competitive for a first-round opponent, but the Trail Blazers had their own issues, illustrated by Wallace throwing that towel in Sabonis' face. The Lakers put them out of their misery in a 3–0 sweep, with Bryant averaging 25 points and 7.7 assists.

Sacramento looked more formidable, having won 55 games to their 56, but the Lakers ran over them, 4–0. O'Neal had two monster games in Staples and then, when the Kings focused their defense on him, Bryant finished them off with two monster games in Sacramento.

San Antonio, their opponent in the West Finals, looked like a true match, opening at home after finishing number one in the West. Two years before, the Lakers had lost the first two games there and had been swept. This time, they won the first two in San Antonio, en route to a sweep of their own.

Showing things had changed, after Bryant scored 45 points in Game 1, O'Neal came to the press room and announced, "I told Kobe that he was my idol." Big kidder that he was, everyone waited for the punch line.

"I'm serious," O'Neal insisted. "He's playing phenomenal. I think he's the best player in the league, by far."

Games 3 and 4 in Staples were fearsome beatings, the Lakers winning, 111–72 and 111–82. Before anyone asked a question in the final press conference, Spurs coach Gregg Popovich likened himself to Gen. George Custer, riding blithely into the Battle of the Little Bighorn.

"Custer had no idea," Popovich said. "That's my statement. Figure it out."

The Lakers were 11–0 in the playoffs, and people were talking sweep and perfect postseason, but the banged-up 76ers stunned them, 107–101, in overtime in Game 1 of the Finals, with Allen Iverson going for 48.

"I'm glad nobody bet their life on it," said a grinning Iverson, "because they definitely would be dead right now."

Gutty little massive underdogs that they were, Larry Brown had his Sixers single-cover O'Neal to keep Bryant from going off and Derek Fisher from dropping all those open three-pointers, as they had against the Spurs. It almost worked. Fisher, who'd gone 0–4 in Game 1, missed all his shots in the first half of Game 2, looking like a choke wasn't out of the question. The 76ers cut a 12-point deficit to 89–86 with 2:22 left, but then, in the shot that turned the series back around, Fisher dropped a three on them to put it away. So much for the interesting part. The Lakers then flew back to Philadelphia and asserted their superiority, winning Games 3, 4, and 5.

Mutombo, the reigning two-time defensive player of the year, had been up for the challenge of playing O'Neal, sniffing, "He is not a monster or a tank where he will destroy you, shoot you, or kill you. He's a human being."

O'Neal was a huge human being, though, and he kept laying Mutombo out, leading with a tightly coiled elbow when he turned into the lane. By the end, with stars and birds twirling around his head, Mutombo acknowledged, "He's a monster, man."

Having overcome their demons just in time, the Lakers had showed how awesome they could be. Their core players were in their prime, except for Bryant, who hadn't even started his yet.

Not that anyone was that confident about the new peace between O'Neal and Bryant.

"We became even stronger than we were. So I don't see that being a threat at all," said Bryant, grinning. "But I'll let you know in October . . . November . . . December . . . January. . . . We're happy to be winning until next January, when people start talking about trading one of us."

■　■　■

In a big surprise, peace was really at hand.

Well, between O'Neal and Bryant, anyway. Amazing everyone, they would coexist easily for the next two seasons without a single flare-up. O'Neal wouldn't even do his code number, in which he alluded to all the dumb shots they were taking from the outside, instead of throwing it in to him.

The Golden Child, Kobe Bryant, as a 17-year-old senior at Lower Merion High School, already had the flair.

Orlando's Shaquille O'Neal had the world on a string in June 1995, laughing as he talked with reporters about his impending free agency amid reports that the Lakers would go hard for him.

Part I: what could go wrong now? Shaq, Kobe, Elden Campbell (No. 41), and Eddie Jones (No. 6) in January 1999, en route to their third consecutive disappointing season at the start of the Shaq-Kobe era.

Dennis Rodman, in one if his attention-getting tricks, takes his shirt off and gives it to a child in the crowd after getting ejected. In the greatest debacle in Lakers history, he came, saw, torpedoed their season, and was cut in 51 days.

Phil Jackson, looking as unconcerned as ever. His serenity helped him last five seasons and win three titles as the third and last coach of the Shaq-Kobe era.

Shaq and Kobe, often at odds during the season, always worked it out at the end, as they're doing here in Game 6 of the 2000 Finals, minutes from their first title.

It wasn't always tense between Shaquille O'Neal and Kobe Bryant, who played together in peace for two seasons before Kobe's arrest in 2003 and Shaq's perception that he no longer needed Kobe changed everything back again.

Happier times: Phil Jackson, Kobe Bryant, and Jerry Buss at the 2000 trophy presentation—the first of three in a row.

Part II: what could go wrong now? Derek Fisher, Devean George, Brian Shaw, John Salley, and Shaquille O'Neal at the 2000 parade, the first of three in a row.

No one enjoyed parades more than Shaquille O'Neal, the rap star, laying it down in 2000. Rick Fox holds the trophy aloft and Mark "Mad Dog" Madsen shows he has even more heart than anyone knew by trying to dance in public.

This is what it's all about: the 2002 championship ring with eight brilliant-cut diamonds across the bottom for their eight titles in Los Angeles. Unfortunately, they never got to nine.

Fans demonstrate support for Bryant, who was suspended for two games for fighting Indiana's Reggie Miller in 2002 (inset). A year later, Bryant, with wife Vannessa addressing sexual assault charges, had worse problems.

Karl Malone (left) and Gary Payton are discreet most of the time, but they can't believe what they've gotten themselves into. As Payton sputtered at the 2003–2004 midseason: "I didn't sign up for this s***."

It was fun while it lasted. The Big Four, all future Hall of Famers—Karl Malone, Gary Payton, Shaquille O'Neal, and Kobe Bryant—at the 2003–2004 opener against Dallas. Days after blasting Shaq in the press, Bryant is the odd man out.

Once it was the Shaq-Kobe era. Now it's just the Kobe era, as he welcomes Lamar Odom, Caron Butler, and Brian Grant, who were all the Lakers could get in trade from Miami for Shaquille O'Neal.

Now, O'Neal's problem became Jackson. O'Neal had accepted Jackson's jibes at first, calling Jackson "my white father," but that was when O'Neal was still in the 325-pound range. Now he was coming in heavier every fall and taking half the season to play himself into shape.

At the end of the 2001 season, he had vowed to come back at his rookie weight, under 300, as a lean, mean rebounding machine. Instead, he spent the summer tending to foot injuries and came back closer to 400.

"I thought about it," O'Neal said in the standard entertaining rationalization. "I decided I'm not going to lose 30 pounds and be a skinny-head. I like being big. I'm the NBA's best NFL player. I got a football body, baby. People can focus on my weight if they want but I've been eating a lot of chicken and fish. Honest."

Of course, Jackson had his fun at O'Neal's expense. ("I think if Shaq got on one side of a teeter totter and we put all the rest of our big guys on the other side, it wouldn't work.") So did others like NBC's Bill Walton, who noted, "Shaq is a virtual house," and, "If Charles Barkley can get on a scale on national TV, why can't he?"

Replied O'Neal: "I'll do that when Bill Walton takes off his toupee."

When he was told Walton didn't wear one, O'Neal tried, "Look, doesn't matter how much you weigh when you can play. . . . How many rings did Bill Walton get anyway?"

The answer was two in the NBA and three more in the NCAA.

"Bill's got two, too?" said O'Neal. "Oh, I didn't know that."

More trouble followed. Given permission to take a day off for the birth of his daughter, O'Neal took two without calling in, and Jackson announced he'd be fined.

"I'm taking care of business," O'Neal said when he rejoined the team. "When it comes to family, I don't have to call anybody. I'm not calling him. And that fine? That motherf***er knows what he can do with that fine. You write that too."

The way O'Neal saw it, he had come back early after his foot injury for the team's sake, which Jackson had conveniently forgotten. After scoring 30 points in the next night's game, an overtime win in Houston that pushed their record to 7–0, O'Neal announced, "If I was a knucklehead, I could see getting dogged out, but hey, I thought I did everything right—especially the last two years. But there's no loyalty in this league. None at all."

213

By then, it was becoming clear enough this wouldn't be your ordinary powerhouse. Nevertheless, there were some things you could count on. Bryant was headstrong and often on his own planet. O'Neal was insecure and measured his effort, according to the threat and the time of year. Jackson wouldn't confront them directly before the playoffs but, in the meantime, he would fill up the newspapers letting them know what he expected of them.

At the end when it looked like all was lost, they would come together. They didn't like each other enough to stop squabbling, but they didn't dislike each other enough to stop competing.

There was a new problem now: having flipped a switch at the end of the 2000–2001 season, the Lakers thought they could do it again. It was human nature and they were as human as humans could be.

So—surprise!—they proceeded to punt another season.

They started the 2001–2002 season with a 16–1 run, making them 39–2 since the preceding April 1. This, of course, started greatest-team-ever talk, which they extinguished by leveling off, going 42–23 the rest of the way. Everyone waited for them to flip their switch late in the season, but the room stayed dark. O'Neal was still taking it easy. Before an April 2 win in Washington, someone asked Jackson if Shaq had been pacing himself for the last five or six games.

"Fifty or sixty games?" said Jackson, smiling.

They eased to a number three finish in the West, making it two years in a row the defending champion couldn't win its conference. This time they didn't even win their division, finishing three games behind the 61–21 Kings in the Pacific.

Of course, everyone just knew they'd turn it on in the playoffs, but everyone was still wrong. The Lakers eliminated Portland in the now-traditional 3–0 first-round sweep but weren't impressive. They were no better in the second round against the Spurs, who opened without the injured David Robinson. After the Lakers eked out an 86–80 win in Game 1, Jackson, realizing this wasn't going to be the expected romp, said he had "never had a worse performance for a half out of a basketball club in the playoffs."

Imagine his reaction in Game 2 when his basketball club trailed by 21 before halftime, presumably another new low, and lost, 88–85. It was 1–1 going back to San Antonio with Robinson coming back.

Jackson was so worried now, it even showed. He talked to O'Neal, who'd scored 19 points with seven rebounds in Game 2, about turning it up, but their discussion didn't go well. Using the press to press O'Neal, Jackson announced, "I had a heated conversation with Shaq, actually, about getting actively involved in chasing the ball down. . . . He said, basically, his toe [hurt]."

O'Neal was boycotting the press, as he had been for weeks. When one of the beat guys followed him as he walked to his he car, O'Neal told him, "Ask Phil, he knows every other f***ing thing."

Game 3 in the Alamodome was a nail-biter in which the Lakers nearly bit each others' heads off. In the second quarter, Malik Rose took two offensive rebounds over O'Neal. In the next timeout, Jackson said something to O'Neal, who smirked and waved him away. Moments later, as Jackson tapped his clipboard with a marker, O'Neal turned away again; this time Brian Shaw stepped between them.

"Phil knows how to push Shaq's buttons," Shaw said. "I saw that Shaq was about to lash out. . . . Shaq needs to hear that from time to time. And Phil's really the only guy bold enough to do it."

O'Neal wound up with 22 points and 15 rebounds. Bryant took over at the end, scoring 11 of his 31 in the fourth quarter, and the Lakers won, 99–89.

They won Game 4, too, 87–85, with O'Neal, who was blocked out by Danny Ferry, reaching over him to keep a key offensive rebound alive late in the game.

"I knew I had to get it," O'Neal said. "I didn't feel like hearing Phil's mouth."

The Lakers won Game 5 to end the series but they hadn't seen nothing yet. The West Finals pitted them against the free-wheeling Kings, whom the Lakers had long delighted in keeping down. Jackson called Sacramento fans "semicivilized rednecks" and "barbarians." The rednecks proceeded to turn every subsequent visit into a night of living hell by clanging cowbells in Jackson's ear, or as close as security would let them get.

The Lakers thought the Kings were softies who couldn't execute in the halfcourt, and whose best shot at defending O'Neal was a Vlade Divac flop. Actually, the Kings were an offensive highlight reel. With point guard Mike Bibby emerging, they had won the Pacific, finishing three games ahead of the Lakers, and they were at the top of their game.

The teams split the first two in Sacramento but, serving notice they were for real, the Kings upset the Lakers in Game 3 in Staples, setting up a must-win Game 4 for the home team. O'Neal, taking it right to Divac, scored 10 points in the first quarter. The Kings were flying so high, they didn't even notice. They led, 40–20, at the end of that first quarter and 48–24 early in the second. The Lakers fought back furiously, if not effectively. They weren't making shots but they substituted frenzy for skill and made it suffice, trailing 99–97 when Divac made one of two free throws with :11 left.

Bryant drove the ball to the basket but missed a runner over Divac. O'Neal got the rebound, but his follow shot missed. No one could get control of the second rebound, which Divac managed to bat out of there. The ball rolled right to Horry—the only one of the 10 players on the floor who hadn't gone crashing into the lane pursuing it,—who spotted up perfectly on the three-point line. Horry's shot left his hand and arched toward the hoop as the clock went to 0:00.0, dropping cleanly into the net like an arrow through Cupid's heart.

For years, it would stand as the most dramatic moment of the Shaq-Kobe era, but at the moment, it only tied the series, 2–2. The Kings then won Game 5 in Arco Arena, so more would be required of the Lakers.

Finally, O'Neal took over. He was moving better than he had against the Spurs but had been in foul trouble throughout the series. Divac was taking a charge or two a game, but the real problem was Bibby, who kept penetrating on pick-and-rolls, challenging Shaq at the basket or retreating behind the screens to knock down three-pointers. By Games 6 and 7, however, O'Neal had cleaned up his repertoire. Knowing Divac would flop on contact, O'Neal stopped contacting him, beating him on quick spins rather than shoving his way to the basket.

This was O'Neal at his zenith, the best Shaq anyone would ever see again. He had 41 points and 17 rebounds in a 106–102 win in Game 6, and 35–13 as the Lakers prevailed in overtime, 112–106, in Game 7 in Sacramento. It was the best playoff series of the post–Jordan Bulls era. The final game drew a 19 rating for NBC, the highest-rated game since Mike left Chicago.

It was also tantamount to crowning the Lakers for the third season in a row. The East winner, New Jersey, was small and worse, used to single-covering opposing centers. It hadn't worked for Larry Bird's Pacers in 2000 or Larry Brown's 76ers in 2001 and, with rookie Jason Collins matched up against O'Neal, it had no chance for Byron Scott's Nets.

O'Neal averaged 36 points and won his third Finals MVP in a row. The Lakers swept the Nets, 4–0. They were at three and counting. They were a dynasty now, if an entry-level one, one of three NBA teams to win three in a row. The Celtics had won nine, and the Bulls had won three twice. Now came the Lakers, just entering their prime. No one could stop them, not even them.

■ ■ ■

Live by the miracle, die by the miracle. The 2002–2003 season was almost like a recap of 2001–2002 with one major difference: Horry's three-pointer rimmed out.

The pattern was the same. O'Neal had foot problems over the summer, came in heavy, took months to get in shape, and got mad at Jackson. The Lakers struggled until the postseason when they got it together.

This time, however, they dug too deep a hole, dropping in the standings for the third season in a row—this time all the way down to number five in the West—sending them out on the road throughout the playoffs. One more thing changed: this time when they got it together, they weren't good enough.

O'Neal was like a horse who runs in handicap races; when he won, he'd show up the next time out, carrying another 25 pounds. He had meant to come back in better shape, but the problem started, as usual, in the summer, which he didn't like to interrupt for things like surgery. So he took his time getting ready for a procedure on his little toe, intending to have it done in August. Then he got sick so it had to be pushed back to September 21, eight days before camp opened. He missed the first 12 games, as they started 3–9. Of course, by then everyone knew the script. As the *San Antonio Express-News'* Glenn Rogers wrote, "This would be considered a disastrous, perhaps fatal, start for any other contender . . . but not here. Why? Because it's all BS: Before Shaquille O'Neal."

This time, the Lakers had more problems than just getting O'Neal back in shape, even if it took the usual six months. The West was loaded, and the great powers kept jockeying to get ahead of each other, becoming even more powerful. San Antonio brought in Manu Ginobili, Speedy Claxton, and Kevin Willis. The Kings, already bursting, added Jim Jackson and Keon Clark.

The Lakers stood pat. A year before, they had acquired Samaki Walker, Mitch Richmond, and Lindsey Hunter, none of whom was a conspicuous success. Now, after sweeping the Nets, they were so happy with themselves, they couldn't think of one thing they needed. They had a $4.5-million exception, but instead of pursuing a big man like Willis or Clark or Charles Oakley, they gave it to Devean George.

The backup center they wanted so they could cut O'Neal's minutes turned out to be a willowy 7'0" free agent named Soumaila Samake. Samake started on opening night, quickly showed he was out of his league, and was gone by Thanksgiving.

By then it was obvious the Lakers were so undermanned, Shaq's return might not be enough. Bryant fumed at teammates, especially George, his protégé, during their 3–9 start, and when Kobe chilled out, O'Neal returned and began treating the little guys like dirt.

O'Neal, also known among the Lakers as the Big Moody, was usually a fun guy, but the princess who felt the pea under the 37 mattresses she slept on wasn't any higher-maintenance than he was. Since press obligations were always the first thing he jettisoned, he made publicist John Black so crazy, Black blamed his heart surgery on Shaq-related stress.

Not that O'Neal's pique at teammates came as any surprise after Shaq vs. Kobe, Shaq vs. Phil, Shaq vs. Del Harris, Nick Van Exel, Fred Hickman, Brian Hill, Penny Hardaway, et al. It was almost like there was a pattern. However, if O'Neal was mad at everyone else, he and Bryant were fine. Still, Lakers fans were getting concerned with the Lakers at 13–19 on January 1, number 10 in the West. It took an 11–4 run to avoid the embarrassment of being under .500 at the All-Star break and having to spend the weekend getting asked about it.

They went 26–9 after the break, allowing them to believe they were still OK . . . even if they were number five, which meant they would be on the road throughout the West draw, starting with their first-round opponent, the 51-win Timberwolves.

As in days of yore, the Lakers broke through to win Game 1 in Minneapolis. Showing the days of yore were over, the Wolves won Game 2, surprised the Lakers by winning Game 3 in Staples, and scared them half to death, taking a 16-point lead in Game 4 before the Lakers rallied to pull it out. The Lakers won in six games, but it had been a harrowing series, and now they had to start all over, on the road again in San Antonio.

The Spurs were in a continuing process of transition, with 21-year-old Frenchman Tony Parker at point guard and Ginobili, an exciting Argentine rookie. They still had the Tim Duncan–David Robinson tandem to send at O'Neal. Noted stretch runners, they had gone 27–5 after the All-Star break. They were already deeper than the Lakers before Fox was hurt in the Minnesota series and George went out in Game 1. The Spurs won, 87–82, with their bench outscoring the Lakers subs, 28–4. The Spurs won Game 2, too, starting the usual Lakers-are-done talk, until the Lakers bounced back to tie it, 2–2.

Laid-back Lakers fans were in an ugly mood, watching their faves getting beaten up on the road at the start of every series. Unlike other fans, they couldn't complain the league was out to get their team since everyone knew the Lakers were the league's favorite, as suggested by their huge differential in free throw attempts. Nevertheless, in Game 3, Jack Nicholson sprang out of his courtside seat to do a full H-E-R-E'-S JOHNNY! on referee Mark Wunderlich and got a standing ovation. TNT, showing the game, alertly showed file footage of Jack at his most deranged in *The Shining.*

Before Game 4, Jackson learned he needed an emergency angioplasty after tests showed a 90 percent blockage, putting him at risk of a heart attack. He watched from a hospital bed with assistant coach Jim Cleamons in charge as the Spurs went up 16 before the Lakers rallied to win, 99–95. Said Cleamons of his boss afterward: "Let's say if he survived this, he's OK." Jackson was actually fine, feeling better than he had in years as he rejoined the team for the trip to San Antonio, saying he had a new lease on life. It was his team that was endangered.

The Lakers fell behind by 25 before staging one of their vintage rallies, coming all the way back to within 96–94, with a chance to win it as time ran out when the ball wound up in the hands of—who else?—Horry, unguarded at the three-point line.

This was how it had gone for three seasons, since Horry hit his big three in the 15-point comeback against the Blazers in 2000, and the never-to-be-forgotten one against the Kings in 2002. The ball seemed to follow him around the court and seek him out at the end. This spring however, with the pressure of being expected to stage his annual miracle transformation, Horry was struggling. He had tried 34 three-pointers in the playoffs, missed 32, and was now running away from his shots. He stepped right into this one, however. It looked good coming off of his fingertips, straight and true, with good rotation while everyone in the arena and at home watching on TV thought the same thing.

"It's something like a giant gulp," said Spurs coach Gregg Popovich, looking on in horror. "A lowering of the heart toward the belly. Those are his shots. We've all seen him make them."

This one seemed to go in, even going below the level of the rim, according to Lakers people, who watched the replay several dozen times . . . before spinning back out.

"I'm supposed to be known for that kind of shot," said a disconsolate Horry. "I thought it was on the money. I wanted the ball. I did everything right. I got my feet set, it just didn't fall."

The Lakers were not conceding anything. They were still the Lakers, after all, they'd go home, win Game 6, and see how the young Spurs held up in the pressure of a Game 7. Instead, the young Spurs wiped the Staples floor with them, scoring on 15 of 17 possessions in the second half to break it open, making the Lakers look old and tired, terminating their dynasty with a 110–82 pounding.

Tears rolled down the faces of Bryant and Fox, sitting on the bench, watching their time run out. The Age of Miracles was over. Real life was back.

Chapter 13

REALITY BITES

I sit here in front of you guys, furious at myself, disgusted at myself, for making the mistake of adultery.... I'm a human being. I'm a man, just like everybody else. I mourn. I cry. Just like everybody else....

If I could just turn back the hands of time.... I have a lot at stake and that's not, that has nothing to do with the game of basketball. That has nothing to do with endorsements, nothing at all. This is about us. This is about our family.

—Kobe Bryant, July 18, 2004

■ ■ ■

So MUCH FOR WAITING until next season.

Before this one even started, it had been overshadowed by the events of the preceding summer, when all who knew Kobe Bryant were shocked to hear he had been implicated in a rape case and would stand trial for sexual assault. In the beginning, it didn't even feel right to care about a game under such circumstances, although the impact of real life ebbed and everyone would go back to caring about the games, even Bryant.

With the media descending upon them as if all the world's paparazzi had been flown in for the occasion, the Lakers embarked on the Preseason from Hell, which was then followed by the Season and Postseason from Hell, with everyone strung out like violin strings.

The Lakers were now not just big, they were notorious. The rest of the league barely existed, as demonstrated by the 2003 Finals, which were tied, 2–2, before the Spurs beat the Nets. This made it the most competitive Finals since Michael Jordan left the Bulls, but TV ratings crashed through the floor to 7.5, the lowest since the tape-delay days on CBS.

It was little wonder that Commissioner David Stern would joke before the 2004 playoffs that his perfect matchup would be "the Lakers against the Lakers." However, Stern didn't like it at all when the madcap Dallas owner, Mark Cuban predicted—correctly—that Bryant's arrest would actually help the league's ratings since people hung on "train-wreck television." Stern was even obliged to reply to the notion that Bryant should be barred from playing. Or, as the commissioner put it, "No Patriot Act here."

For the Lakers, who were riding that train, the season would be an ordeal. By the spring, when they were considered long shots getting longer after losing the opener of their second-round series in San Antonio, publicist John Black, looking unusually chipper, was asked what he was so happy about.

"I can see the light," said Black.

"Which way are you rooting?" he was asked.

"I'm rooting for the light," he said, laughing.

■ ■ ■

The summer got off to a great start, they thought. Glamour team though they were, for years when the Lakers had gone looking for help, they had been led on and let down, but everything was breaking spectacularly right. Intent on landing a real power forward, they found that Malone, a free agent after 18 seasons in Utah, not only wanted to come but would play for peanuts, compared to the $19 million he'd made in his last season. He was taken care of for the rest of his life, and his agent, Dwight Manley, who lived in Orange County, advised him to go where he wanted to go rather than follow the money.

The Lakers were over the salary cap and could only offer their midlevel exception, $4.5 million, never daring to hope it would be enough. Over the years, players like Charles Oakley and Kendall Gill had told them they'd love to come for that, but as soon as they got a bigger offer, they took it. Malone said he would not only come for that, he'd take half of it if they found another good player to take the other half. That turned out to be Gary Payton, another sure-fire Hall of Famer, who wound up getting the whole $4.5 million with Malone volunteering to take the $1.5-million veteran's minimum.

Enthralled Lakers fans hung on the latest development in the negotiations, right up until the moment a story broke out of some place called Eagle, Colorado, that Bryant had been arrested in a sexual assault case. Eagle was next to Vail, home of the prominent Steadman Hawkins Clinic, where Bryant had arrived June 30 for arthroscopic knee surgery, checking into the posh Lodge & Spa at Cordillera. There he had met the 19-year-old woman at the front desk, whom the press would refer to as "the accuser."

She wouldn't be identified in newspapers and mainstream media, but was given away by the grocery store tabloids. Months before the trial, Google listed seventy thousand results for her name.

The facts soon became as familiar as the Pledge of Allegiance. The young woman had acknowledged feeling "chemistry" with Bryant, had shown him around, and had then gone with him to his room. She said he forced her to have sex with him. He said it was consensual.

The next day, she filed a criminal complaint. On July 4, the Eagle County sheriff issued an arrest warrant for Bryant, who had gone back home. Bryant turned himself in and was released after posting $25,000 bond. It would take two weeks for the young Eagle County D.A., Mark Hurlbert, to determine whether to file charges. Meanwhile, everyone tried to go back to their lives which, in the Lakers' case, meant signing Malone and Payton. On July 17, the two new Lakers were introduced at a press conference in the sparkling Arena Club overlooking the floor in the Staples Center.

On July 18, there was another press conference at Staples after Hurlbert announced that Bryant would be charged with sexual assault. This one was in the unadorned press area on the event level, down the hall from the dressing rooms. There Bryant made his first comment since his arrest, with Vanessa sitting next to him, holding his hand, her gaze frozen on him as he grimaced through a halting four-minute statement, his voice trembling and cracking, anything but the poised icon everyone was used to.

223

He insisted he was innocent. ("I didn't force her to do anything against her will.") He was contrite. ("I sit here in front of you guys, furious at myself, disgusted at myself for making the mistake of adultery.") He pledged his love to Vanessa. ("You're a blessing. You're the beat of my heart, the air I breathe. You're the strongest person I know. And I'm so sorry, having to put you through this, having to put our family through this.") He even thanked fans for standing by him. ("I appreciate everybody out there for their support, and we're going to need support and prayers now more than ever.") But he missed one thing. This wasn't a game. Even Lakers fans couldn't automatically stand behind him now.

From the start, the story had a life of its own. A typical day that summer, as charted by *Sports Business Daily*, included stories on ABC's *World News Tonight*; MSNBC's *Lester Holt Live*, *Countdown with Keith Olbermann*, and *The Abrams Report*; CNN's *Wolf Blitzer Reports*, *Newsnight*, and *Larry King Live*; CNNfn's *The Flip Side*; Fox News' *Fox Report*, *Hannity & Colmes*, *The O'Reilly Factor*, and *On the Record*; CNBC's *The News with Brian Williams*; *ET*; *Inside Edition*; FSN's *Best Damn Sports Show Period*; and ESPN's *SportsCenter* and *ESPNews*.

The story ranked with the war in Iraq and the Laci Peterson trial. At Bryant's press conference, a correspondent from *ET* told a colleague from the *Los Angeles Times* that the syndicated show had the Bryant story scheduled for saturation coverage over the coming year, à la the O. J. Simpson case. From a media standpoint, this was Simpson II. Like the O.J. case, it had sex, race, beauty, fame, tragedy, and best of all, suspense. If this one had a live complainant instead of two dead victims, it also had a professional athlete who was still active and in the spotlight, instead of one who had been long retired.

In this case, the athlete couldn't get out of the spotlight if he wanted to, and seemed ambivalent about it. The day before Bryant flew back to Eagle to be booked, public records showed that 9-1-1 medics had treated a woman at his home in Newport Beach. Records also showed a prior call to 9-1-1 in March.

On July 16, Kobe and Vanessa made a splash, attending the ESPY Awards in Los Angeles. On July 18, Hurlbert announced Bryant would be charged. On July 20, Bryant appeared at the Teen Choice Awards, wearing a black Martin Luther King T-shirt, posing with a multicolored surfboard as he paraphrased Dr. King's statement, "An injustice anywhere is an injustice everywhere."

The court case–turned-circus just kept growing. Bryant bought Vanessa a $4-million, eight-carat diamond. This delicious item, carrying the suggestion he was paying her off for backing him up, was disclosed by *People* magazine and breathlessly reported in advance in a *New York Post* gossip column. When Bryant went back to Eagle to be arraigned, girls in the crowd outside the courtroom cheered him shrilly, as if he was a touring rock star.

The press, mainstream and tabloid, descended upon Eagle, turning the young woman's friends into instant celebrities. Several disclosed that she had twice taken overdoses in the last six months, distraught over the end of a relationship. Her friend, Lindsey McKinney, told the story to *Orange County Register*'s Marcia Smith and Heather Lourie. *The National Enquirer* then offered McKinney $12,500 for her story. *The Enquirer*'s Michelle Caruso was even filmed at the front door, making the offer, assuring Lindsey's father, "It's more than I've ever seen them pay for anything. Stories on Julia Roberts only pay five grand."

This was becoming the press' favorite kind of story, about itself. Some newspapers sat on the overdose story, feeling it violated Colorado's rape shield law. *The Register* played it both ways, following the news with a sympathetic feature, also by Smith and Lourie, headlined, "His money, fame and power place much of the focus on Bryant, not his accuser, whose life has been invaded."

For fans of the gothic, there was a scary column by *Sports Illustrated*'s Rick Reilly, speculating what Colorado's draconian rape laws would mean if Bryant were found guilty:

> While he is awaiting sentencing, he will likely be given a penile plethysmograph test, in which an electric measuring band connected to a computer will be placed around his penis. He will then be shown pornographic, deviant and sex-abuse images, and the device will record his level of arousal. The results of the test will be used to determine the course of his rehabilitation treatment.

"It's all very Clockwork Orangeish," says Dan Recht, former head of the Colorado Criminal Defense Bar. . . .

Over the last five years convicted rapists in Colorado have received "indeterminate" sentences—four years to life. Only when they are deemed safe to re-enter society are they allowed out. . . .

There will be a bus ride, likely to the Colorado State Penitentiary in Canon City, where for the first year, "he will be in a cell 23 hours out of 24," says [Denver trial lawyer Bob] McAllister. "He's famous so the guards will make sure there's no appearance of favoritism. They'll probably be harder on him, full-body cavity searches, just to show him he isn't anything special."

Best case . . . Bryant will be paroled in six years. . . . but he won't be living his old bling-bling NBA life. He'll be required to inform his parole officer of his every movement, by contacting the officer or by electronic bracelet or GPS device. Some sex parolees are not allowed to be around anyone 18 or under. Under Megan's Law anytime Bryant changes his address, he will have to register with the police as a sex offender and his name will be placed on a list that is available to the public.

After 10 years Bryant might be off parole and a relatively free man. He would be 41 years old.

Bryant's endorsements dried up. The Italian hazelnut company, Nutella, dropped him right away. McDonald's waited a few months before dropping him quietly. Nike, which had just signed him to a $48-million deal, kept him on the roster but didn't bring out a Bryant shoe.

Hurlbert got death threats. A Swiss bodybuilder named Patrick Graber was arrested by undercover policemen in El Segundo after he allegedly offered to murder the young woman for $3 million. A University of Iowa student, who was said to have been drinking all day at a golf tournament, was sentenced to four months in a federal prison for leaving an obscene death threat on her answering machine. Before the trial would begin, she would move four times to escape harassment.

It was madness on a daily basis and it wasn't going to lighten up if Bryant came out to play.

■ ■ ■

The surprise was that Bryant wanted to play.

Playing meant exposing himself to the giant horde of press trained on him, which included *ET*, *Access Hollywood*, and that peculiar creation of the O.J. phenomenon, *Celebrity Justice*, a syndicated TV show devoted entirely to the thrilling sight of stars on trial.

This was a living hell for Bryant with his highly developed sense of privacy. Before, the local papers and TV stations had followed the standard practice of honoring the separation between his professional and personal life, even giving him extra room, according to his particular sensitivity, as when everyone went light on the story of his marriage. Now, all the old bets were off. The 9-1-1 calls from his house made the newspapers. Stories on the Laine family alluded to the court documents in the divorce between Vanessa's parents, detailing Kobe's gifts, down to the dollar. Vanessa was now part of the story. By bringing her to his press conference, demonstrating she was by his side, Bryant had made her part of his legal strategy and, as such, a key figure in the case.

The attention represented the torture of one thousand cuts to Kobe, who circled the wagons as never before. His inner circle was now down to Vanessa, his lawyers, and his agent, Rob Pelinka. For months, Bryant wouldn't return calls from Lakers officials or teammates. He holed up in his Newport Beach house inside a gated village over the summer, with internal as well as external security. Two cars pointed outward sat in his driveway to keep any possible intruders away. There was often a tarpaulin thrown over the gates to his driveway.

Nevertheless, he always intended to rejoin the team, even if he had mixed feelings about it. He didn't actually feel like playing and, although he would always deny it, he was scared of the reception he'd get. It showed in the relief that gushed out of him months later when he learned he was the leading vote-getter for the West All-Star squad. ("Phew! I really don't know how to quite explain it. So, thank you. Just, thank you, man. I really appreciate it. . . . I don't know quite how to describe it. It's very unexpected. Man, it just goes a long way with me.") But that wouldn't be until mid-December and he would go through a lot before then.

Right up until the start of camp, he went back and forth. Once the most dedicated of players, he had been idle all summer, making plans with his lawyers. He wanted his old life back and that meant basketball. Not only would he play, he would do it the way he had before. Most stars talked to the press selectively, after some games and a few practices, but Bryant had almost always been available—and would be now.

There were a lot of things you could say about Bryant. He was headstrong, didn't have enough caution to fill a thimble, and didn't know as much as he thought he knew. No longer the boy next door, he had begun showing diva tendencies. He once said he could never get into the jewelry thing, but now he got into a lot of it. He spent lavishly, in general. Corporate partners now found him booked up, out of time, and often difficult. He was so upset with Adidas, he bought out his contract, paying cash. A new shoe deal took a year to negotiate, with Reebok officials becoming so upset at Pelinka's imperious demands, the company went to the trouble of making an announcement when it dropped out. With only Nike left, it took months to make the $48 million deal. Nike officials complained about Pelinka, too; one told the *Times'* Tim Brown: "He really talked down to Phil [Knight, Nike CEO] in the meeting."

Pelinka did what Bryant told him to, to a fault. Arn Tellem had been more like a mentor but had been moved to the side, along with Bryant's parents. Pelinka wasn't going to make that mistake.

The sneaker deal was a tender spot for Bryant, since it represented his cachet—which was now behind that of LeBron James, the new liason to puberty who got a $90 million deal. Bryant got so upset at the *Times'* story, he had John Black call sports editor Bill Dwyre to request a sitdown. Before arrangements could be made, however, Bryant went to Eagle for knee surgery.

For all his faults, however, Bryant was no coward.

"I didn't want to feel like I was running and hiding," he told *ESPN Magazine*'s Tom Friend. "I have absolutely nothing to hide. And I didn't want to feel like I did. I didn't want my family to feel that way. So I said, 'I'm gonna go out there and do my job. This is my job. I'm gonna go back to work.'"

■ ■ ■

Of course, nobody said it was going to be easy . . . or fun . . . or endurable.

Camp opened October 1 at the University of Hawaii with only the rookies and free agents there. With nothing else to do, the huge press corps, much of which was unfamiliar with the territory and didn't know the veterans reported later, asked the young Lakers, like the number one pick, Brian Cook, what they thought of Bryant's predicament.

The veterans arrived the next day, except for Bryant. In the over-heated atmosphere, the team had to announce this didn't mean he had decided not to play. Pelinka had told them he was "just not feeling well." Coincidentally or not, there were hearings coming up in Eagle, in which his defense team was trying to get the young woman on the stand in an attempt to end it right there and then. Bryant didn't show up the second day, either. Lakers officials couldn't even reach Pelinka until that night to find out when Kobe was coming.

Meanwhile, on the charter flight over, O'Neal entertained teammates with jokes at Bryant's expense. Continuing in a similar vein the next day, when O'Neal was asked how he felt about Kobe's absence, he said, "The full team is here." So much for the interlude in the feud.

O'Neal and Bryant had been fine for two seasons, but their dynamic had changed dramatically. O'Neal was now looking at a long season of being swarmed over by the press and he hadn't done one thing wrong. It would be the worst of all worlds; all they were going to ask about was *Kobe*.

If theirs was always a marriage of convenience, Bryant was now inconvenient. With two all-time greats like Malone and Payton there, Shaq figured he no longer needed Kobe to win. Meanwhile, Phil Jackson, in midseason form, mused about getting Michael Jordan out of retire-ment if Bryant turned out to be unavailable. This set off another great flapping of wings until Jordan rejected the possibility the next day. (By then, the press corps was checking out Internet gossip that Bryant had fired Pelinka and that Magic Johnson was dying. In both cases, the rumors turned out to be exaggerated.)

For his part, Bryant wasn't feeling too warmly toward O'Neal, either. If Bryant hadn't returned a lot of calls over the summer, he knew who had rung up and who hadn't, and he said O'Neal hadn't. O'Neal said that he had, but had gotten the machine and left a message. O'Neal's public comments had been cool, expressing support in a pro forma way, adding pointedly the judicial process had to run its course. Worse, Bryant heard O'Neal was gossiping about his case. Bryant was no longer bulletproof. His confidence was no longer a given and his pose no longer infinite. O'Neal's feelings had once been a matter of indifference to Bryant but now he came in steaming, telling Jackson even before they went to camp that he wasn't going to take any more of Shaq's BS.

And the BS just kept coming.

Upon arrival, two days late, Bryant looked frail and wan, shocking everyone who knew him, who had become used to the notion that he could handle anything without looking like he was even trying. Having bulked up to a formidable 220 pounds, he was now back down around 200. His complexion was ashen. The young man who had never acknowledged fear in any context now said he was "terrified" on behalf of Vanessa and their infant daughter, Natalia. The young man who had always scorned tattoos now had a large one on his right arm—an image of Vanessa over butterfly wings and a reference to Psalm 27.

"Going through something like this humbles you and you understand that the ultimate purpose here is to do God's work," Bryant told the press swarm in the sauna-like gym. "It's not about the money, it's not about the fame and all that other stuff. It's about going out there and doing what I do best and having a good time doing it.

"To be honest with you, I'd much rather play basketball and not be famous. I'd much rather do something else that I love doing and getting paid well to do it and being able to be married to my wife and raise our children without anybody bothering us when we go out in public, or everybody scrutinizing every little detail, everybody making up rumors about our lives. I'd take that."

Unfortunately, that wasn't being offered. He was clearly hanging on by his fingernails, so far behind in his rehab from knee surgery, he couldn't even practice with the team in the two weeks it was in Hawaii. He wouldn't play until the last two exhibitions.

His presence should have been a reminder that had everyone else counting their blessings, but O'Neal had his own problems. No matter what else was going on, and how dire its implications, he was focused like a laser on getting an extension when his contract expired, even if that wasn't until 2006. The Lakers had always put every dollar on the table and locked him up as far into the future as soon as the rules allowed. Now, however, he was 31, he had mushroomed in size as well as stature, and the dollars were staggering. Due to make $30 million in the last year of his contract, he wanted two more years at that level. Buss was hoping to get away for $22.5 million, so they had something to talk about.

O'Neal did what he always did when he didn't get what he wanted, when he wanted it. In an exhibition against Golden State before they broke camp in Honolulu, he punctuated a dunk, yelling "Now you gonna pay me?" loud enough for Buss, sitting courtside to hear.

"I didn't mumble," O'Neal told the press guys afterward. "You read my lips and you read them clearly."

The Lakers weren't even back on the mainland yet, and Bryant was upset at O'Neal, who was upset at Bryant and Buss. Everyone else was just exhausted. As omens went, this wasn't promising. If they had been smart, they would have turned toward Tahiti instead of Los Angeles and started paddling.

■　■　■

Of course, as things turned out, the problems that surfaced in Honolulu were just a tuneup. On media day, the organization set up a picket line outside the El Segundo practice facility and barred some members of the media, hoping to lessen the hysteria. Perhaps thinking he could redirect the media, like Moses parting the Red Sea, Jackson reminded them there were more important things, like Iraq, going on. Of course, without press coverage that was disproportionate to the importance of what he did, Jackson wouldn't be making $6 million annually. In any case, the press didn't melt away.

Every day, Black announced Bryant would only take basketball questions, but it was the reporters' job to ask other questions, and Bryant often answered them. When a CBS producer asked Bryant about that day's events in court, Black lifted her credentials on the spot. After

Newsweek's Allison Samuels wrote a tough cover piece, she couldn't even get credentials.

For his part, Jackson regarded this as the usual hysteria, like that which he'd turned to his own advantage in Chicago. He jauntily told the press he would show players "how to dodge questions that you guys present," and said Bryant's situation might actually be a "boon" that brought them together. Everyone else in the organization was considering alternative careers.

"Just assume this is the season from hell," someone told Black, "and anything that doesn't go wrong is a bonus."

"I just didn't know the flames would be so hot," said Black.

Four days later, O'Neal, sitting out an exhibition in San Diego, said he was doing it because "I want to be right for Derek, Karl, and Gary." In case anyone had missed the significance of what he'd said, he repeated the list of players he wanted to be right for, which didn't, of course, include Bryant.

Bryant was now venting in front of teammates, vowing to leave at the end of the season when he'd be a free agent—free, that is, to get away from O'Neal. Of course, that got back to O'Neal, who got even madder at Bryant. The feud was back on and spiraling toward a showdown.

Everywhere they went, the press corps, which included so many members who cared little about basketball, followed. Before an exhibition at Staples, a TV guy doing a courtside remote asked a local writer, "Which one is Payton?" In Las Vegas, a TV woman entering the dressing room greeted Derek Fisher with a breezy, "Hey, Deron!"

Bryant finally began practicing on October 18. The veterans had the day off, so it was just Kobe, looking like he was enjoying himself, and the young guys on a quiet Saturday afternoon in El Segundo.

"Some days must be better than others," someone suggested to Bryant afterward.

"Every day is a bad day," he said.

Bryant played his first exhibition in the next-to-last one, against the Clippers in the Pond of Anaheim, on October 23. He was rusty but brash as ever, getting up 14 shots in 32 minutes and missing 10. The sideshow was better than the show. Mike Tyson attended to show support for Bryant. Two security people ushered Vanessa into the press room and made sure the ladies room was clear before she entered. Vanessa wore a top with "Fashionable Motherf***er" written on it.

The next night in the exhibition finale in Las Vegas, Jackson, fretting at the loose play he'd seen in the preseason, mentioned the possibility of "implosion." Bryant went 3–10 in that one. Afterward, O'Neal suggested he pass the ball more while he was getting in shape. The next day, Bryant, who never used to react, reacted.

"I know how to play my guard spot," he said. "He can worry about the low post. I'll worry about mine."

Replied O'Neal: "Just ask Karl and Gary why they came here. One person. Not two. One. Period. So, he's right, I'm not telling him how to play his position. I'm telling him how to play team ball. . . . He doesn't need advice on how to play his position, but he needs advice on how to play team ball. As we start this new season, s***'s got to be done right. If you don't like it, then you can opt out next year. If it's going to be my team, I'll voice my opinion. If he don't like it, he can opt out. . . . I ain't going nowhere."

O'Neal and Bryant had never had an exchange like that. The nonconfrontational Jackson had to step in, telling both players to knock it off. Everyone else went back to the usual practice of pretending it had never happened.

"It's all resolved," said Payton the next day at practice. "We're talking about basketball now. That's all we're going to talk about. We're talking about basketball. We're not talking about who's saying this and who's saying that. Everything is fine here in our camp and that's the way it's gonna be."

"It's not going to continue," said Malone. "Trust me."

What did the new guys know? Everywhere else, this would have been more than enough. Here, it was only the opening act. Bryant, still burning, went home and called Jim Gray, the ESPN reporter who was a longtime confidant, dumped all over O'Neal, and told Gray to say he had said it all on the air.

On O'Neal: "There's more to life than whose team this is, but this is his team so it's time for him to act like it. That means no more coming into camp fat and out of shape when your team is relying on your leadership on and off the court. It also means no more blaming others for our team's failure or blaming staff members for not over-dramatizing your injuries so that you avoid blame for your lack of conditioning. Also, 'my team' doesn't mean only when we win. It means carrying the burden of defeat just as gracefully as you carry a championship trophy.

"Leaders don't beg for contract extensions and negotiate some $30-million-plus deal in the media when we have two future Hall of Famers playing here basically for free. A leader would not demand the ball when you have three of us besides you, not to mention the teammates that he's gone to war with the past three years. . . . By the way, you also don't threaten not to play defense and not to rebound if you don't get the ball every time down the floor."

On playing in pain: "I don't need Shaq's advice on how to play hurt. I've played with IVs before . . . with a broken hand, a sprained ankle, a fractured tooth, a severed lip, and a knee the size of a softball. I didn't miss 15 games because of a toe injury that everybody knows wasn't that serious."

On their relationship: "He is not my quote-unquote big brother. A big brother would have called me up over the summer."

On that note, the Lakers started the 2003–2004 season.

Chapter 14

LAST TANGO IN LA-LA LAND

I think when you decided to be on the Lakers, you realize it's going to be a circus over there. You're on the Lakers, you're in Los Angeles, you have Shaq and Kobe. Even minus all the problems going on right now, the whole nine years I was there, there was always something going on. . . .

You get numb to it, especially living in L.A. It's a different world. A lot of those guys love that spotlight. Guys on that team want to be movie stars. Guys want to be rappers. They love the spotlight. It doesn't seem to affect them at all.

—Former Clipper Eric Piatkowski

■   ■   ■

AT THE MADMEN'S BALL, the hour is getting late.

If this was the Lakers' last time around the floor, a possibility that loomed from the beginning with Kobe Bryant and seven more of them about to be free agents and Phil Jackson's contract running out, they would go out the way they had come in.

The music got louder and louder and the dancers whirled faster and faster, right up to the surprise at the very end. None of that boring, time-consuming fading into the twilight for them. When they went, it would be in a thunderclap, which would catch everyone by surprise, following the most dramatic postseason even these maniacs had ever known.

Everyone had always known something like this was out there, waiting for them. They just didn't know what it would look like when it arrived. As Jackson joked early in the season, after a storm slowed traffic to a crawl and made everyone late for that night's game, "I know the apocalypse is around the corner but maybe not tonight." But soon.

This season would have it all, the highest highs, the lowest lows, the worst fights, the most dramatic comebacks, the most miraculous shots. It was as if the gods decided they wanted to Shaq and Kobe one last time and had them replicate the entire era.

Even for the Lakers, this was different, with the real—represented by Kobe Bryant's court case—juxtaposed with the trivial that was treated as if it was real—represented by the basketball season.

The word that kept coming up in camp was "surreal," as when Bryant flew in from Eagle the morning of media day in El Segundo, hurried to the facility, donned his jersey, and taped drop-ins for upcoming telecasts. Smiling as if nothing was wrong, he read off cue cards that said, "Lakers basketball is coming up next," and, "You best get out of our way because we're coming after you."

Nothing worked the way it had before. In the hallway leading to the gym at the practice facility hung framed photos, and the first one, taken after the their 2002 title, showed O'Neal and Bryant with their three championship trophies, wearing those custom-made varsity jackets that cost thousands of dollars, smiling hugely.

It was hard to look at it without thinking how innocent Bryant and the Lakers had been and how recently. Someone in the organization must have thought so, too, because at midseason, it came down.

■　■　■

The season hadn't even started and everyone was wrung out. Publicist John Black almost resigned on the spot at the exhibition game in Las Vegas, dismayed at being told the *Times* was about to run a story that mentioned his new role as media censor. Shaquille O'Neal came in the day after Bryant barbecued him on *SportsCenter* with steam coming out of his ears like a walking Mt. St. Helens. He looked like he hadn't slept a wink and smoldered for a week, while everyone dove out of his way. The Lakers had seen O'Neal upset but never like this. He got unhappy enough at tiny slights and could go a long way to find one. Having just taken one for the ages between the eyes, no one thought he would ever get over it. Bryant was hurt, pouting, or both. Having just played in two exhibitions, he now scratched himself for the opener, saying he wasn't ready.

So they started 18–3. If the end of the season always brought out the best in them, so did the beginning, as they put away their own agendas, and theirs was very good, indeed.

With the game's greatest tandem and two more sure-fire Hall of Famers, they now had the greatest starting lineup ever assembled, and the new guys fit perfectly. Malone and Payton were tenacious, grind-it-out competitors. Payton's aggressiveness gave them a fast-break dimension they didn't have with Derek Fisher. Malone's professionalism made him the leader they needed, particularly O'Neal, who doted on the Mailman and would accept it when he told him to get his big ass in gear.

Malone, an underrated shooter and passer, could play the high post with O'Neal down low. Representing about six hundred pounds of muscle between them, Shaq and the Mailman gave them a scary-looking front line. "That sealed it for me," said the newly retired David Robinson when he heard Malone was going to the Lakers. "I thought, 'This is a pretty good seat over here.'"

Malone and Payton were in heaven, having come from declining teams they could no longer carry to this powerhouse, where all they had to do was help. No one even blamed them when things went wrong; that still fell on the Big Three. Both Malone and Payton had been reluctant interviews in recent seasons, but now they burbled away happily and at length. They were like Yoda and Gandalf. Their presence got everyone past the Shaq-Kobe blowup, with everyone adopting a new mantra: "Karl and Gary didn't give up all that money to come here for this." Even O'Neal zipped it up and kept it zipped all season.

They won their opener at home, walking on the Mavericks. Bryant stayed in the dressing room in the first half but came out on the bench in the second, sat down next to O'Neal, and tapped him on the leg. Shaq didn't as much as turn his head in acknowledgment. He didn't owe Karl and Gary that much.

Bryant was back for the second game in Phoenix, still rusty, but the Lakers won anyway, out-rebounding the Suns by 14. After that, they were off to the races, with their old taboos falling and their cup running over.

In Dallas, where owner Mark Cuban favored edgy promotion, the Mavericks put an image on the scoreboard video screens of O'Neal's head, superimposed on Fat Albert's body, going, "Hey, hey, hey!" O'Neal looked over to the Lakers bench, laughing, and everyone broke up. They led by 19 before winning, 114–103, and the rest of the West knew fear again.

"On the same team, they got four of the best players in the league at their position," said Mavs coach Don Nelson. "Hello? Anybody home?"

"Anybody who said they couldn't play together is foolish," said the Spurs' Gregg Popovich, after the Lakers stepped on his defending champions by 16 in Staples. "They're hell on wheels right now. . . . They're maybe the most talented team I've seen in my life."

■ ■ ■

December traditionally had a meaning of its own among the Lakers and it wasn't about Christmas cheer. Six weeks into the season, their usual fast start would lessen any sense of urgency. They would level off, with personal agendas resurfacing. They were like a grizzly, going into hibernation, not to be bothered until spring. So it was again with O'Neal growing bored as usual and Bryant isolated and distracted.

Bryant's legal team, had run into a brick wall trying to get the young woman on the stand in the preliminaries when Judge Frederick Gannett rejected the motion. Bryant's attorney, Pamela Mackey, had then proceeded to use the woman's name on six occasions in the hearing, with Gannett reprimanding her each time, claiming lamely she kept forgetting. Finally Gannett told her, "I could get you a big muzzle."

However, under Mackey's cross-examination the next day, Det. Doug Winters testified the woman had told him she expected Bryant "to put a move on her," and hadn't said anything about telling him to stop in their first interview.

A review of the physical evidence showed she had one small bruise on her neck, which, Winter testified, he hadn't even noticed. The yellow panties she wore during the incident were found to contain semen that didn't match Bryant's DNA.

Gannett ruled Bryant must stand trial but took a skeptical view of the prosecutor's case, noting, "Almost all the evidence produced at the preliminary hearing permits multiple inferences which, when viewed either independently or collectively, and upon reasonable inference, do not support a finding of Probable Cause."

Legal pundits said the prosecution was out-classed. *Vail Daily News* Managing Editor Don Rogers called on Gannett to dismiss the case right then and there. Describing Bryant as a "brat [who] has been living a great big lie with his McDonald's–fit wholesome image for celebrity-sick America," Rogers wrote, "I just don't think there's a case the prosecutors can honestly prove. . . . We don't get to just send Mr. Bryant to prison because we think he committed a crime."

Bryant's life on the court was now getting more attention than his life in court, with preliminary hearings dragging on and no trial date in sight. If he understood the import of the trial, Lakers fans seemed to regard it according to its impact on their favorite team.

There was a lot going on in Los Angeles that winter, with wildfires threatening the San Fernando Valley and a grocery-store strike. When sportscaster Fred Roggin told his radio talk-show audience about his wife and children evacuating their home, a listener sent in an e-mail, asking him to get back to Shaq and Kobe. Moving down the dial, a caller to the *McDonnell-Douglas Show* said if Bryant opted out and left, he hoped he would be found guilty.

Bryant was now a plaything for the popular culture. During a game at Staples, TV personality Nicole Richie, interviewed by a Fox-TV side-line reporter, said, "I want him to have sex with me." *Saturday Night Live* did a skit with Vanessa berating Kobe when they were alone. A Baltimore Ravens receiver named Travis Taylor and his wife, Rashidah, went to a Halloween party dressed as Kobe and his accuser.

There was nowhere to run, nowhere to hide. Since radio was entranced by Howard Stern, or at least his ratings, knockoffs were every-where, so now on the local oldies station, KRTH, you could hear Harvey Levin of *Celebrity Justice* interviewed about Bryant's latest court appear-ance by DJ Gary Bryan. If this was more than you bargained for between the Ronettes and Gladys Knight and the Pips, it was obviously the way to go. KLSX, the local classic rock station, hired a deejay named Jonathan Brandmeier, who did *his* comedy take on the Bryant case, in which he pretended to be the young woman, musing, "I'll go have sex and then turn myself in," in a falsetto voice.

■ ■ ■

In a coincidence with dire implications for the Lakers, Bryant was not only going to be a defendant but a free agent. His free agency began to get more attention, too, as the press began to understand he was serious about leaving.

The Lakers' roll lasted into mid-December. Bryant and O'Neal, speaking again, seemed to be getting along better than they ever had, but insiders said it was a surface jocularity that changed nothing; Bryant told a confidante he was "wide open" to leaving. He even asked Black, the closest man in the organization to him, to come to the Clippers with him. Bryant needed a lot of slack in the best of times, and these, when he felt besieged and even more wary of the outside world, weren't them. He treated the beat writers like paparazzi and sometimes fumed about leaving in front of teammates. The more it looked like Bryant was leaving, the cooler teammates were. This just made Bryant madder and more determined to leave, which made them even cooler, in a continuing spiral toward divorce.

A process of disinvestment was already well under way on both sides. Bryant's anger at O'Neal led to his vow to leave to get away from him, which got back to Shaq, prompting his announcement that this was his team and, "If he don't like it, he can opt out."

Arrangements were already in the works. Bryant's agent began signaling Kobe's interest to the Clippers in no uncertain terms. Agents were always scurrying around, doing things that constituted tampering, but Pelinka went farther than most. The *Times'* Tim Brown reported Pelinka had been overheard telling a Clippers official, "Save your cap space."

Not coincidentally, the Clippers began saving their cap space, passing up players who could have helped to make sure if Bryant actually wanted to come, they'd be far enough under to give him a maximum offer.

Bryant was now even more inclined to ignore teammates' feelings and take over games at the end. Players complained that Bryant was chasing the ball all over the floor, but he was a commanding presence. When he demanded the ball, they gave it to him, Payton and Malone, included. It wasn't uncommon to see one of them hand Bryant the ball with five seconds on the shot clock so that he had to shoot it, just to complain about him afterward. As one player—not O'Neal—said after Bryant led a November 21 comeback win against the Bulls, "What are we, robots?"

On December 19, Bryant spent the day in Eagle, jetted back after court adjourned, got to that night's game against the Nuggets in the second quarter, missed nine of his first 13 shots, then hit a dramatic game-winning 20-footer as time ran out. O'Neal, Malone, and Payton stomped away afterward without talking to the press. Normally, the Lakers weren't into hiding their feelings, but that was how this season would go, ominously silent. Players ripped Bryant off the record, but no one said anything for publication.

Jackson, who had always liked to get things out in the open to make his players deal with them, was now covering up for Bryant. Before, Jackson had been tough on Bryant, trying to keep him with the program. Now, Jackson sensed Bryant needed a lot of room, so whatever Kobe did, Phil acted as if it was OK. It didn't work. Bryant, who had also co-existed easily with Jackson for two seasons, now decided he didn't like Phil, either.

Their good times soon ran out. Malone, who had missed only six games due to injury in 18 seasons, sprained his right knee in a December 21 win over the Suns that made the Lakers 20–5. He was expected to be out for a week but it turned out to be until mid-March. O'Neal, running low on enthusiasm right on schedule, joked with Payton about faking an injury so they could go on the injured list together. Luckily for O'Neal, he popped a calf muscle in a January 2 loss in Seattle and got to take the rest of the month off.

On January 4, Bryant scored 44 points, but the Lakers, now in the midst of a four-game losing streak, lost, 101–98, to the Clippers. A fan got on the scoreboard video screens, holding up a red Clipper No. 8 Bryant jersey. Asked about it afterward, Bryant concluded the Q&A, musing, "On that note, I'll call it a night."

Two nights later, the Lakers got their doors blown off in Minnesota, and Payton fumed, "I didn't sign up for this s***. This is bulls***."

Payton didn't like Bryant's gunning, or Jackson's triangle offense, or the fact that Jackson often played Fisher, who actually knew the offense, in crunch time. However, Payton preferred to let his agent, Aaron Goodwin, do his complaining, which Goodwin finally did, announcing that Gary was sorry he came.

Payton then went into his diplomatic act. "In Seattle, if he would have come to my team," he said of Bryant the next day, "I probably would have been dominating the ball too."

On January 12, 10 days after O'Neal was hurt, Bryant went out for two weeks with a shoulder injury. The Lakers were now starting Payton, Devean George, Slava Medvedenko, Kareem Rush, and Brian Cook. This, at least, allowed Jackson to claim the rest of the season that their problems were due to injuries, although no one knew the real deal better than he did. At midseason, the What-Me-Worry Kid was so concerned about Bryant's state of mind, he talked privately about asking Kobe to take a leave of absence.

By then, Jerry Buss was working on a leave of absence for Jackson, otherwise known as the rest of Phil's life.

■ ■ ■

At first, it looked like management would ignore the stuff in the news-papers in the standard denial number—*Kobe, leave us for the Clippers?* They were the Lakers, after all. Players wanted to come to play for them, not the other way around.

However, Buss soon figured out the possibility that Bryant would walk was real. On February 1, Super Bowl Sunday, with the team on the East Coast and Bryant out, the owner went down to Kobe's Newport Beach home to talk to him. Bryant insisted later he didn't say anything bad about O'Neal or Jackson, but the three weren't best friends at the moment, so who knows what might have slipped out?

Buss immediately broke off extension talks with Jackson. These had been considered routine in the fall when Buss was just happy to learn his daughter's boyfriend would coach for another two seasons. However, when Jackson asked for a raise from $6 million to $12.5 million, Buss asked for time to think it over. Jackson's agent, Todd Musburger, said later they were near agreement when Buss pulled the plug, but after that, the Lakers never wanted to talk again.

Dialing it up on the bizarre scale, Black was then detailed to inform the press that negotiations had been halted. The Lakers were, in effect, turning their coach into a lame duck to signal Bryant. Everybody started running around, getting reaction from everyone else. Bryant, who had just rejoined the team in Houston, was asked what a departure by Jackson would mean for his own decision.

Said Bryant: "I don't care."

This was interpreted as an expression of disdain, sufficient to set off a feeding frenzy at the All-Star Game media availability back home, two days later. However, Buss's visit, a secret which wouldn't leak out for weeks, had impressed Bryant, who insisted he wanted to stay for the first time, even sounding like he meant it. Not that anyone believed him, or should have. The Lakers could offer him more years (seven versus six) and bigger raises (12.5 percent to 10 percent) than other teams and had the money on the table. If he wanted to stay, why was he still saying he would opt out?

However, the Bryant who came out of the All-Star break was nothing like the Bryant who had gone into it. The rest of February, he averaged 30 points and 8.3 assists. Of course, after that, he had his share or regressions into Me-First Land, and teammates did their share of rolling their eyes behind his back, but nothing too bad happened . . . until April 11, the third-to-last game of the season.

In Sacramento for what was thought to be the game that would decide first place in the Pacific Division, the Lakers staged a team no-show. O'Neal picked up two quick fouls and finished with 10 points and five rebounds. The Lakers were behind by 19 at halftime, and Bryant had taken only one shot. Payton was heard, asking him, "You going to play today or what?"

The Kings were double-teaming Bryant when he came off screens, so he was looking for the open man. In the last three games, his shot totals had been 26-23-23, and there had been the usual muttering about it, so he might have been looking for the open man to a fault, just to show what happened when he gave it up the way everyone always wanted him to. Bryant went home, thinking this was just one more bad team performance, not realizing he was being singled out. By the next morning, he knew different. Walking off the floor at El Segundo after practice, he snapped, "Can I have some room to breathe?" as the press approached him and kept going.

In the next days' *Times*, columnist Bill Plaschke wrote Bryant had "tanked" at Sacramento, perhaps as a negotiating ploy to show Buss who was more important, Kobe or Shaq. A Lakers player who didn't want to be identified—but was not O'Neal—told the *Times*' Brown, "I don't know how we can forgive him."

At that point, it was also an open question if Bryant could forgive them, either. He stormed into the practice facility the next morning and polled teammates, one by one, demanding to know which one of "you motherf***ers" had been the source of the quote. All denied it just as heatedly. As a Lakers official put it, "Kobe's melting down."

That night, at home against the Warriors, Bryant had 45 points, eight assists, and seven rebounds, carrying the Lakers to a 109–104 victory. Then he got 37 the next night at Portland. Included was a leaning three-pointer that he squeezed off under the armpit of Ruben Patterson, who was draped all over him, tying the game with 1.1 seconds left in regulation. Then with the Lakers trailing by two and time running out in the second overtime, Bryant launched a high, arching three-pointer over the onrushing Theo Ratliff which fell straight through, giving the Lakers a 105–104 victory. At that point, it didn't seem like it was a good idea to fool with Kobe or Mother Nature.

OK, is everybody ready for the playoffs?

"I wanted to come to a tough situation," Malone said later. "I had to come to a tough situation. Now, I didn't understand, I didn't know all *this* was going to happen. . . .

"When we were going through some pretty tough times, I used to sit in the locker room and I kidded the guys. I said, 'Damn, you guys won three championships with all this going on?'"

■　■　■

Even the Lakers weren't used to this level of chaos, especially this late. By this point, they had always been on their best behavior, no matter what had happened before that. Now it didn't seem like they had much good behavior left in them. Nor did their path look promising. As the number four seed, courtesy of the win in Portland that moved them past Sacramento on the last night of the season, they would only be at home for one round in the Western draw.

Even as they dispatched Houston, 4–1, in the first round, the papers kept pursuing the breakup angles that lay everywhere.

"Here I am, right in the middle, just like what I feared," Jeannie Buss told the *Times'* Jay Adande about the impasse between her father and her guy. "But I think Phil is a professional. My dad is a great owner of a team. I don't think it's been a distraction or as bad as it could have been. There's so many other distractions. It's like a little minidistraction in a world of distractions. . . .

"You look at somebody like Phil, I don't think people think he needs to hear that he does a good job. Because it's like, 'He's self-actualized and he doesn't need any of it.' But I still think that he's an employee and it's important for him to be told he does a good job."

In other words, Jackson was mad at her dad, but with everything else going on, this barely ranked as a problem, since Phil just wanted to be asked back.

Bryant was still wild, and the Lakers still weren't sure what they could do or say about it. In Game 1 against the Rockets, he went 4–19 from the floor. Then with the Lakers trailing, 71–70, in the final seconds, he tried an unusual windshield-wiper move, driving right with two Rockets on him in the sure knowledge he would shoot, reversing direction, and driving back the way he had come in a vain attempt to get open. Finally, he launched an off-balance 27-footer that hit nothing but O'Neal under the basket. Shaq went back up for the game-winning dunk.

"He can make some of those shots he missed," said Fisher, who was still close to Bryant, "but I don't think those are the type of shots that he consistently wants to have to try and take. . . . Pump fake, guys flying by and having to lean in. As talented as he is, it's tough to be consistent doing that."

Shot selection had always been Bryant's problem. He had never shot 47 percent in any season (Michael Jordan shot 52 percent as a rookie), because he had never figured out the part about getting the easiest shot he could. It often seemed his basic shot was a 20-footer on which he fell back so far, he had to jackknife his legs for enough leverage to get the ball to the basket. If Jordan and Larry Bird had been the game's greatest shot-makers, Bryant ranked as the game's greatest impossible shot-maker.

"I mean, Kobe Bryant just amazes me every single time he takes the floor," said the Rockets' Eric Piatkowski. "Just the shots that he makes, the moves that he makes, his professionalism, the way he handles himself, everything about him. I don't know how he does it.

"It's really a treat to watch him play. I'm watching him saying to guys on our bench, 'That's a terrible shot he just took!' But he makes it. He's just amazing.

"The shots where he's taking one or two hard dribbles, and he has guys hanging on him, and he jumps straight back, and he's shooting over Yao [Ming] and all these guys, and he just, bam, he hits it. Not even Michael Jordan hit shots like that."

For better and/or worse, however, the Lakers had become Bryant's team, on the floor as well as in the mind of Jerry Buss. They'd been O'Neal's team in the glory days of 2000–2002, but now, even trimmed down and motivated, Shaq didn't dominate as he once did. His scoring average in the playoffs would drop to 21.5, against a career average of 28. He no longer had the old explosion. Watching him gather himself after taking an offensive rebound and then settle for trying to lay the ball up in the Houston series, a Lakers staffer noted, "Three years ago, he would have torn the basket down."

Stamina was a problem, too. O'Neal faded late in games, which he attributed to not getting the ball. He had trouble coming back on short rest. With two or more days off, he would average 26 points that post-season, but when he only got one, he went down to 18.5. Once, he over-whelmed all other centers and had to be double-teamed or else. Now there was one who could actually stand up to him—the 7'5", 300-pound Yao—and several who could at least contain O'Neal.

O'Neal would only outscore Yao, 81–75, in the series, as Bryant led the way. Kobe hit a runner in the lane to win the pivotal Game 4 in Houston, then capped it with 31 points in Game 5, another of his commuting-from-Eagle specials, arriving at 6:56 for the 7:22 game, so tired he almost fell asleep on the ride over from LAX. His arrival in the garage area in Staples was shown to the cheering crowd on the Staples TV screens. He missed his first three shots but then went 12–18, with 10 assists, six rebounds, and three steals

"This is not a circus," Malone said afterward, angered at suggestions Bryant's performances under these circumstances this were a mere entertainment spectacle. "This is the furthest thing from a circus I can imagine. This is not a circus, this is life. It's been written about so much, it's like, it's a speeding ticket. This is not a speeding ticket. . . .

"What he's done this year, how many guys would have done it? I've known a lot of guys, tough guys, who would not have even shown up. They would have taken the whole year off. I commend him and I'm not ashamed to say it. The guy didn't run and hide. The guy faced it."

■　■　■

In a better place than they had been before the playoffs, at least, the Lakers moved into the second round against their old nemesis, the Spurs, in the new SBC Center.

Jackson was so concerned about opening there, he took advantage of a three-day break between Games 1 and 2 to fly the team back home. Being Phil Jackson, he zinged San Antonio in the process of announcing his decision, noting, "Once you've been there, you've been there enough."

San Antonio was actually a charming place, known as the honeymoon capital of Texas, with its picturesque St. Jacinto River flowing through downtown, lined by hotels, restaurants, and bars. If Jackson wasn't keen on it, his players had always seemed to enjoy themselves out on the town.

More to the point was their opponent, the defending champion Spurs, in the midst of another late-season surge, having finished on a 27–7 run to win the West for the fourth time in five seasons (to the Lakers' one).

Tim Duncan and Tony Parker weren't quite O'Neal and Bryant, but with the brash little Frenchman still coming fast in his third season at 22, they were one of the better duos. The Lakers had more stars, but they had more problems, too.

The Spurs won Games 1 and 2, just as they had done the year before. Parker went for 20 points, torching Payton, "the Glove," who was now being burned so often, insiders joked his nickname should be changed to "the Pot Holder."

The Lakers' day of reckoning had arrived, at last. Only six NBA teams had come back from 0–2 in a seven-game series, and they didn't look like the best candidate to stay together when the going got tough.

Their past seemed to follow them wherever they went. Before Game 2 in San Antonio, O'Neal's stepfather, Phillip Harrison, had told the *San Antonio Express-News*, "Kobe Bryant could be one of the best players that ever played the game if he learned how to play team basketball. The game is played inside out, not outside in. You play team basketball, no problem. You have to establish the inside game first. Shaquille is the most dominant player to ever play the game. You have to pass him the ball. Let's stop the drama and just play ball."

As to their relationship, Sarge said, "They just work together and that's all."

This was more like a golden oldie than news but it still came at an inopportune time—with feelings still tender all around—to be reprising everyone's complaints.

Nor was it a good time for Payton to flip out, but by now, he was a basket case. Unused to being regarded as a weak link, he was now up to his neck in bad notices after Parker outscored him, 50–11, in the first two games. Whether this was the best time to flip out or not, he did anyway.

"Y'all can blame me for everything," he said before Game 3. "Man, I don't care. I don't listen to all that. OK, you're going to put me in one year and you're going to tell me I'm the problem of this situation. Whatever, man. Blame me. I could care less. I'm going to go home and play with my kids and play with my wife anyway, so I don't care. A year ago, you guys weren't talking that crap. 'Gary Payton is still this and that and that.' But now you come and put me on the Lakers, and I'm not having a good year or a good playoff. Oh, I'm the problem now. . . .

"I can't stop Tony Parker. Yeah, OK. That's great. Let me get in the pick and roll 65 times and I bet I'll beat you, too. You can put it on me. Whatever you want to do. Somebody's got to be the scapegoat. But you guys don't want to put it on ol' who-it's-really-supposed-to-be, huh?"

And who might that be?

"You tell me, then," Payton said, laughing. "I don't know."

Of course, it was O'Neal, who hung so far back on pick-and-rolls, Lakers opponents started running them as soon as they got off the plane. In case anyone had missed the fact the apocalypse was finally here, Jackson made it official, spelling out their doomsday scenario, acknowledging a loss would be "pretty much a death knell" for them. He talked about waking in the middle of the night, wondering if this was the end, and making sure his players knew what was at stake.

"We have a team with a nebulous future," said Jackson. "I went down through the list of every single one of them, where they're at, how old they were, what direction they're going to go, and what their future is. We only have four or five guys whose future to remain together here seems even possible. It's a team that has to play for the now, for Sunday's game."

By now, the press corps was in nirvana. The Spurs were the defending champions and led the series, but press people just went to their practices to make sure no one got hurt.

Reports of the Lakers' demise were still exaggerated, even when they were self-generated, as they then proved, winning Games 3 and 4. Game 3 was a wipeout, with the Spurs looking casual, infuriating coach Gregg Popovich. Game 4 was another of Bryant's returns from Eagle. The others had been dramatic enough, but this was one of the best games of his career, scoring 42 points with six rebounds, five assists, three steals, and no turnovers, leading a comeback from 10 points behind at the half.

In a real upset, the Lakers were coming together. As if in a replay from the 2001 series against the Spurs, O'Neal now said of Bryant, "Once again, I have to title him as the best player ever."

What about Michael Jordan? someone asked.

"What about him?" replied O'Neal.

Once more, they went back to San Antonio for the pivotal Game 5.

Before, the Lakers had gone down by 25 and closed to within two before Robert Horry's game-ending three-pointer missed. That was a thriller, but this was a classic.

This time, it was the Lakers who went up by 16 in the third period and the Spurs who came back, taking a three-point lead into the last two minutes. With :11 left, Bryant hit a 20-footer to put the Lakers up, 73–72. With :05 left, the Lakers took a foul, making the Spurs start over. This time, Duncan, taking the in-bounds pass, set a screen for a dribble handoff to Parker, but the Lakers covered it. With O'Neal all over him, Duncan drove to his left, across the top of the circle. Still smothered by O'Neal and unable to even pull up, Duncan launched a desperation shot, going away from the basket.

Bingo!

It fell with 0.4 seconds left, putting the Spurs ahead, 73–72. The dazed Lakers called time out, setting up a last play, for Bryant. The Spurs covered him and option number two, O'Neal, as he rolled to the hoop.

The ball went in to Fisher, who'd been last in line in the four-man stack the Lakers set up in front of the side-court in-bounds pass. With no time and Manu Ginobili flying at him, Fisher threw up a desperate, 19-foot half-hook . . .

That dropped right through?

The Lakers couldn't believe it. The Spurs didn't want to believe it—Popovich called it "the cruelest loss I've ever been involved with"—but it happened.

"Fish's shot went up," said Malone, "and I'm thinking, 'Oh, it's got a chance!' Then I'm thinking, 'Oh, it's got a good chance!' Then I'm like, 'Dang! We won!'

"I was looking around for somebody, but everybody was going crazy, there was nobody to hug. So then I look over and see Shaq. And he's just standing there looking at me like, 'What, that good?'"

They didn't come any better than that, miracle shot answering miracle shot in the greatest finish in NBA history.

For the Lakers, it was only the latest in their series of miracles that dated back five years: the rally from 15 points behind in the fourth quarter of the 2000 West Finals, Horry's shot in the 2002 West Finals, coming from 3–2 behind in the 2002 West Finals. All were now mere prelude for this, the greatest of them all.

Bryant, who'd had to go back to Eagle between Games 4 and 5, staggered through 47 minutes, out on his feet. During one timeout, the team doctor, Steve Lombardo, came over to look at him. Exhausted and dehydrated afterward, Bryant was hooked up to an IV and given two bags of fluids.

The Spurs turned themselves around fast enough to make Game 6 back in Staples competitive, but the Lakers ground them down and won, 88–76.

After all that had gone before, the Lakers were back.

■　■　■

Lakers in love, one more time.

The team that was so divided, coming off a season that had been so horrific, was together once more. There had been signs of a thaw for months, but something bad always happened that put them back where they started, with everyone hiring divorce lawyers. Now, love broke out all over Lakerdom.

Two more series lay between them and their fourth title in five seasons, but no one was worried. Even in Eastern cities, the Lakers-Spurs series was considered the real NBA Finals, as suggested by headlines in the *Boston Globe* ("Lakers-Spurs winner take all") and *Chicago Tribune* ("Rematch may play like Finals.") A *Minneapolis Star-Tribune* headline called the Timberwolves' second-round series against the Kings, "That 'other' semifinal."

Everything was breaking the Lakers' way. They would start the West Finals at Minnesota but would have a week to rest, which their elderly, their large, and even their Kobe needed. Meanwhile, the Kings were taking the Timberwolves to the wall.

The Wolves would wind up getting one day off after winning a tense Game 7, and by then Sam Cassell, the cold-blooded shot-maker who had helped turn them into an elite team, had a bad hip injury. Everyone assumed the West winner would claim the NBA title, as the last five had by a combined 20–6. When the Pistons and Pacers locked horns like two ancient elk in an agonizingly low-scoring East Finals, it looked like the West would get another walkover.

The Lakers quickly turned the West Finals around, taking home-court advantage back by beating the tired Wolves in Game 1. Cassell could only play 32 minutes the rest of the way, and the Wolves succumbed in six.

There wasn't a snit in sight among the Lakers. Bryant, who had insisted all along that whatever else happened, he would opt out, now told a confidante he didn't know if he would. O'Neal was no longer living for the day Bryant left. Before the Finals, Fox said O'Neal told him, "We need to keep this together because when it's gone, it's going to be gone."

O'Neal even said he could handle the new deal, with Bryant leading the offense, although he wasn't exactly enchanted at the thought.

"As long as we're winning," O'Neal said. "If we're winning, all that's fine. If we're not winning, then everybody has a problem, including me."

In other words, even if they stayed together, they had better not get off to a bad start next season or any season. Of course, it had been that way for five years, so what else was new?

"I just point to two guys," said Malone of their turnaround, before the NBA Finals. "And I said it probably about a month ago. Kobe and Shaq, seems like they relaxed and with that, the team has relaxed, as well. So it's no coincidence that happened."

The dynasty was alive and well and planning to run forever.

BRAVE NEW GENERIC WORLD

Shaq is the most dominant player in the game, there's no question about that. The question is, if I wait until he isn't the most dominant player, will I get adequate return on him? Maybe I'm trading him too soon. Maybe I'm trading him too late. I don't know.

—Jerry Buss, July 2004

■ ■ ■

In the end, Kobe Bryant beat the rap but the Lakers didn't.

On September 1, 2004, one year, one month, and 13 days after filing a sexual assault charge against Bryant, Eagle County D.A. Mark Hurlbert filed a motion to dismiss it. Calling it "justice . . . sadly interrupted," Hurlbert said the young woman, now 20, had dropped out, praising her courage. Since she was still pursuing a civil suit against Bryant, this was self-serving and otherwise meaningless.

The prosecution had stumbled for a year, since Judge Frederick Gannett, in the process of ruling Bryant must stand trial, expressed his skepticism at Hurlbert's case. Judge Terry Ruckriegle had subsequently ruled the young woman's sexual history was admissible, and Hurlbert, himself, had dropped out as lead prosecutor.

Bryant released a statement, apologizing to the young woman "for my behavior that night and for the consequences she has suffered in the past year. Although this year has been incredibly difficult for me personally, I can only imagine the pain she has had to endure."

As if to confirm the statement was the result of negotiations between their legal teams, it was handed out to press people in Eagle by the lawyers representing the young woman in her civil suit.

"It clearly is a negotiated statement," Alan Dershowitz, the famed appeals lawyer told the *Los Angeles Times*. "Not a word of that was written by Kobe. You can see the lawyers' hands all over that. It is very artfully done."

If Bryant's ordeal was over, his life would never be the same. If he had been the boy next door when he arrived with the Lakers, he was no longer. Oh, and the Lakers as he had known them were gone, too.

■   ■   ■

Just when the little divas thought they could go on pulling this stuff forever, along came . . . the Pistons?

After the Lakers' heart-pounding journey through the West draw, after all the crises they survived, with their superstars once more united in the nick of time, it was taken for granted they had only mop-up work to secure the fourth title of the Shaq-Kobe era.

The Pistons were just a good team, making it up as they went along. It had only been a year since a palace coup had unseated Rick Carlisle, the coach who had turned their 32–50 club around, but was too brusque for owner Bill Davidson and his lieutenant, Tom Wilson. Desperate, GM Joe Dumars had grabbed the first good coach he could find. That turned out to be Larry Brown, even if they were rebuilding around kids and he was a veterans' coach who always wanted to trade off the kids.

Dumars, himself, was only in his fourth season as GM. Happily, he was a quick learner; he was so far behind the curve when he took over, he was going to go to Wimbledon during the July start of the free-agent signing period.

Typically, Brown kept prize rookie Darko Milicic chained to the bench and didn't take long to decide he didn't like a lot of Dumars' young players, like 6'10" second-year forward Memo Okur. Predictably, Brown begged Dumars to get him a veteran no one else would touch, Portland's troubled Rasheed Wallace. Fortunately, Wallace was not just available, the Trail Blazers, who were in the process of an image makeover, were holding a fire sale. Dumars wound up giving up little to get Wallace from Atlanta, which had traded for Rasheed and kept him for one game.

The Pistons finished on a 20–4 run but still had to dig out of a hole in the second round of the playoffs when they trailed the Nets, 3–2, going back to New Jersey for Game 6. The Pistons then got by Indiana in an agonizingly low-scoring East Finals but didn't look scary doing it. The deciding Game 6, when Indiana led at halftime, 33–27, was typical. Even as the Lakers warned themselves against complacency, Malone mused: "Seems like over here in the West, you score 33 points, you're down by 30 at halftime."

Skepticism was universal, even among admirers. On ESPN's *Sports Reporters* the *New York Times'* Bill Rhoden stuck up for the Pistons, calling them "an excellent team.

"Having said that," Rhoden added, "I think they'll win one game."

So no one got too worried or excited when the Pistons stunned the Lakers in Game 1, 87–75. Detroit stifled everyone but O'Neal, who got 32 points with Brown single-covering him as he had when he was coaching the 76ers in 2001. This time, Brown wasn't doing it with 7'0" Dikembe Mutombo but with Ben Wallace, whose listed height was 6'9" but who was closer to 6'7". Wallace, a two-time defensive player of the year, was known for his hairdos, including his psychedelic-era Afro. Detroit fans waved "Fear the 'Fro" banners, but the 'Fro wasn't quite as scary when it only came up to your chin.

Things seemed to settle into their usual—harrowing, miraculous—pattern in Game 2. The Lakers rallied from six down in the last :36 of regulation. Bryant hit a long three-pointer with 2.1 seconds left and Richard Hamilton in his face, sending it into overtime where they won, 99–91.

However, an alarming problem—energy—had surfaced. Not even an elderly team is supposed to get beaten to the ball every time it's loose, but the Pistons had out-rebounded them, 20–10, in the second half. The Lakers hadn't gotten a single defensive rebound in the last 5:18 of regulation, while the Pistons climbed all over the boards, playing volleyball until they got the ball into the hoop.

Unconcerned as usual, Jackson pooh-poohed it, noting on his players' behalf: "I just think they didn't react to the ball." It was the same round, orange thing they'd been playing with their whole lives. Their reaction time wasn't likely to improve in Games 3, 4, and 5 in Detroit, but that wasn't a concern, either. The home team hadn't swept the middle three since the league went to the 2-3-2 format in 1985.

Of course, there's a first time for everything.

O'Neal, still struggling on one day's rest, was held to 14 points in Game 3 and 20 in Game 5. Bryant, shadowed by the rest of the Detroit defense, got 11, 20, and 24 and shot 32 percent. With Malone sidelined by his knee again and their interior defense kaput, the Lakers couldn't stay in front of the Pistons or keep them off the boards.

During the season, the Lakers out-rebounded opponents by one a game and shot an average of 4.7 more free throws. In the Finals, the Pistons out-rebounded them by eight a game and shot an average of 11 more free throws. None of the games in the Palace was close, and the clincher was a 100–87 laugher after the Pistons led by 27.

The Lakers were officially old, they learned that spring.

■ ■ ■

Within weeks, they were officially history, too.

Jerry Buss told Phil Jackson he wouldn't offer him a new contract, no matter who he was dating. O'Neal was traded to Miami for the NBA equivalent of $24 in wampum and beads. After that, they didn't look much like the Lakers anymore. For the first time in a long time, and for the foreseeable future, they would be just another team, loathed as much but feared no longer.

Bryant would inevitably be blamed for breaking up the Lakers trinity by the other two-thirds of the trinity as well as everyone else, since O'Neal and Jackson thought he had ordered their departures. Jackson was working on a book, due out that fall. Insiders said he would describe Bryant as "uncoachable." O'Neal was being classy but wasn't planning on keeping that up. As he told an ESPN interviewer who asked about Bryant upon Shaq's arrival in Miami: "It's time for that, but not now." That time was only a month later when O'Neal's latest rap album was released with a number called "You Not The Fightin' Type," in which he told DJ Skillz, a Cincinnati deejay, "You remind me of Kobe Bryant trying to be as high as me . . . but you can't . . . even if you get me traded."

The real story was more complicated. By the end, Bryant was OK with O'Neal and Jackson, but Buss wasn't. Months before, Buss had made a simple decision: he had to keep Bryant, period.

O'Neal was dispensable since Buss didn't like the idea of giving him another $60 to $90 million. Buss had gone up to $22 million a season, trying to sign him to an extension, but O'Neal had steadfastly refused to take a pay cut. Since Shaq would make $30 million in the last year of his contract, he wanted $30 million a season on his extension.

Nor did Buss like the price Jackson had given him for two more seasons: $25 million.

Bryant had been furious at O'Neal and Jackson when he and Buss met in February but had softened by season's end. In July, when Bryant finally re-signed, he insisted he would have gladly have gone on with Shaq and Phil, calling Shaq "my partner in crime."

By then, the horses were out of the barn, down the road, and out of sight. The organization had had enough. In the end, with so much ego at play and so many hundreds of millions of dollars at stake, everyone was too worn out to think straight.

■ ■ ■

What the Shaq-Kobe era lacked in longevity, it made up for in entertainment value. During their last five seasons, in which they won three titles, appeared in the Finals four times, and made the headlines a lot more than that, there was never anything like the Lakers, not the Charlie Finley A's or the Bronx Zoo Yankees or Da Bears or Da Bulls. A lot of us who covered them prayed for their breakup daily so we could get a little rest, but the moment they were gone, we missed them.

This was how close they came to prolonging the madness. If they had won the title that seemed dead ahead, Buss would have brought everyone back. Instead, the owner flew home from Detroit, fuming at O'Neal. This was a tip-off to what was coming because O'Neal hadn't been any worse than any of them, including Bryant.

If it came to a choice, Buss had to go with the 25-year-old, ferociously competitive Bryant over the 32-year-old, not-what-he'd-been O'Neal, but the trick was to try to avoid choosing. Even a fading O'Neal was irreplaceable. With the conditions he put on them—the Pacers would have given up Jermaine O'Neal but Shaq wouldn't play in Indiana—they couldn't get anything close to his value back.

At the very least, Buss should have asked Bryant how he felt about O'Neal at the end, but it never came up. Buss said it was a business decision; he didn't want to extend O'Neal.

"At some time, we know his value is going to decline," Buss said. "That's completely obvious. . . . We offered to make him the highest-paid player in the NBA for perhaps the rest of his career. He turned that down. . . . We certainly negotiated in good faith. We did not call off those negotiations. He's the one who called off those negotiations."

Gloom and fear hung over the organization for weeks, but Buss wasn't around. He took off for his annual vacation in Italy, leaving GM Mitch Kupchak to handle things as best he could, checking with him long distance. Of course, the hard-partying Buss could be hard to find. The year before, Malone's signing had been held up a week because he wanted to talk to the owner, who was overseas, and they kept missing each other. Meanwhile, the Spurs kept calling Malone, offering five times more than the Lakers. Malone finally settled for a welcoming message from Buss on his answering machine.

The days when Hall of Famers came for minimums to try and win titles were over, not that Buss seemed worried. He made his comments about letting O'Neal go in a conference call from Italy. As he noted, greeting the beat writers: "What could I tell you? The pasta's great and the wine is flowing."

And the era was ending. *Bon voyage,* greatness.

■ ■ ■

On July 14, it became official: O'Neal went to Miami for the bargain basement price of Lamar Odom, Brian Grant, Caron Butler, and a No. 1 pick. Rudy Tomjanovich, a Rocket for all 34 of his years in the NBA, became the new Lakers coach. The new center would be an old friend, Vlade

Divac, signed as a free agent at 36 after a season in which he had averaged only 28.6 minutes a game.

Incredibly, they almost lost Bryant, who looked like he was Clippers-bound, reportedly telling their delegation in a meeting at the Four Seasons in Newport Beach, "I want to be a Clipper."

The Clippers, with Elton Brand, Corey Maggette, and a big, young front line, had the better supporting cast. However, they also had madcap owner Donald T. Sterling and the rules limited their offer to $105 million over six seasons to the Lakers' $136 million over seven.

Bryant agonized until the night before he was to announce his decision, making up his mind on a late walk with Vanessa. At that point, even Rob Pelinka didn't know which way he'd go. On July 15, Bryant re-signed with the Lakers. With the bill for his legal defense reportedly in the $4-million range, a career to re-establish, and West, his old mentor, advising him to stay, Bryant decided to bank the extra money and Lakers tradition.

Not that he was in any doubt that the good times were over.

"It's not even close," Bryant said. "We know that. Everybody knows that. . . . We don't have the most dominant player in the game so that's going to change things drastically. It's going to be more of a struggle for us. We know that."

Derek Fisher, who had been their conscience, like Jiminy Cricket, signed with Golden State. Rick Fox, their calming influence, was traded to Boston with Gary Payton. Jackson was in Montana. West was in Memphis. Chick Hearn was in the Big Pressbox in the Sky.

Nothing is forever, the Lakers learned that summer.

INDEX